LLEWELLYN'S

2018

Magical Almanac

Featuring

Barbara Ardinger, Elizabeth Barrette, Mireille Blacke,
Blake Octavian Blair, Deborah Blake, Deborah Castellano,
Dallas Jennifer Cobb, Monica Crosson, Raven Digitalis,
Ellen Dugan, Michael Furie, Ember Grant,
Justine Holubets, James Kambos, Sandra Kynes,
Tiffany Lazic, Najah Lightfoot, Lupa, Jason Mankey,
Melanie Marquis, Estha K. V. McNevin, Susan Pesznecker,
Stacy M. Porter, Suzanne Ress, Rev. J. Variable X/0,
Charlynn Walls, Tess Whitehurst,
Charlie Rainbow Wolf, and Natalie Zaman

Llewellyn's 2018 Magical Almanac

ISBN 978-0-7387-3779-9. Copyright © 2017 by Llewellyn Publications. All rights reserved. Printed in the United States. Llewellyn Publications is a registered trademark of Llewellyn Worldwide Ltd.

Editor/Designer: Lauryn Heineman

Cover Illustration: © Tammy Shane

Calendar Pages Design: Michael Fallon

Calendar Pages Illustrations: © Fiona King

Interior Illustrations: © Elisabeth Alba: 45, 48, 75, 77, 80, 202, 205, 260, 265; © Chris Down: pages 57, 58, 100, 103, 236, 240, 289, 291, 293; © Kathleen Edwards: pages 36, 39, 41, 84, 89, 210, 213, 216, 267, 269, 272; © Wen Hsu: pages 7, 20, 23, 25, 67, 68, 71, 189, 192, 194, 197, 199, 251, 253, 257; © Mickie Mueller: pages 9, 11, 15, 115, 117, 120, 245, 248, 296, 300, 302; © Eugene Smith: pages 51, 54, 94, 97, 221, 223, 227, 276, 280; © Amber Zoellner: pages 28, 32, 62, 65, 109, 112, 231, 233, 283, 286

Clip Art Illustrations: Dover Publications

Special thanks to Amber Wolfe for the use of daily color and incense correspondences. For more detailed information, please see *Personal Alchemy* by Amber Wolfe.

You can order Llewellyn annuals and books from *New Worlds,* Llewellyn's catalog. To request a free copy of the catalog, call 1-877-NEW-WRLD toll-free or visit www.llewellyn.com.

Astrological data compiled and programmed by Rique Pottenger. Based on the earlier work of Neil F. Michelsen.

Llewellyn Worldwide Ltd.
2143 Wooddale Drive
Woodbury, MN 55125

Table of Contents

Earth Magic

The Magic of Mundane Garden Creatures

by Sandra Kynes

Yes, this is about bugs. Unlike the animal world, where we find many creatures to which we can relate, the insect world can seem rather alien. However, throughout human history insects have been considered important enough to appear in mythology, folklore, and sacred writings. While some insects are admired for their ingenuity and beauty, others represent desirable qualities.

So why should Pagans and Wiccans care about insects other than to acknowledge that they have a place in the natural world? To paraphrase the wizard Gandalf: the smallest of things can hold a great deal of power. But don't worry; you don't need to handle them in order to use them for magic or ritual. Symbolism, energy, intention, and visualization provide the means to call on the power and influence of insects. For example, you can place a picture or figurine of an insect on your altar to draw in its energy for ritual. In fact, insects can even represent the elements: a butterfly for air, a dragonfly for water, a cricket for earth, and a lightning bug for fire.

Write a spell on a picture of an insect, and then visualize its energy boosting your willpower. Wear jewelry shaped like one to call on its particular qualities for divination sessions, astral travel, or other practices. Go outside and watch them—observation is a good way to tune in to their energy.

Garden Insects

For simplicity, I am using the term insect even though some of the creatures mentioned here are classified differently. Now, let's take a stroll through the garden and history to explore the power and meaning of these creatures. Of course, we will also discover how they can be our magical allies.

The Butterfly

We'll start with the enchanting butterfly, which has been one of the greatest symbols of transformation throughout the world. If you associate it with glitter and unicorns, think again because this delicate creature is no lightweight. Associated with the Great Goddess, it symbolized her power of regeneration. Since then it was used in many cultures to represent spirit, the souls of the dead, and more specifically, ancestors.

In Eastern Europe there was a popular belief that a butterfly was the embodiment of a witch. In fact, the Slovenian word *véšča* means both "witch" and "butterfly." In Russian, the word *baba*, which was derived from *bábočhka,* "butterfly," refers to a female ancestor. Elsewhere in Europe during the Middle Ages, witches and fairies were believed to disguise

themselves as butterflies to steal milk and butter, which may be the basis of their common name.

For Pagans and Wiccans, the butterfly can be an aid for love spells and dream work. It also helps in working with the fairy realm and contacting spirits. As a symbol of change, the butterfly provides support for renewal. It shows us how to foster confidence for finding opportunities and personal freedom. With its help, we can bring fidelity and happiness to relationships. Also, wear a piece of butterfly jewelry as a reminder of its association with witches. If one alights on you, whisper a wish to it before it flies away.

The Bee

The bee, more specifically the honeybee, is another garden visitor that has had great significance and a long relationship with humans. In Neolithic times, the Great Goddess was occasionally depicted as a combination of woman and bee. The bee's ability to produce honey echoed her power and role as provider and nurturer.

Honey was the universal sweetener in the ancient world and a preservative. In fact, in Egypt it was used in the embalming process, which may have symbolically added sweetness to the afterlife. A highly valued commodity, honey was used as an offering to deities. Across many cultures, the bee symbolizes abundance, community, and fertility.

Also closely associated with the Goddess's power of regeneration, bees represented the quickening force of life. In the temples of some deities—most notably Artemis and Demeter—priestesses were called *Melissae*, which means "bees." According to mythology, souls existed as bees until the Melissae gathered them to be born into human form.

Magically, the bee can lend us a great deal of power and support. The spiritual dimension of the bee draws us into a closer communion with the Divine. Like the ancients, we can show esteem for our chosen deity with an offering of honey. In spellwork, the energy of the bee can help attract prosperity and abundance, unify the family, and strengthen a relationship. It also aids in sparking romance. In addition, the bee can give us a boost when we need to get motivated. Finally, along with its association with the afterlife and as a symbol of the soul, the bee aids us at Samhain to communicate with loved ones who have passed from this world.

The Spider

The next garden creature is a creepy-crawly that does not fly (thanks be to the Goddess). As a gardener I have made my peace with spiders, but I could never bring myself to intentionally touch one. While the spider plays an important role in the ecosystem and is part of the army of "good bugs," it does not engender warm, cuddly feelings as does the butterfly. However, its ephemeral web is a source of endless fascination, beauty, and metaphor.

In various Native American tribes, Spider Woman or Spider Grandmother is regarded as a benevolent being who guides and provides. She is also considered a supreme creator. In Hindu myth, the spider symbolizes the goddess Maya. Representing a divine creative force, she is a goddess of illusion, wisdom, and intuition. Spinning the web of fate, she is associated with magic and witchcraft. Likewise in Europe, a number of goddesses are associated with the

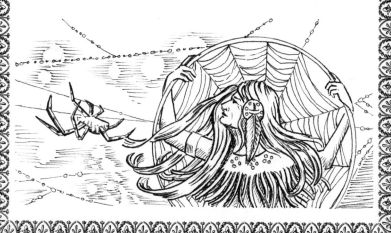

magical craft of spinning and weaving. Both the spider web and weaving symbolize magic because from seemingly nothing, something is brought into existence.

As for magic, we can visualize the energy we send out as a web of magic that weaves together our ideas and their manifested outcomes. We can call on the energy of the spider to fire up and support our creativity and to develop the skills we need to express it. The spider also helps us in creating or renewing connections and communicating with other people. It can help us recognize opportunities and have the patience to wait and work on desired goals. Known for its aggressiveness, the spider can teach us how and when to employ assertive power that is guided by wisdom.

The Dragonfly

With shimmering, metallic colors and fleeting, darting flight, it is no wonder that dragonflies have been regarded as mysterious and magical. Dragonflies are ancient creatures and one of the earliest to appear in the fossil record. Early depictions of them have been found in Egypt and other locations worldwide.

In a number of cultures, dragonflies were associated with warriors because of their speed and quick, agile maneuvers. In Romanian folklore, the origin of the dragonfly was associated with the devil and black magic. The name dragonfly is believed to have come from the Romanian word *drac*, which has the dual meaning of "devil" and "dragon." In one tale, it was referred to as the devil's horse. In Portuguese lore, the dragonfly was called a witch's horse. Likewise in Italy, dragonflies were linked with witches.

Also associated with shamans, the dragonfly itself is a shape-shifter. Most of its lifespan, which is more than a year, is spent in the realm of water in the nymph stage. When it is ready, the nymph emerges from the water at night under the protection of darkness to begin its transformation to the realm of air.

When you see a dragonfly cruising through your backyard, take time to watch it. Let its movement and energy mesmerize and enchant you. Afterward, take time to ground and center your energy and jot down a few notes about what you felt or thought. Magically, call on the dragonfly for support in dream work, especially to interpret its meaning or message. The dragonfly is also helpful in meditation when seeking introspection, clarity, and truth. Of course, it is instrumental to both initiate and deal with change. Carry a picture of one when you need to bolster courage.

The Firefly

Another amazing winged creature in the garden is the firefly, which is also known as a lightning bug. Its twinkling bioluminescence can turn any backyard into a magical display of lights. Like many people, I have fond childhood memories of catching and releasing them.

In Maya legend, fireflies served as a metaphor for the stars, while Aztec myth portrayed them as fire-throwing witches. According to Apache folklore, the original source of fire was a mythical campfire started by fireflies. Quite naturally, the firefly can aid us anytime we seek illumination and inspiration. Representing hope, it can also help when we need guidance. For spellwork, include the firefly when you need to remove negativity or any metaphorical darkness in your life. As an activator, this bug adds power to spells. We can also call on it to get our own energy moving to help us achieve our goals. In addition, the firefly can give our creative expression a big boost.

The Moth

Sharing many of the butterfly's associations, especially with that of the soul, the moth is mostly nocturnal and very elusive. In Europe, moths were regarded as restless souls longing to return to the earthly plane. A moth attracted to a candle flame is a symbol of the soul seeking truth as well as transcendence. The moth is also regarded as a symbol of knowledge.

In addition to being considered an oracle, the moth was often regarded as a witch. In fact, there are two species with the common names of white witch moth and black witch moth. The black one is also known as the butterfly of death even though it is not harmful. Both white and black moths were believed to be the spirits of ancestors. Another species is called the death's head moth because its markings resemble a skull and crossbones. In European folklore, this moth was also called the death bird and was regarded as an omen of death and a symbol of immortality.

Associated with the Moon, the moth is the perfect symbol for an esbat altar and lunar magic. Employ its energy in spellwork, especially for defense. The moth can also help in understanding omens and messages received through divination. Because of the perfect symmetry in its patterns and shape, the moth represents balance and can help bring our energy into balance. Associated with transformation, the moth can be called upon to usher in changes that you want to make in your life.

The Cricket

Another nighttime creature to look for is the cricket. Actually, it is more appropriate to listen for it. Held in high esteem in antiquity, the cricket was an emblem of happiness and good luck. In China, crickets were often kept in ornate cages for their pleasing chirping sounds and to bring luck to the household. The Greeks and Romans also kept caged crickets in the home.

Throughout the folklore of various countries, the cricket could bring good or bad luck. Also, its presence in the house could forecast rain, death, or the return—for better or worse—of a lover. However, imitating the chirp of a cricket was considered dangerous, as it could bring negative consequences. In England and America, the cricket was

regarded as the personification of the house spirit. Similarly in Ireland, they were regarded as old, wise house sprites whose enchanted singing could keep away mischievous fairies at night.

As a symbol of cheerfulness, we can use this creature in spells to invite happiness, luck, and security to our homes. The cricket can also help us develop and learn to trust our intuition. It is especially helpful for guidance in knowing when to bring situations or relationships to an end and find renewal. The cricket is also instrumental in sharpening communication skills. Hold a picture of one while you sit outside and listen to their chorus. Visualize the picture absorbing the sound and energy of the crickets, and then use it to boost the energy of a spell or ritual.

The Ladybug

Last but not least is everyone's favorite, the ladybug. Regarded as having a supernatural origin, almost all folklore about the ladybug associates its presence with good luck and killing it with bad luck. In addition, it was considered especially lucky if one landed on you.

In German lore, the ladybug had a role similar to the stork in delivering babies. Italian legend regarded it as a sort of tooth fairy leaving coins for children. Known as the ladybird in the British Isles, during the Victorian era it became associated with romance. Perhaps because its red spotted pattern somewhat resembles the fly agaric mushroom, Finnish folklore portrayed the ladybug as a helper and guide for shamans.

For modern spellwork, invite the energy of the ladybug to help attract luck, happiness, and romance. Also call on it for support in reaching goals. If you find one in your home, thank it for the blessing it brings. For shamanic or astral work, ask the ladybug for guidance and help in interpreting any messages you receive. Also, carry or wear a ladybug image as you traverse the realms.

~

By learning all we can about the natural world—including mundane garden creatures—we join the ranks of the wise folk who have gone before us. Like many things in nature, when we invest a little time to learn more than a few cursory details, a whole new world of magic and meaning can open to us. You can start by finding out about the species of insects in your area. Their characteristics and behavior may reveal ways in which they can support and contribute to your magical practices.

If you have a garden or just a few flowerpots on a porch, grow at least a couple of native species of plants to support the pollinators and other "good bugs." Observe the ones that you attract because they may bring special messages for you.

Resources

Alcock, Joan Pilsbury. *Food in the Ancient World.* Westport, CT: Greenwood Press, 2006.

Bronfen, Elisabeth. *Over Her Dead Body.* Manchester, England: Manchester University Press, 1992.

Datlow, Ellen, and Terri Windling, eds. *The Beastly Bride.* New York: Viking, 2010.

Davies, Hazel, and Carol A. Butler. *Do Butterflies Bite?* New Brunswick, NJ: Rutgers University Press, 2008.

Kritsky, Gene, and Ron Cherry. *Insect Mythology.* Lincoln, NE: iUniverse.com, Inc., 2000.

Mitchell, Forrest L., and James L. Lasswell. *A Dazzle of Dragonflies.* College Station, TX: Texas A&M University Press, 2005.

Oliver, Harry. *Black Cats & Four-Leaf Clovers.* New York: Perigree Books, 2010.

Roud, Steve. *The Penguin Guide to the Superstitions of Britain and Ireland.* London: Penguin Books, 2006.

Schlaepfer, Gloria G. *Butterflies.* Tarrytown, NY: Marshall Cavendish Benchmark, 2006.

Stankiewicz, Edward. *The Slavic Languages.* Berlin, Germany: Mouton de Gruyter, 1986.

Werness, Hope B. *The Continuum Encyclopedia of Animal Symbolism in Art.* New York: Continuum International Publishing Group, 2006.

Earth Beat

by Monica Crosson

Early spring is one of my favorite times of the year to be outdoors in the Pacific Northwest. I am witness as the Maiden unfurls her magick slowly, allowing us to savor each and every moment of her awakening, from the black cottonwood that parades some of the first haze of green and seduces our senses with its resinous perfume, to the first bright blossoms of trillium, flowering currant, and Indian plum that dot our fairy-tale forests. I can't help but be in love with my Pacific Northwest home, where forty species of ferns grow with wild abandon and moss covers anything that stands still.

It was on such a morning, almost twenty years ago, when I was out in the garden carefully breaking up the soil that would soon play womb to our seeds, that my son, Joshua, came up to me. "Mama," he said, "dirt makes you happy, doesn't it?"

I put my broad fork down and sat beside him in the dark loamy soil. "How can you tell?" I asked.

"Because when you're in the dirt your eyes smile." I picked up a little of the soil and rubbed a bit on his cheek. He giggled.

"Looks like dirt makes you happy, too."

Joshua playfully threw himself into my vegetable bed and pushed his arms and legs back and forth.

"Are you making a dirt angel?" I asked.

"No, Mama." He stood. "I'm making the Goddess."

"She's beautiful," I said.

"Do you wanna give her a hug, Mama?"

Though I felt a little silly, I leaned into the dirt and gave Joshua's artistic interpretation of the Goddess a hug. He was soon lying beside me. The scent of fresh earth and Joshua's own scent, a mixture of both sour and sweet, infiltrated my nose, and at once I remember feeling strangely comforted—as if all my fears, in that instant, had been lifted as I lay content within the arms of the Mother.

"Mama," Joshua whispered.

My eyes still closed, I answered, "Yes, sweetie."

"Does the Earth have a heartbeat? I think I hear it," he said.

I remember the faint buzzing of insects just around my face, the sensation of the soil beneath my cheek, the scent of new grass, and the distant drumming of a woodpecker. The vibrations of Mother Earth speaking, breathing, and moving all around us. "Yes, Joshua," I said. "Her heart beats strong and wild. A lot of people just don't take the time to stop and listen."

"I like the sound," he softly breathed. "Can we listen for just a while longer?"

"Of course, Joshua, of course."

The Element of Earth

I tend to work with the element of earth the most in my practice. For me, magick is more than elaborate ritual or a quick spell found in a book or on the Internet. It is working hands-on with the natural world. I listen for its secrets that echo through the forest. I feel its rhythm in a meandering stream and experience its bliss in the chance meeting of wild animals that we share this world with. Magick is written within the petals of a flower and rises with the scent of rain.

As the oldest form of magick, earth magick is about discovery. Finding that unity between human beings and the earth. Unearthing inner peace, learning stability and understanding the rhythms of our own bodies. Earth is solid, enduring, grounding, and serene. Use the element of earth when manifesting your ideas, for prosperity and fertility magick, for grounding, and for attuning with the natural world. Its direction is north and its season is winter. To experience earth's calming power one needs to only go outdoors. Take a walk in the park or sit under a favorite tree. Plant seeds in the garden, build a sand castle on the beach, or make mud pies with the kids.

People whose signs are Taurus, Virgo, and Capricorn were born under signs of earth. They are self-disciplined and persistent and can easily reach any goal they set up for themselves. Magickally, earth signs make excellent herbalists or Kitchen Witches. They are well attuned to their natural surroundings and may enjoy garden magick or working with rune stones or crystals and gems.

Goddesses Connected with the Element of Earth

Gaia: A Greek mother goddess and the personification of the earth itself. She stretched out, at the beginning of time, laying out the land and providing sustenance for all her people. Zeus determined the site of Delphi by locating the naval of Gaia, or as the Greeks believed, the center of the earth. Invoke Gaia in spells for abundance and the harvest, ecology and healing of the land, divination, and parenting.

Demeter: Greek goddess of the harvest and the underworld, marriage, sacred law, and the life and death cycle. She is the mother of Persephone, who was kidnapped and taken to the underworld. Demeter's mourning for her daughter causes the world to become cold and barren for six months, only to rejuvenate in the spring upon her daughter's return. Call upon Demeter to bless the land, for fertility magick, for wisdom, when dealing with legal matters, or when "birthing" a new creative endeavor.

Cel: An Etruscan earth goddess whose name means "earth" or "soil" and comes from the Etruscan root, *kel,* meaning "to grow." Also a goddess of the underworld and of fate, she was called upon when interpreting omens. Invoke Cel at Mabon to bless your meal of thanksgiving, as the Etruscan month Celi (our September) was named for her. Also call upon Cel for divination, growth, and wisdom.

Danu: The most ancient of the Celtic deities, Danu was known as the "Flowing One." An earth goddess connected with the faery hills, she is the grand creator who birthed all things and mother of the Tuatha Dé Danann. Call upon her regarding enlightenment, fertility, luck, wisdom, and inspiration.

Five Ways to Experience the Element of Earth
Barefootin'

I was a bit of a wild child growing up. My hair blew tangled about my face and my knees were perpetually scraped. Summer was my favorite time of year, not only because school was out, but because I was allowed to sleep outside and run around barefoot all of the time. Remember summers spent barefoot? How delightful was the sensation of warm sand pressing against the soles of your feet as you played at your favorite beach or the way the grass tickled as you ran through the yard on cool summer evenings? Well, it's time to reawaken that inner wild child by going barefoot once again!

The act of simply slipping off our shoes and spending a few minutes barefoot in the grass or on a sandy beach reawakens a very basic connection to earth, creating a bond with the Mother that has become lost to most of us with modernization.

Make Friends with a Tree

Do you have a favorite tree that you feel connected to? If not, go into your yard or a favorite park and get to know a tree. Maybe you are drawn to maples for their connection with love, prosperity, and longevity. Or what about the mighty oak (the classic Druid's tree), used magickally for protection, fertility, and luck? There is always the apple tree, also known as the "Silver Bough," long used in love spells and divination.

I have made a strong bond with a willow tree that gracefully watches over our property. Willow is connected to the Moon and my watery soul. She guards against evil and has allowed me use of her branches for both my wand and a besom.

Making a connection with a tree is simple. First, go into your yard or favorite park and find a tree that resonates with you. Visit the tree a few times—maybe take a book or a set of tarot cards with you, or just meditate and enjoy its calming energy. Once you've settled on the perfect tree, mentally ask the spirit of tree to be your teacher and guide.

Working with plant allies is a wonderful way to gain a deeper understanding of earth magick. Take advantage of their wisdom and transformative powers.

Beat a Drum

Many Native American tribes likened the beating of drums to the heartbeat of Mother Earth. This powerful instrument is used in ritual to raise power, to heal, to send messages to the spirit world, to aid in meditation, and for social ceremonies.

Drumming is a great way to connect with the earth's natural rhythm. The low, constant beat reverberates through your feet (remember—go barefoot) allowing one to enter a relaxed state and move one's consciousness into that inner world where our spirits are fed.

Don't worry if you don't have a traditional native hand drum, you can use an old cookie tin or oatmeal container to get yourself started. Rhythmically striking a large rock with a strong stick works, too. You may also consider joining an established drum circle or forming a new one with your circle or coven.

Plant a Garden

If you are lucky enough to have a piece of land (even a small yard or containers on a balcony), utilize that green space by growing your own herbs and flowers for spellwork and maybe a few fruits and vegetables for your family to consume. Plunging your Witchy hands into the soil is not only a great way to make that connection with the element of earth, but it reminds us of the wise women and cunning men before us who gleaned medicine and magick from their gardens.

This is also a great way to get the kids involved in the earthy fun. Infuse your garden with magickal energy by having the kids paint pots with magickal symbols, create a faery house, or make magickal mosaic stepping stones. When your garden is complete, why not dedicate it to the elves?

Bring the Element of Earth Indoors

Having a few potted plants or natural found objects in your home lends a wonderful green energy to your living space. When our children were small, our family's altar/nature table would fill up seasonally with found treasures, including hag stones, cones, leaves, driftwood, antlers, hazelnuts, and interesting rocks. Their

placement designated a quiet haven where the kids could go to reflect on nature's gifts.

If you feel you're not equipped with a green-enough thumb to conquer an outdoor garden, give indoor gardening a shot. Choose houseplants for your home whose energy you would like to project. Maybe a little protective magick is what you seek—try a nice cactus near your front door or hang potted ivy near your windows. Would you like to promote a harmonious home? Try the lovely peace lily. Want to test your skills at Kitchen Witchery? Set up a few favorite herbs in a sunny window in the kitchen. Some of my favorites include:

Basil (*Ocimum basilicum*): This member of the mint family is used heavily in Mediterranean cooking. Magickally, use basil for protection, wealth, and to encourage love.

Sweet Marjoram (*Origanum majorana*): This herb is related to oregano and makes a suitable replacement in cooking. Magickally, use marjoram in dream pillows and in spells for love, peace, health, and happiness.

Sage (*Salvia officinalis*): This woody perennial is a favorite in holiday cooking. Magickally, use sage in spells for wisdom, purification, intuition, and abundance.

Rosemary (*Rosmarinus officinalis*): One of my favorite herbs, this Mediterranean herb lends itself well to sauces and pork and lamb dishes. Use rosemary in spells for remembrance, love, mental powers, purification, and protection.

Decorate a few small pots (or one large one) with Witchy symbols, words of power, runes, etc. Use your newly decorated pots to plant your herbs using a really good potting soil and then place in a sunny window. Bless them by saying,

> *Like the wise women (cunning men) of old,*
> *I will work my spells with these gifts of the earth*
> *To give comfort, to heal, to nourish, to give mirth.*
> *Bless these herbs with the power of three*
> *As I weave an earthy magick—so mote it be!*

Gentleness and Grace: Deer Wisdom

The element of earth's wisdom and teachings can come to us in many ways. Working with the land teaches us thankfulness and responsibility for the next generation. Seasonal change teaches us to embrace change in our own lives. From trees we learn the importance of being well grounded, and from the earth's varied landscape we learn to appreciate beauty in all its forms.

Animals associated with the element of earth also have lessons to share. Bears are protective and intelligent. They remind us to be strong and courageous. Coyote is the classic trickster, teaching us adaptability, playfulness, and resourcefulness. The wolf helps us discover freedom and trust our instincts.

But it is the wisdom of the deer that I most often seek. Maybe it's because they are most commonly seen at the edge of a wilderness setting, representing a bridge between the wild and the tame (much like myself). In Celtic mythology, deer were able to move between the worlds, and hunting a stag represented the pursuit of wisdom. A stag's antlers were representative of a tree, and because they were shed and regrown every year, they were a perfect symbol of rebirth.

A deer's gentle spirit and swift, delicate movement remind us to have grace under fire. Their innocent nature teaches us to find that lost childlike quality within ourselves and to use that ability to look at things from another perspective. The deer spirit can also be used to help develop your intuition and refine psychic abilities. Magickally, the deer spirit can be used in spells for renewal, life's mysteries, grace, intuition, and peace.

Animal Spirit Meditation Beads

An animal spirit guide is much more than just an animal whose qualities we admire. It is the embodiment of our subconscious mind and a guide to help us acknowledge those aspects of our lives that need to be transformed, inspired, or comforted.

There are several ways to cultivate a connection with an animal spirit, including observing nature and keeping track of repetitive sightings of a specific animal, shamanic journeying, dream work, and meditation. Animal spirit meditation beads can work as an aid in focusing your intention on a specific animal spirit while in a meditative state.

You will need:

13 beads to represent the lunar months (use turquoise, peridot, hematite, or another earthy stone)
3 beads representing the triple Goddess
Spacer beads of your choice (wood is nice)
A charm representing whatever animal spirit you connect with
Beading string

Lay out your beads in a way that is pleasing to you. String them onto your beading string and knot it securely at both ends.

Strong and Wild

That scruffy little blond-haired boy who taught me to really take the time to hear the heartbeat of the earth is now all grown up. Between college classes, his job, and social activities, I don't spend near as much time with him anymore. But just a few months ago, in the quiet of the evening, when the wind had stilled and the bullfrogs had hushed their throaty song, I watched him sitting on the side porch, alone, his head tilted.

"What are you doing?" I finally asked.

He held up his index finger to silence me, waited a moment, and smiled. "I know you can hear it, Mom," he spoke low.

I listened. I could hear the movement of a toad searching for grubs beneath a daylily, the restless movements of swallows in a birdhouse near the window, and the creak of branches deep within the surrounding forests. "Her heart beats on," I said. "Strong and wild. Can I hang out here with you awhile and listen?"

He smiled. "Of course, Mom, of course."

Resources

McKosato, Harlan. "Drum: Heartbeat of Mother Earth." *Native Peoples Magazine*, July/August 2009. Accessed on October 5, 2016. http://www.nativepeoples.com/Native-Peoples/July -August-2009/Drums-Heartbeat-of-Mother-Earth/.

Took, Thalia. "Cels." The Obscure Goddess Online Directory. ThaliaTook.com. Accessed on October 5, 2016. http:// www.thaliatook.com/OGOD/cels.html.

The Well-Stocked
Magical Cupboard
by Ember Grant

The idea of a Witch's cupboard is the subject of many imaginative and artistic representations—old wooden shelves overflowing with ancient, dusty books and ornate bottles with peeling labels, adorned with spider webs and accented by skulls, bubbling cauldrons, strange objects floating in liquid, eye of newt, wing of bat, and so on—hardly (usually) what our real cupboards look like. It's right out of the Halloween apothecary decor aisle at your local department store. Of course, if that's the look you want, go for it.

I love finding old, decorative bottles for storage and making my own labels. But perhaps we should avoid the dust and cobwebs and keep our cupboards clean (and somewhat organized). When it comes to the real practice of our Craft, we need practical storage and a ready supply of ingredients for our spells.

Planning Your Cupboard

When creating your own magical cupboard, there are some organizational strategies to keep in mind. If your magical items and spell ingredients are scattered or disorganized, your magic may become that way as well. Even if you already have a well-stocked cupboard, maintenance is always essential. You may even need to keep a formal inventory if you have a large storage space. Whatever your situation, here are some guidelines to assist you in planning and stocking your cupboard.

First, consider if your magical cupboard will simply store herbs and spices or contain all your magical items, such as tools, candles, etc. Of course, the space you have allotted and the size of your cupboard may determine this. And speaking of that, what will you use as a cupboard? Do you already have an empty cabinet? Do you need to buy one or can you repurpose something you already own? Size and space will naturally dictate how and what you store. Some people are lucky enough to devote an entire room of their home or an entire basement or attic to their Craft; others must be content with the corner of a room or a closet.

Personally, I keep nearly everything I need in one large cabinet—an old entertainment center that has a closed storage space in the bottom, an open area for books in the middle (I just keep handy reference guides here), and a space with glass doors on top to hold my jars and bottles. I still need a separate space for all my candles and holders (of which I have an excessive quantity, since I make candles), but this unit works well for everything else. It even has a lighted shelf that serves as a mini altar. In addition, I do keep a small storage ottoman for objects that I only use a few times a year. Furniture with built-in storage is great for small spaces. Look for storage benches and coffee tables that also keep your supplies hidden from view.

If you prefer a cabinet with doors, you can use a free-standing pantry, china hutch, or armoire—check resale shops. Otherwise, a simple bookcase may do the trick. Other options include chests, trunks, and stackable storage containers and shelves that hold baskets. You need to be comfortable with your choice and its location in your home. Equally important, it should be convenient and not be a hassle every time you need to use it.

Now that you have a cabinet, what do you put in it? Let's start with herbs and spices. I keep my magical ingredients separate from the ones I cook with. This just makes things easier. It's also more convenient and safe. I know that anything in my kitchen is safe to eat, and if I'm doing kitchen magic, I keep those herbs there. Things in the magical cabinet may even be poisonous (for example, my dried foxglove flowers).

Next, consider containers. Again, you can repurpose. And if you're not going to mix your edibles and nonedibles, the type of container won't matter (some containers are not suitable for food storage). You can use old jars from candles, spices, jams, etc. Glass is typically the best choice. If you use clear glass, be sure to keep your items stored out of direct sunlight. This will help extend the life of your herbs. And be sure to dry fresh herbs completely before storage. You can also dry slices of fruit, like oranges, lemons, and apples. Don't forget to clearly label everything. If you have lots of jars, organize them on a spice rack.

Speaking of storage, how long should you keep your ingredients? That depends. Unlike cooking herbs, it's probably okay if you keep these a bit longer. However, I recommend replacing them after a year or so. There are some exceptions. For example, I grow many herbs in my garden, and so I replace my stock each year. But some items, like dried rose petals and thorns, I keep indefinitely. Salt will keep a long time as well, and so will items like acorns and leaves. Still, it's a good idea to examine all your supplies regularly just to make sure something hasn't spoiled.

Herbs and Spices

If you're feeling overwhelmed by all the options—like the thousands of plants listed in herbal encyclopedias—start small with basic culinary herbs and spices. These are easy to obtain or grow, and they're inexpensive. I've included some suggestions here, but undoubtedly others will come to mind that you consider essential. This is a basic start-up list that covers a wide range of uses. Add as many more as you wish to your cupboard. For more information on the metaphysical properties of plants, I recommend *Cunningham's Encyclopedia of Magical Herbs.*

Herbs

Try basil (love, prosperity, and exorcism), bay leaves (protection, purification, psychic powers, healing, and strength), catnip (beauty, love, happiness, and cat magic), chili pepper (love, fidelity, and breaking hexes), clover (protection, wealth, success, love, fidelity, and exorcism), daisy (love and lust), dandelion (divination, summoning spirits, and wish fulfillment), dill (protection, money, and passion), lavender (love, chastity, protection, sleep, longevity, and happiness), peppermint (purification, love, sleep, healing, and psychic powers), rosemary (protection, passion, intelligence, exorcism, healing, sleep, and youthfulness), sage (longevity, wisdom, protection, and wish fulfillment), and thyme (healing, sleep, psychic powers, purification, love, and courage).

Spices

I recommend cinnamon (success, spirituality, healing, psychic powers, passion, and protection), cloves (protection, love, exorcism, and wealth), ginger (love, power, success, and money), and, of course, salt.

Flowers, Foliage Plants, and Trees

Most Witches enjoy working with plants and flowers in magic and ritual, and many tend their own gardens. Again, this depends on your personal space. I do recommend always having roses on hand, even if you simply buy some long-stemmed roses from a shop and dry them. Save the petals, leaves, and stems with thorns. In addition, if you can, try to grow plants native to your specific location. Trees, too, will depend on where you live and what's available to you. Of course, many supplies can be purchased online. These lists, again, cover popular plants that are relatively easy to find or grow.

Flowers and Foliage Plants

Stock foxglove (protection; *foxglove is poisonous*, so snapdragons are a good nontoxic alternative), geranium (fertility, love, health, and protection), holly (protection, luck, and dream magic), ivy (healing and protection), lilac (exorcism and protection), marigold (protection, legal matters, psychic powers, and dream magic), rose (psychic powers, love and love divination, protection, healing, and good fortune), violet (wish fulfillment, good fortune, healing, love/passion, and protection), wormwood (psychic powers, protection, love, and summoning spirits; *wormwood is poisonous*), and yarrow (love, courage, psychic powers, and exorcism).

Trees

Try cedar (purification, money, healing, and protection), elder (exorcism, protection, healing, prosperity, and sleep), hickory (legal matters), maple (love, longevity, and wealth), oak (protection, money, health, luck, and fertility), pine (protection, exorcism, healing, money, and fertility), and walnut (health, mental powers, wishes, and infertility).

Miscellaneous

Depending on where you live, always keep your eyes open for "collectibles." These are things you find in your yard or in public areas. When collecting, be sure to get permission first, if necessary. Items to look for include feathers, shells, nuts, seeds, leaves, pine cones, stones, acorns, and even broken egg shells from birds' nests—these are wonderful for fertility and spring rituals. These gifts from nature should always be found naturally and never taken from a protected area or a living creature. The only exception would be taking a small plant cutting; be sure to thank the plant.

What else should you store in your cabinet? Random things you find interesting, even if you're not sure when or how (or why) you would use them, and special items you find in metaphysical shops or festivals. It's also good to have items related to the elements: feathers to represent air, for example, and nuts and seeds for earth. If you like to practice cat magic, save naturally shed cat claws or whiskers. And speaking of naturally shed animal items, look for snake skins, antlers, and so on. If you purchase something, always try to be knowledgeable about how the item was obtained. Be prepared for all situations and seasonal celebrations or rituals. Keep your tools and altar cloths handy as well, along with your book of shadows and other reference materials.

Here's a list of other items in my magical cupboard: essential oils, incense (dried woods and resins, sage wand), fossilized mammoth tusks (purchased at a gift shop in Seattle), graveyard dirt (respectfully collected by someone I know), spring water (collected locally myself), fossils (part of my stone and crystal collection), mini-cauldrons, assorted statues, mortar and pestle, tarot cards, and all my ritual tools. I also save scraps of leather and ribbons and pieces of fabric for making bundles. Of course, I keep my collection of crystals and stones nearby—this is another topic entirely.

~

You can certainly have that mystical cabinet with the ornate and mysterious bottles if you desire. Your magical cupboard should reflect your personality. Whether you keep it secret, keep it purely functional, or want it to be the classic Witch's apothecary, make it special, make it beautiful—make it magical. Ultimately, the contents, and how you use them, are what matters most.

The Five Celestial Animals of Feng Shui

by Mireille Blacke

According to *Dragon: The Bruce Lee Story*, when the legendary martial artist was still a child in Hong Kong, his father placed three *bagua* mirrors nearby to keep him safe from harm. Octagonal bagua mirrors are used in feng shui (Chinese geomancy) to protect and repel negativity. Years later, Lee placed three baguas near his newborn son, Brandon, for the same reason. As *Dragon* unfolds, we watch as male generations of the Lee family are terrorized by an armored samurai in dream sequences. During a massive rainstorm, Lee is ultimately victorious as he kills this relentless foe to defend young Brandon. Shortly after, in July of 1973, Bruce Lee dies at the age of thirty-two while filming *Game of Death*. Viewers learn that a typhoon dislodged a protective bagua from its long-term location at Lee's ancestral home.

In 1993, two months before *Dragon*'s release and twenty years after Bruce Lee's death, the life of twenty-eight-year-old Brandon Lee ended due to the negligent handling of a squib-loaded prop gun while filming *The Crow*, a gothic thriller set in perpetual rain. It was difficult to bury this fact while watching prescient dream sequences of the elder Lee desperately trying to protect his only son from a seemingly unstoppable killing force in *Dragon*. Could a misplaced mirror really contribute to the demise of a family's legacy? Despite attributing these deaths to logical explanations, bad luck, or simple human error, the memory of those eight-sided mirrors never left me, and my interest in feng shui was born.

As the years passed, I found some overlap in my own practice of Wicca and the principles of feng shui. As feng shui is the Chinese practice of living in harmony with one's environment, it is practical and useful in creating a peaceful setting for meditation, ritual work, and spiritual growth, regardless of your belief system. One method to do this involves the five Celestial Animals of feng shui.

Celestial Animal Basics

In Chinese geomancy, the shape and contours of the landscape are analyzed. Practitioners of the Form school of feng shui observed that certain natural locations were more lush and preferred by animals to build homes or nests. In these areas, practitioners felt a harmony of energy (chi), and attributed this to balanced and appropriate amounts of sun and shade, warmth and cold, wind and water, yin and yang. Characteristics of these areas included typically a higher hill and a glade with two lower sides, fronted by an opening through which a distant view was visible. The shape of the landscape resembled certain animals, in physical form as well as function. From this observation, the theory of five Celestial Animals was created.

When creating sacred space, avoid negative chi by implementing feng shui remedies to block or redirect it. "Poison arrows" of negative chi include sharp or jutting edges of the furniture or room. Common remedies include mirrors, aquariums, fountains, plants, wind chimes, crystals, and statues.[1] When creating sacred or ritual space within the home, such remedies can transform negative or blocked chi to foster a peaceful spiritual retreat.

Black Turtle

Associated Direction: North
Element: Water
Season: Winter
Color: Black
Energy: Yin
Meaning: Stability, security

In terms of the Celestial Animal hierarchy, the Black Turtle holds the greatest influence and is considered the most important. The turtle represents protection, security, and stability, and it brings a solid foundation to the home environment. Turtles are long-lived animals, and their armor seems indestructible. When a turtle retracts into its shell, it is calm, safe, and protected. Consider the turtle's outer shell to be a shield that "has your back," in a sense. Appropriately, the turtle corresponds to the back of or area behind the home and is aligned with the color black and the direction of north. If your natural landscape is missing Black Turtle energies behind your home, incorporate tall trees, arbor vitae, or fencing as substitutions.

Consider the Black Turtle first when using feng shui to create sacred space in the home, to fortify its protection and security. To avoid the turmoil which may result from unknown, uncontrolled situations existing "behind our backs," implement turtle-like protection by making your back less vulnerable. Choose a seat with your back to a wall. Within the desired room, enhance the Black Turtle's important protective position by using a wall, shelf, plant holder, or chairs with high backs. A fountain, certain flowers (lavender, daffodil, tulip, iris), artwork, figurines, or even an aquarium with live turtles near the wall opposite the room's main entrance are recommended.

Green Dragon

Associated Direction: East
Element: Wood
Season: Spring
Color: Green
Energy: Yang
Meaning: Wisdom, strength, spirituality

The dragon is common in Chinese art and celebratory customs. In the context of the five Celestial Animals, it symbolizes the flow of chi and protection on the east side. From the perspective of inside the home, with the Black Turtle behind us (to the north), the Dragon will reside to the left side of the turtle. The adjective "green" links the Dragon to aspects of the direction of east—strength, wisdom, and growth.

The ideal Green Dragon site will be slightly lower than the plateau of the turtle's hill in a natural landscape. The Green Dragon is generally situated on the left of the house in the form of a rolling hill, porch, green tree, or any structure that wraps or curls. Substitute for the Dragon with objects at least as tall as the house (tall, green trees, an adjacent building, a high fence).

When creating sacred space, Green Dragon energy protects the left side of the room (as a long wall, curved closet, tall plant, or shelf) and promotes wisdom and personal growth. Artwork or figurines depicting dragons may also help invoke its energy, as would an arrangement of marigold, hyacinth, or wolfsbane. A decorative wine bottle holder in the form of a dragon works for me.

White Tiger

Associated Direction: West
Element: Metal
Season: Autumn
Color: White
Energy: Yin
Meaning: Natural strength, force

Tigers are powerful, majestic, alert, and ready to quickly respond. In feng shui, the tiger represents force and daring. This Celestial

Animal appears opposite the Green Dragon and is associated with the color white.

The White Tiger resides in the west, which is often associated with intuition, diplomacy, and feminine wisdom; the west is linked with the use of magic versus the rationality or logic from the east. From the vantage point of the home, with the Black Turtle behind us, the White Tiger paces to our right.

The White Tiger partners with the Green Dragon, on the right and left sides respectively, in a balanced relationship between emotion and logic. Thoughtful, controlled reflection (associated with the Green Dragon) often dominates instinctive, visceral decisions based on force and impulse, which are the domain of the White Tiger. Therefore, the White Tiger's protective stance (and yin properties related to energies involving the dead) is linked to hills or substituted slopes that are lower than the Green Dragon's

territory (yang energies involving the homes of the living). The hill of the White Tiger may be substituted by trees, a shed (lower in height than the house), a white stone façade, or a see-through fence.

. In the setting of sacred space, the White Tiger balances impulses with natural strength and allows connection with our departed ancestors. Symbolize the White Tiger with a piece of furniture shorter in height than that of the Green Dragon. Substitute peonies, asters, wisteria, wind chimes, bronze statues (reflecting the metal element), or small and long but flat objects (e.g., white stones) to enhance the area of the White Tiger.

Red Phoenix

Associated Direction: South
Element: Fire
Season: Summer
Color: Red
Energy: Yang
Meaning: Vision, introspection

The Phoenix is a mythological bird associated with resurrection and rebirth, corresponding to the view from the front of the house and the direction of south. As such, a symbol of this Celestial Animal should be placed on the opposite side of the Black Turtle: at the front door, front part of the house, or doorway of a room. The Phoenix embodies the color red, a revitalizing color of good fortune, happiness, and prosperity.[1] In contrast to the immobility and protection characteristic of the Black Turtle, the Red Phoenix needs an open space to receive energy. A home or building with its front entrance facing a brick wall, mountain, or similar structure blocks Phoenix energy and interferes with the full reception of chi. Trees should ideally not block your front entrance and a desk should not face a wall.

After the Black Turtle, the placement of the Red Phoenix is the most important for the home's harmony. The bird soars high, allowing us to see far and wide. A clear view in front of us is desired, without obstructions. If your view is obstructed (e.g., facing a wall), improvise with a panoramic picture of a sunrise or a mirror, which reflects the space. Neutralize negative chi in a room by adding sunflowers, tiger lilies, lamps, or wind chimes,

symbolizing the Red Phoenix. An entirely open front entrance is not advised, as the Red Phoenix must attract the flow of chi from the sun, roads, or water sources in a controllable way.

Within the setting of sacred space, a sense of protection and peace of mind prompts greater clarity to make informed decisions. The Form school of feng shui links the Red Phoenix with predicting the future; a greater understanding of our options from an open vantage point may help us access "veiled information" needed to reach our goals.

Yellow Snake
Associated Direction: Center, oneself
Element: Earth
Season: (None)
Color: Yellow
Energy: Receptive
Meaning: Knowledge, stability, calm

The snake corresponds to the center space, surrounded and protected by the four other Celestial Animals but also in control of them. The snake is associated with the color yellow and the element of earth to ground the central position. The Yellow Snake is extremely receptive and sensible, remaining alert and perceptive in its surroundings. Its location in space depicts the point where all energies meet and a view from which the space is best seen. The position of the Yellow Snake reflects us: it is our own vantage point.

In a room designated for ritual work or sacred space, keep the center as clear as possible. To symbolize the Yellow Snake, place a meditation figure (e.g., Kwan Yin), a crystal, a globe, sage, geranium, lilac, or flowerpots of clay or ceramic as a centralized point of focus.

The Animals at Work

Ideally, creating sacred or ritual space in the home should involve all five Celestial Animals. In the Celestial Animal hierarchy, the Black Turtle is most important, followed by the Red Phoenix. If you adapt your home or room in just these two areas, great improvement to the flow of chi may be expected.

The Black Turtle energy is maintained with high headrests and armrests of chairs and high headboards of beds. Avoid situations where your back points to a doorway, hallway, or window, as this is not the ideal pathway for the flow of chi. The Red Phoenix should remain in front of the Yellow Snake, similar to a coffee table or red footstool in front of a couch. Artwork of an open air scene near your front door can enhance the energy of the Red Phoenix (though pink flamingoes on the front lawn may be pushing it). When seated at a table or in general, it is preferable to see the home's front door or the main entrance to each room, where those entering the room are most visible.

Encourage the protection of Dragon and Tiger on each side of the Yellow Snake with a solid sofa or a comfortable armchair. Arrange the Celestial Animals in a horseshoe-shaped configuration to enhance the flow of chi in a particular room. When you are seated, protect your right side to shoulder height, to increase feelings of control in most situations.

Incorporate elegant depictions of the White Tiger with artwork or suitable feline figurines according to your belief system (e.g., the Egyptian goddess Bastet). Maintain the alert and grounding properties of the Yellow Snake in the center of a room, with a corresponding figurine, a framed image, or perhaps a yellow-based centerpiece with similar features (coils, twists, braiding, etc.).

Balance between the five Celestial Animals is critical. When the energy of one Animal is lacking or excessive, it can negatively impact the energy of the others. As so aptly depicted in *Dragon: The Bruce Lee Story*, Turtle's excessive watery influence crippled the mighty martial artist known as Dragon.

Feng Shui Remedies in Sacred Space

According to feng shui, the bagua mirror is commonly used to create harmony and good fortune, and also to reflect or transform negative chi when establishing ritual or sacred space. An eight-sided bagua mirror reveals a central point surrounded by eight trigrams, each corresponding to a different life area. Hang a bagua mirror on the wall of a home or room above furniture or a doorway to enhance a particular life area or to harmonize a room. Place its mirrored side facing the negative source to reflect or transform negative chi ("poison arrows"). Ideal placement is near the room's center, but a side wall will also work. To purify and energize an object, place it on top of a flat bagua.

When creating ritual or sacred space, the room's center (domain of the Yellow Snake) should be free from clutter to permit optimal flow of chi.[2] Clean and dust the area weekly, discard dead or wilted flowers (stagnant chi), and replace blown light-bulbs quickly. This will benefit guests or visitors, including discarnate or spirit energies you intend to welcome into your ritual space.

A bagua mirror, chime, or crystal may be placed in any sector when necessary, along with symbols of the Celestial Animals. If forced to sit with your back to the room's entrance, place a bagua mirror on the wall facing you so that the energy of others entering is "caught" by the mirror. Add a representation of the Black Turtle if a piece of furniture lacks adequate back support for those who sit there, and symbolically add protection for the right and left sides (e.g., chair arms). When creating sacred or ritual space in a bedroom, move each bed's headboard against a wall, but not in front of a window or doorway. If possible, raise the sides of each bed to enhance the Dragon and Tiger energies.

In creating sacred space or simply a peaceful environment, the Celestial Animals of feng shui promote balance, increase harmony, and reduce chaos. Choose animal representations that resonate with you. Adding a few bagua mirrors or other feng shui remedies probably wouldn't hurt either, depending on the forecast. After all, variable weather patterns reflect the chaos, challenges, and changes of life.

Just remember: it can't rain all the time.

Notes

1. Richard Webster, *Feng Shui for Beginners: Successful Living by Design,* (St. Paul, MN: Llewellyn Publications, 1997).
2. Karen Rauch Carter, *Move Your Stuff: Change Your Life.* (New York: Simon & Schuster, 2000).

Powwows and Why You Should Attend Them

by Najah Lightfoot

A proud Native American man brushes past you. You try not to stare, but your mind is having a hard time placing the beauty and majesty of his clothing. Your gaze lingers over the bright plumes adorning his head. His legs are wrapped in deer hide. You hear the sound of many bells ringing as he walks by.

From the corner of your eye you spy a young Native American girl. She is dressed in the colors of her tribe. She is wearing a jingle dress—a dress made with layered tin cones that sound like chimes when she dances. Another girl wears a brightly colored shawl with fringes that almost touch the ground.

You wind your way through the crowd into the arena. The announcer is calling for all the dancers to get ready for the next contest. The next drum group gets ready. They beat the drum so deeply that your heartbeat matches its rhythm.

Not ready to settle down, you return to the vendors, to shop for sage and sweetgrass, precious works of arts, and magical flutes. Along the way, you decide to get in the line for fry bread or Indian tacos. Where are you? You have entered the world of the Native American powwow, a gathering of tribes from across North America. A meeting place filled with Native American women, men, and children, as well as non-Native people who come to partake in the festivities.

If you've ever lit a sage bundle or used white sage for cleansing and purification (known as smudging), then at least once in your life you should attend a powwow. Go as an homage to the peoples whose traditions have been mainstreamed into spiritual culture with little regard or respect for their time-honored practices.

While most of us practice traditions and rituals that stem from European ancestry, here in North America, we live, move, and breathe on soil that was first settled, honored, and revered by Native American people. Smudging is usually one of the first practices we learn as magickal people. Some of us may have attended a sweat lodge ceremony. By attending a powwow you come face to face with the people and the culture from which those practices are derived.

Ancient Ancestors

In the spring of 2016 I was blessed to journey to Mesa Verde National Park. For years my husband and I had wanted to make this trip. A journey to Mesa Verde is a pilgrimage within itself. Mesa Verde is the land of cliff dwellings. It is the home of the ancient Anasazi people, who are more accurately known as the Ancestral Pueblo people. Mesa Verde is located forty-five minutes west of Durango, Colorado. The city of Durango sits in the southwest corner of Colorado, about an eight-hour drive from the bustling metropolis of Denver. Once you make the entrance to Mesa Verde National Park, you must then drive approximately one hour up steep, windy roads to get to the cliff dwellings of the Ancestral Pueblo people.

After you arrive at the parking lot, a steep and treacherous path awaits your footsteps. But it is truly worth the journey.

When your eyes land on the homes of these ancient people, your spirit senses the reverence these ancient ancestors had for nature. Circles are incorporated into their dwellings or ceremonial rooms, known as *kivas*. Petroglyphs of spirals and mysterious symbols mark cliff dwelling walls.

The Ancestral Pueblo people inhabited Mesa Verde from 550 CE to 1300 CE. No one knows exactly what happened to them or why they left their homes after centuries of habitation. But we do know their descendants are the Native people who migrated to Arizona and New Mexico and also remained in the southern part of Colorado.

Attending a Powwow

Denver, Colorado, hosts one of the largest powwows in the nation. The Denver March Powwow is held around the time of the spring equinox at the Denver Coliseum.

I try never to miss a Denver March Powwow. As the light returns to the Northern Hemisphere and fresh green plants begin to emerge from the ground, I know powwow time is right around the corner.

My soul surges and my spirit soars as I sit in the arena and watch the colorful dancers. As they spin and dance to the beat of the drum, I sometimes find tears sliding down my cheeks. I cry because I know Mother Earth smiles as her children remember her with dance and song. The flurry of colors and the spinning of dancers reminds me of the Pagan song "She's Been Waiting" by Paula Walowitz.

For those of us who drum, you cannot beat the power of the drum at a powwow. Groups of ten or more people are gathered around a single enormous drum. They beat the drums and sing for the contests and the dancers. The arena is lined with so many drums, you can hardly walk around the perimeter. Many people stand at the edge of the drum circle, while the drummers drum and the singers sing, to feel the rhythm and the heartbeat.

As you watch the dancers compete in the highest levels of competition, you too may feel called to join in the dance. And while the competitions are reserved for tribal members, several times throughout the powwow, the announcer will call for the "intertribal." This is where non-Native American people can join with the dancers in full regalia on the floor and dance to the drum. Dancing the intertribal is an ecstatic experience! You may find yourself going around the floor, trying to mimic the steps as young and old alike step to the sound of the drum. Once you've danced the intertribal, you will always want to return to the Powwow.

Powwows are held in Canada and North America. The website www.powwows.com is a great resource for finding powwows in your area. Albuquerque, New Mexico, hosts the Gathering of Nations Powwow, the largest powwow in North America.

Here is a short list of Powwows held in North America:

Denver March Powwow—Denver, CO
Gathering of Nations Powwow—Albuquerque, NM
Cherokees of Alabama Spring Indian Powwow—Arab, AL
Choctaw-Apache Tribe of Ebarb Annual Powwow—Noble, LA
Monacan Indian Nation Powwow—Elon, VA

Rules of Etiquette

- The clothing is called regalia. It is insulting to refer the clothing as a costume.
- Don't stare. You will see jaw-dropping beauty, but do your best not to stare.
- Ask politely if you may take a picture. Some people may be okay with having their pictures taken; others may not.
- Follow the cues from the announcer. They are instrumental in conducting the flow of the powwow, and you just may learn a thing or two.
- While lots of vendors come to the powwow, try to buy your items from Native American vendors. This is a good way to pay respect for your sage, sweetgrass, and trinkets. Plus your dollars will go a long way in helping tribes and families.
- In addition to the dancers, Native Americans hold an enormous place of honor for veterans and members of military. While their numbers may be small in terms of demographic data, Native Americans have the highest number of enlisted men and women for their population in the United States. Show respect and stand during the Grand Entry, while the men and women who have served their country enter the arena.
- There are also many booths that deal with current issues specific to Native American people. You can buy tapes and CDs of drum music, donate to a cause, and purchase T-shirts with Native American sayings.
- Finally, have fun! Wander around and meet some new people. Take time to speak with the vendors and offer a handshake. Find the one item you've been searching for but didn't know you needed.

If you can't make it to a powwow this year, put it on your calendar for next year. Hold it in your mind that someday, somehow, you will make it to a North American powwow.

The living hoop of the powwow allows us to touch ancient beliefs and practices similar to our own. It is good to honor the people from whom we use so many things, to keep and honor the Old Ways.

Magic without Candles

by Michael Furie

Pick up almost any book on magic or read just about any article or web page on the subject of spells, and you are very likely to run across the instruction to light candles. Most formal spellwork involves the use of candles or fire in some form. It is a powerful means of changing the atmosphere and releasing energy, but what if you cannot (or choose not to) strike a magical flame for your working? What do you do as an alternative to using candles if it is during the heat of summer or your smoke alarm is too sensitive or you're just out of candles?

The four physical elements of magic (air, water, earth, and fire) each have their own qualities and mechanisms of action, but all are capable of transmitting energy and intention. Though fire is expansive and light-emitting, thus transferring its message at a fast pace, the smoke of incense can be just as effective. Incense has been used since ancient times to carry our prayers and intents to the gods, and while this may not be the focus of every form of magic, this principle can still be applied. If the incense, whether raw, homemade, or store bought, is infused with the energy of your specific magical intention and then lit to smolder and release the smoke and the magic directed toward your goal, this can be as effective as any candle working. The power of fire is still being utilized in this scenario, as it is the catalyst for the incense smoke. If your desire is to move away from the fiery element altogether, effective magic can still be worked through the other elemental forces, such as harnessing the power of water.

Water

Witches cooking up a brew in a cauldron situated over a fire is a classic magical image and, while a bit of a stereotype, is still a legitimate practice. Infusing the essences of perfectly aligned herbs into pure water and combining this mixture with your intention can be a great way to unleash magic toward your goals. The resulting brew can be poured out onto the land or in a moving body of water to send its power out to manifest the magic. Brews, blessed pure water, and salt water can all be used as anointing liquids as well. Dabbing a bit of the liquid on the person or object to be affected can transfer the magic directly to them through the power of the water element. Anointing a symbolic object that is then used as a talisman can be an effective means of manifesting something physical without using formalized ritual. The power of water in all its forms is one of motion, adaptability, feeling, and magnetic change; water greatly helps draw things in as its means of manifestation.

Earth

The earth element, however, is related more to solid stability and physicality—the completed power of elemental condensation. In most magical thought, the earth element is the final formation, its solid nature being born of the other three forces. This nature usually means that earth is the slowest element to bring manifestation but that it also can be the most complete and satisfying in its scope. Here are two powerful methods of utilizing the power of earth in your magic.

Make a Bundle

The first option is to make a bundle, sachet, or charm bag to suit your intention and bury it in the ground to release its energies into the earth to manifest the magic. Filling a biodegradable pouch with herbs and items that correspond to your magical goal, charging the bundle with your intent and gifting it to the land to release the magic is a powerful means of spellwork that is less often discussed today.

The main focus tends to be in burying the remnants from other types of magic as a final task, but this method is the complete method of magic. A key point is to make sure that the items going into the bundle are safe to be placed in the ground. Adding a bunch of salt, toxic ingredients, or synthetic fabrics would not be advisable. Simply make sure that all the ingredients align with your goal, such as basil and sage leaves with some marjoram and mint, brought together in a gold cloth pouch for prosperity. With your need written on a piece of paper, add a coin, seal the bag, and bury it in the ground. This technique can be used for any purpose. Change the herbs, items, and fabric colors to suit the goal and proceed as usual.

Stone Magic

A second means of tapping into the power of the earth element is by way of stone magic. With this technique, you have the choice of selecting a crystal or gem with traditional properties corresponding to your goal, using a clear quartz crystal in your magic, or enchanting a "regular" stone from your local area.

Choosing a crystal that carries a natural alignment to your goal, such as rose quartz for love or green aventurine for prosperity, can help to speed up the transmission of your magical intention and can be a great option if you have the necessary stone on hand. If, however, your crystal supply is limited or your goal is more complex and spans multiple intentions, a clear quartz stone is an ideal choice. The energy of clear quartz is wide-ranging and useful for projecting any and all intentions. When the magic is related to locality, the spirit of place, safety, return travel, and so forth, a stone gathered from your local area can be invaluable. In a similar manner, if you desire to move or travel back to a specific place, a stone from that area can be charged as a talisman of your desire; the only caution would be to avoid taking anything from a protected, private, or dangerous area.

To charge the stone, hold it in your hands and visualize (and/or remember) the land you seek, filling the stone with this energy. Focus strongly upon your intention and mentally transfer this into the stone. Carry this stone with you as a talisman or send it to someone you know in that area (if any cooperative people are available) and have them keep it as a magical beacon to draw you back to that place.

Substitutions for Candles

Finally, if you already have a spell or ritual in mind that would normally require candles and you need to modify it (for whatever reason) and substitute for one or more candles, there are a few simple options from which to choose. Flowers emit a strong energetic power and can sit in place of a candle if needed. A single red rose, carnation, or tulip, for example, can replace a red candle in a spell. Small pots (or bundles) of fresh herbs can also be used as stand-ins for candles. The herbs can be chosen according to their alignment to your spell's goal, or a single plant can be utilized. One such herb is mullein (*Verbascum thapsus*). Old folk names for mullein include "candlewick plant" and "hag's tapers," and these names are related to its prior use as wicks in early candle making. Pieces of the stalk used to be occasionally made into

wicks for candles, but the plant itself can also be used as a substitute for the whole candle. The stalks can be charged as if they were candles and set on the altar in their place (unlit, of course) to hold the energy of the spell.

One last option for casting a spell without the use of traditional candles is a thoroughly modern method: the use of artificial candles. Though these electronic, battery-operated lights are not the same, since they have been crafted to resemble candles and do generate an ambient glow, they can be used to help lend the appropriate atmosphere to magical workings. Some Witches, such as the late Marion Weinstein, have used them in instances when regular candles would not be safe or advised, such as outdoors or around small children or animals. There are some types that are coated in actual wax and have a "realistic" flicker to them, and these are the best to use for magical purposes. They can actually be charged with intent and though they might not function in the same way, the electric candle will still emit the energy of our intent out through its light.

Even though candles and, indeed, the power of fire in general are critical components of most spellwork, having an open flame (or several) is not always feasible for a variety of reasons. Even if we cannot kindle a magical fire, that need not be a stumbling block to the casting of spells. Magic is a gift that is not strictly tied to a single practice or procedure. We have the power of innovation and experimentation on our side, and with these abilities we can develop new avenues for our magical expression so that our power to manifest our goals remains strong.

Magickal Crafting

by Melanie Marquis

Magick is a craft. It's a hands-on, creative, and personal practice much like knitting, painting, woodworking, or any other crafty or artistic endeavor. If you like magick and you also enjoy crafting, combining the two creates a powerful medium for expressing and manifesting your most heartfelt wishes and intentions. When we're making something, be it a piece of folk art or a fancy dinner, the physical action of our hands at work unites with the creative ability of the mind and the emotional aspects of the spirit, completing a circuit that brings our personal power to full capacity and allows this energy to flow freely throughout the body and into the object being created.

Despite the effort and concentration required, creative work—like magickal work—is usually invigorating and exhilarating rather than exhausting. This is because with crafting or with magick, you are putting energy into a closed, complete system rather than into an open-ended system where the return from your efforts may never materialize. The energy you put into a magick spell or into a creative work yields definite and apparent results. Something new has been created, and the power inherent in this new creation is equal to or even greater than the energy expended to create it.

For people who have trouble staying focused or really getting into it when casting spells, magickal crafting can be an effective way to stay engaged and interested in the magickal process. As you craft, a spell is woven, and the end result is a tangible item that will anchor and fortify the magick all the further.

Turning Crafts into Magick Crafts

There are many ways to infuse magick into the crafting process, from enchanting the tools of your craft to empowering your final creation. The particulars of your craft will suggest specific ways to bring magick into the process, but there are a few things anyone can do that will transform any crafting project into a creative act of magick.

One way to infuse magick into your arts and crafts is to enchant the tools and supplies you'll be using for your project. You can do so through a process called "empowering" or "charging." Everything on earth, including your crafting supplies, has an electrical pulse or vibration. When you empower or charge an object, you are altering, magnifying, and focusing this pulse so that it resonates in harmony with the energetic vibration of your magickal goal.

For instance, if you were planning to embroider a magickal charm for prosperity, you might choose to use green thread, as this color is often associated with wealth and abundance. To further align the thread with your intentions, you could empower it by holding it in your hands as you envision a great flow of wealth and conjure in your heart the emotions that this prosperity will bring. Send these emotionally charged thoughts into the thread, and it's fully charged and ready for use in your craft.

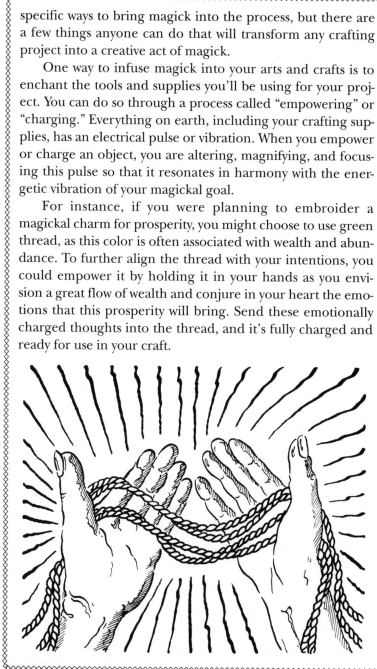

You might prefer instead to write down your intentions on a piece of paper and place the supplies on top of the paper to absorb the energy of your intentions.

Or you might choose to empower each of your crafting tools and supplies to represent different aspects of your spell. If you were to build a porch swing to encourage and support family unity, you might, for example, empower the nails and screws with the energy of unbreakable bonds, enchant the wood to magnify its naturally strong and tenacious energies, and infuse the chains with a vibe of flexibility and cooperation.

Dedicate Your Tools

If you have any primary tools of your craft that you expect to use again and again for many magickal crafting projects, you might consider empowering these tools to be in perfect harmony with you, rather than aligning them to specific magickal goals.

You might design a personalized ritual in which you dedicate yourself and your special crafting tools to the highest pursuits you can dream of achieving. Are you a painter who

wants to create art that inspires psychic sensitivity? A moon-lit ritual with just you and your paintbrushes might be the perfect setting for affirming your ambitions. Do you knit hats to share with those in need of warmth and comfort? A customized ritual in your cozy living room surrounded by friends could be a great way to enchant your knitting needles with an energy of loving friendship. However you choose to enchant them, your crafting tools will impart their energies into whatever you create.

As you work on your craft, think of yourself as a master of magick, assembling just the right pieces to create the circumstances, opportunities, and resources you desire. When it's finished, reaffirm your intentions and consider your creation a physical representation of your magickal goal.

Taking Care of Crafts

Take good care of your magickal crafts, noticing them often and keeping them in good repair. Once the original aim of the spellcraft has been accomplished, you can reprogram the craft with a new magickal purpose. Simply clean it gently to clear away the old magick, then infuse it with your emotionally charged thoughts so that it resonates with your new intention.

◦◦◦

You might consider making magick crafts to mark the change of seasons, or make it a regular hobby that you do daily or monthly to relieve stress and keep your skills fresh. You might create magickal crafts to help you connect with desired energies or to give yourself an extra little push toward success. Magickal crafts also make wonderful gifts to share with very special friends and loved ones.

Magickal crafting doesn't require a whole lot of artistic expertise, so don't be afraid to give it a shot even if you don't consider yourself the artistic type. All that is needed is the desire to try out a new mode of magick and an open mind.

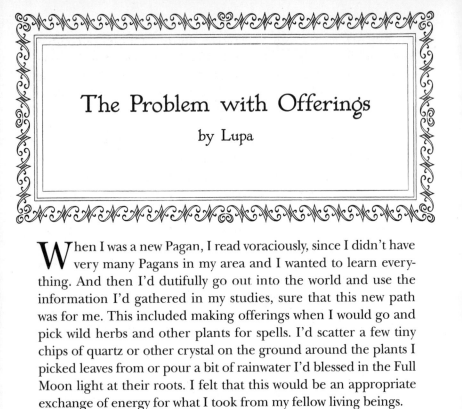

The Problem with Offerings

by Lupa

When I was a new Pagan, I read voraciously, since I didn't have very many Pagans in my area and I wanted to learn everything. And then I'd dutifully go out into the world and use the information I'd gathered in my studies, sure that this new path was for me. This included making offerings when I would go and pick wild herbs and other plants for spells. I'd scatter a few tiny chips of quartz or other crystal on the ground around the plants I picked leaves from or pour a bit of rainwater I'd blessed in the Full Moon light at their roots. I felt that this would be an appropriate exchange of energy for what I took from my fellow living beings.

It wasn't until I was older that I began to think more about this sort of spiritual supply chain. Where, for example, did those quartz crystals come from? Who mined them and under what working conditions? What effects did the mining have on the environment nearby and downstream? How many hundreds or thousands of miles were they transported before they got to me, and how much fossil fuel did that transport cost? If the crystals were drilled and strung on cord, who did all that arrangement and where did the string come from? If I was using small quartz chips in a small glass bottle, what was the background of the bottle, and so forth?

And that got me wondering whether I should be thanking more than just the plant I took leaves from. Should I thank the quartz and the land that gave it to me, and the people who helped it get into my hands? And then what of the cotton string that held the strand of crystals together, should I thank the cotton plants and the people who wove its soft fluff into a fine line?

You see where this is going—the world is a lot more complicated and interconnected than I initially assumed. And it really shook my conception of offerings and how they worked. Was it really a proper offering if I was taking something from one piece of land to give it to another in thanks?

What Are Offerings, Anyway?

Let's start with the concept of an offering in spirituality. One interpretation is that a spirit, deity, or other being has done something for you or given you something that you value, and you want to do or give something in return in gratitude. Another way to look at it is trying to achieve balance: you want to replace as much as you took, to the best of your ability.

Pagans often like to give food as an offering. It's one of the most easily obtained forms of energy, it's something that we value, and the tradition of offering food to the spirits is likely as old as spirituality itself. While store-bought food certainly won't be turned down, we're encouraged to make the food ourselves from scratch, with bonus points if we can grow or raise at least some of the ingredients.

And that answers the basic problems an offering supposedly solves: honoring a being who has helped you with a gift and giving back as much as you have received, albeit in a different form. But food isn't the only option. Artisans may give pieces of their craft, particularly if a permanent shrine or altar is involved. Those who don't feel comfortable making something by hand may give up part of their income to buy items made by others to offer up.

What happens if we don't give offerings? Well, the spirit, deity, or other being may feel miffed and be less likely to help out next time. (We've all had those people in our lives who take, take, take and never give back!) And we may end up feeling guilty and wrong, as though we aren't observing our path properly.

And really, a lot of the offerings we make are about making ourselves feel more right in the grand balance of the universe. But that can lead us to a very self-centered way of thinking of offerings, which is where I ran into problems so many years ago when I was making them without thinking about what I was giving and what its greater impact was.

Unweaving a Web of Connections

The way I counteracted that self-centered tunnel vision was to really look at how everything was interconnected, starting with my offerings. I started with a loaf of bread. It's a fairly simple thing when made at home—flour, water, salt, yeast, and whatever other extras I might like to add in. Let it rise for a while, then put it in the oven and let the heat bake it.

But it gets more complicated. Let's look at the bulkiest ingredient, flour. In order for flour to be procured, you need wheat. In order to grow wheat, you need a field. And that field is made from a wilderness place in which all the native plants and animals have been violently displaced, the soil turned, and the fungal mycelium disturbed, and these days the land soaked in pesticides, herbicides, and other chemicals. Huge amounts of water are poured on the field every day, taken from local waterways and aquifers.

Next, the wheat must be harvested. Small farms may do all the work themselves, but bigger operations may hire migrant laborers at low rates to help with larger yields. Harvesting machinery kills many small animals as it gathers the wheat. And the trucks that then carry the wheat to be stored or processed release greenhouse gases into the air, burning petroleum ripped from the earth with plenty of pollution as a side effect.

Processing the wheat into flour is similarly energy intensive. White flour is made when the bran, or outer covering, of the wheat is removed (along with many important nutrients), creating a product with less flavor and nutritional value. And then it needs to be packaged and transported again to the store. I go to get it (usually by driving), take it home, and use even more energy in the oven to bake it into bread.

Where do I even start with my gratitude to the many beings and lands that are part of the path my bread has taken to get to me? Yes, my intent was to bake the bread as an offering to a deity, but in the process I've contributed to environmental degradation, habitat loss, and the deaths of animals, plants, and fungi along the way.

I could just get frustrated and throw the bread outside for wildlife to eat as a way to make up for my impact. But then the wildlife would become more habituated to humans as sources of food, and bread isn't really good for a lot of animals to eat, and I might have made them sick. Can I possibly do anything to make this all right?

Some Potential Solutions

As you can probably tell, there's no easy answer to the offering conundrum. However, I'd like to offer a few possible ways to mitigate your impact while still being able to meet the goals of an offering (honoring someone who has helped you and restoring balance).

A Daily Thank-You

Every night when I go to bed, I say the following prayer:

> *Thank you to those who have given me this day,*
> *Those who have given of themselves to feed me,*
> *Clothe me,*
> *Shelter me,*
> *Protect me,*
> *Teach me,*
> *And heal me.*
> *May I learn to be as generous as you.*

It's an acknowledgment that I couldn't be in this world without the combined contributions of many, many beings. It doesn't automatically fix the imbalances caused by my taking things from the land, but it at least reminds me to be mindful of the impact I make and to find ways to minimize it while still allowing myself to practice my spirituality.

Giving of the Self

Technically I don't even own my own body; it's made of molecules drawn from the environment through the food I ingest, and when I die it will all go back to be turned into something else. But for the purposes of this article let's say my body is the one thing I know I have to offer freely.

That means that my efforts are there for the offering. I can create songs and poems to those who have given things to me, I can dance in their honor, and I can even dedicate the effort of one of my long-distance runs to them.

But I can also take my time and offer it in more concrete ways. I can volunteer time to clean up litter and other pollution, plant native species and remove invasive ones, create wildlife habitat, and reduce my consumption of fossil fuels and other destructive resources. I'm even able to tailor these offerings to the beings I'm giving them to. If I harvest herbs in the wild, I can also take time to improve the land they grow on. If I receive a blessing from a deity of the ocean, I can volunteer time with a nonprofit working to clean up marine habitats.

Time can also be translated into money. If I don't have the time to volunteer, I can take what money I can afford to put aside and donate it to organizations doing the sort of restoration work I'd love to support.

Stop Giving Offerings

This may seem counterproductive, but stay with me here. When we make offerings, we're trying to balance out or honor very specific interactions we've had. This puts our giving back into distinct chunks of time and effort. Unfortunately, it's all too easy to live selfishly the rest of the time, because you're trained to only give when you've already received or when you otherwise have a specific reason for making the offering.

What if you lived as though every moment was worth reciprocation? What if you walked every path, every day, full of gratitude for what you have received? What if you kindled an awareness of every being that contributed to the very air you breathe?

The goal is not to wallow in the guilt of never being able to truly give back to every spirit, deity, and living being that has had a hand in your existence. Instead, it's to cultivate gratitude and a desire to pass it on to others. Walk lightly on the earth, help those in need, express your thanks to those who help you, and pay it forward without expecting anything in return. Be an active, aware part of your community, human and otherwise.

Perhaps that life of reciprocity and interconnection is the greatest offering you can give the universe and all who share it with you.

Air Magic

Greek Handkerchief Magic

by James Kambos

The humble handkerchief has played an important role in civilization for centuries. In ancient Rome, games and races wouldn't begin until a handkerchief was dropped to the ground. During medieval times, knights would tie a lady's handkerchief to their helmets before battle as a sign of devotion and for luck.

From catching a tear to making a fashion statement, handkerchiefs have been part of our lives for over a thousand years. In his play *Othello*, however, it was Shakespeare who gave the handkerchief magical significance. Then the day came when I learned that my Greek ancestors from the Aegean Islands also had their own magical beliefs about handkerchiefs.

My Lesson in Greek Handkerchief Magic

It was a sunny autumn afternoon many years ago that I learned how an ordinary handkerchief could be used magically. I had taken a weekend off work to visit my mother. After arriving I settled into a chair in her den. On the table by my chair was a houseplant. That wasn't unusual. But there was something in the flower pot along with the plant that was unusual: a handkerchief. Pressed into the soil was a yellow handkerchief, and it was tied into a knot. Part of the knot couldn't be seen because it was covered with soil. How odd, I thought to myself.

I had no idea, but I was about to learn some family history and be initiated into the family tradition of Greek handkerchief magic.

I reached out to examine my bizarre discovery.

"What in the world is this for?" I asked.

Giving me a sharp look, my mother answered, "Don't touch it! Just leave it alone."

I continued, "But why in the hell do you have a handkerchief stuck in a flower pot?"

"If you promise not to touch it, I'll tell you." She began to chuckle. "It's what my mother used to do when she lost something."

Now it made sense. My mother's mother, Katina, was skilled in the art of Greek folk magic. She had spells to remove the curse of the evil eye and could tell your future by reading tea leaves. To bless the house, she'd combine olive oil and smoldering cloves, and then while saying a secret charm, she'd sprinkle the oil mixture around the house. When she left Greece for America, she brought her magical traditions with her. So now I was about to learn another of her folk magic traditions.

My mother began to explain that the day before she had misplaced a gold pendant. To help her find it, she decided to use a Greek folk magic charm my grandmother had taught her. She said when her mother would lose something, she'd take a handkerchief, roll it, bring the ends together, and tie it in a knot while thinking of the lost object. Then she'd usually press the knot into the soil of a houseplant or outside in the garden. The loose ends of the handkerchief would be left exposed above the soil.

In a day or two the item would turn up. So, following these steps, that's what my mother had done. In a few days my mother found her pendant. It seems she had wrapped it in a tissue and dropped it into her purse. In a day or so after performing the handkerchief spell, she said she had a feeling she should look in her purse, and that's where it was.

After learning all I could from my mother that weekend about this old magical tradition, I began to use it myself. As I found out on many occasions, it does work. I've recovered my checkbook, keys, and even an important file at work using Greek handkerchief magic.

What follows are detailed instructions about how to make Greek handkerchief magic work for you.

How to Perform
Greek Handkerchief Magic

Greek handkerchief magic is easy to do. All you need is a handkerchief. Use one you've had awhile; that way it's imbued with your energy. It's always performed when something has been lost. You can use it to find jewelry, a missing document, eyeglasses—anything you can think of.

After searching for your lost item, if you can't find it, then select a handkerchief. It can be white, colored, plain, or fancy. It can be lace, cotton, silk, or linen. Any hankie will do.

Begin by thinking of your lost item as you run the handkerchief through your hands a few times. Now, roll the handkerchief up. Bring the ends together and tie the handkerchief into a knot. The knot should be about in the middle. Visualize the lost item in your mind as you tie the knot. At this point I say,

> *I won't untie you until you bring my* (name of item) *back to me!*

If you wish, you may press the knotted handkerchief into a houseplant or garden soil. (Why this was done I never discovered.) Or do what I do: place the knotted handkerchief where the lost object was kept. For example, if you lost a ring, then place the handkerchief in your jewelry box, and so on.

Now, leave the handkerchief undisturbed and go about your daily routine. For me, usually in an hour or

two it suddenly dawns on me what I was doing when I was last holding the item. I retrace my steps, and I find the misplaced item. It may be hard to believe, but it works.

When you've found your lost item, thank the handkerchief and untie the knot. If you had your handkerchief in soil, wash it.

Now you have a new magical tool. It must now be used only for this purpose. Keep your handkerchief on your altar or tucked safely in a drawer.

A Few Tips

How does handkerchief magic work? I don't know. But many experts in human behavior say we never really lose anything. Somewhere in our subconscious we know where "lost" things are. I feel that at the moment you tie the handkerchief into a knot, it must help trigger your memory.

Here are a few things to remember when you perform Greek handkerchief magic:

- Let the handkerchief do the work. Don't stress trying to remember where something is. Don't be surprised if you get a feeling or suddenly know where something is. I've known people who've tied the handkerchief into a knot and immediately just knew where their lost item was.

- Also, if you're ever in a pinch and find yourself in a situation where no handkerchief is available, use a paper towel. It's happened to me, and it worked well.

- It's hard to believe that a simple piece of cloth we call a handkerchief could possess such power. But remember Othello's words as he described the fabric of his special handkerchief to Desdemona— "There's magic in the web of it."

Daily Dowsing

by Charlie Rainbow Wolf

I have to admit that this was one of the most challenging articles I've written in a long while, not because of the subject matter but because this is such second nature to me that I kept having to backtrack and go over things that may not be familiar to a newbie. Just what is dowsing, anyway, and why should you make it part of your daily magical practice? Let's start with the basics.

Dowsing can either be a noun or a verb. As a noun, dowsing is a method for locating something—water, for example. The technique involves using some kind of a tool (sticks, rods, and pendulums are popular dowsing tools) and observing how that tool moves in response to different energies or influences that are not seen or understood. As a verb, dowsing means to use one of these tools to search for something.

For people who have heard of dowsing, the first thing that comes to mind is when country folk would "witch" for water using a forked stick or dowsing rods in order to locate where to dig a well. My own nephew found our septic tank by dowsing for it just last year using a forked willow stick. My father-in-law had two L-shaped metal rods that he used for dowsing in order to avoid plowing up a water pipe or digging into a sewer drain on the farm. He would loosely hold one in each hand, with the long part sticking straight out, perpendicular to him and parallel to the ground. The rods would cross in front of him when he located whatever he was seeking. I never knew the rods to fail him in all the years I spent on the farm.

Dowsing Pendulums

My preferred dowsing tool is a pendulum. It all started with Galileo, when he realized that pendulums swung independent of the width of their swing and therefore could be used as timekeepers and more. This is why they're used in clocks—but care must be taken to compensate for changes in temperature, which also influences the swing of the pendulum. The Earth's gravity affects a pendulum's movement, too, and if you really want to get into the physics of things, read up on the Foucault pendulum, which works with the oscillation of the Earth's orbit as well as with gravity. In the meantime, I'm going to continue with something less mathematically complicated!

Pendulum dowsing for personal use takes more than just gravity and the Earth's rotation, though. It also takes the power of thought. You have to use your intention to determine what information you want your pendulum to find—as in the earlier dowsing rods example. There are some who say that just thinking something doesn't make it happen—and to some extent I agree with them. However, as science continues to catch up with established spiritual beliefs and practices, who's to say that the link between what we think and what happens won't one day be understood? Psychologists have long understood the power of the mind. It's no longer pseudoscience.

So let's look at the different kinds of dowsing pendulums. They seem to be available in all shapes and sizes and materials, and it's confusing for the beginner who doesn't know where to start. I have two hints to offer to you here. The first is to choose something uncomplicated. Yes, the "chakra wands" that are long sticks with the different colors on them are very pretty, but I wouldn't recommend them for the beginner. Choose one color. It can be something that you like, or if you are experienced in working with color magic or gemstones, choose something that resonates with what you're doing. The second tip I'd offer is to go for something natural. Some pendulums are made of gemstone dust that has been artificially reconstituted. Some of the composite pendulums may have plastic or resin decoration on them or other items glued onto them. There are those folks who don't find this a problem, and that's great, but for me it seems to get in the way of the natural energies into which you're tapping when you're dowsing.

My own personal favorite is a copper dowsing pendulum on a copper chain. The copper resonates with the element of earth—and it's the energies of the earth that you're tapping into when you're dowsing. My dowsing pendulum has the copper rising up it in a spiral—again, mimicking the spiral helix of DNA and giving the energy a natural path up which to travel.

Dowsing pendulums also come in polished gemstones, too. These are better than the composite types, where the gemstone dust has been molded into a pendulum shape. (A merkaba seems to be popular at the moment—like everything else, the popularity of different designs comes and goes in cycles.) It's possible to get spheres that have a point on one end and a hook and chain on the other, and some of these are absolutely beautiful. I've heard people say that the crystal has been traumatized by being polished into a pendant shape. Others believe that polishing births the crystal forward into its true purpose. That all gets a bit New-Agey for me! If you like it and if it feels right, use it. If not, then don't. (The older I get, the simpler my magic becomes!)

If you're a tree-talker and resonate with the spirits of the forests, look into the wooden dowsing pendulums. Many of them aren't as heavy as metal or stone, but they're still wonderful companions. I know people who have dowsing pendulums made from their tree totem, and this works very well for them. If you're passionate about a particular wood or you want to incorporate it into your daily practice, then using a natural timber that has been carved into a pendulum is a good way for you to go. I've seen the most beautiful shapes—but remember not to get too complicated or ornate. It's also possible to carve or burn runes or other insignia into a wooden pendulum, but this is probably for more advanced work.

Starting to Use Your Pendulum

Now that you've chosen your pendulum, what do you actually do with it? Well, like any companion, before you launch into a really deep conversation, you need to get to know each other first. Call me old-fashioned, but I like to attune my new magical tools to me first, to get rid of the energies from all the people who handled them and get it used to me. (And if you think this is rather New-Agey, then ask yourself, do you have a favorite pen when writing or a favorite spoon when cooking? Same principle.) You can go online and find all different ways of cleansing and programming your pendulum, but I think some people want to make it complicated in order to make themselves appear wise and magically enlightened. All I do is throw my pendulum under my pillow for a month. It works for me, but your mileage may vary.

Once the pendulum knows that it's yours, the next thing to do is to strike up a conversation with it. In my work as an astrologer I abhor it when people try to play "test the psychic" and ask me things to which they already know the answer, but this is exactly what you need to do when attuning your pendulum. Some sources will tell you that back and forth is yes and side to side is no, but the truth is that this is a subtle language between you and your pendulum, and there is no one meaning that applies to all people and all pendulums. You need to find what your pendulum does when it says yes, what it docs when it says no, what it does when it says maybe, or what it does when the answer is not to be determined.

There isn't one right way to hold your pendulum, but you do need to follow a few loose guidelines. Make sure it's free enough to swing; you don't want to hold it too close to your hand. The chain or cord needs to be straight, so it's not influenced by your hand movements, but it also needs to be secure, so you don't keep dropping your pendulum. My favorite way is to pinch the chain between the ball of my thumb and the outside of my index finger and let the pendulum drape over the back of my hand. If the chain or cord has a bead or knot at the end, it's possible to pinch this between your fingers where they join onto your palm, and let the pendulum dangle freely underneath your hand. Find what works for you and do it.

You always need to ask your pendulum questions that can be answered either yes or no, so start by asking it silly questions to which you know the answer: "Am I wearing shoes at

the moment?" or "Is it raining in my living room?" See which way the pendulum swings. Be consistent! Ask it a string of questions to which the answer is yes, so there's no doubt in your mind that this is what the pendulum is answering.

Repeat this exercise with questions that should be answered no. Ask several questions and get a real feel for the negative response. Don't be surprised if your pendulum starts to get very animated, either. The more outrageous the question, the more vehement the answer is likely to be! Make this fun, but take it seriously, too. You're bonding with a new tool, and while this doesn't have to be dour, it's not a game.

Once you've got your definitive yes and your definitive no, ask the pendulum questions that may be subjective. "Is it raining?" It's not raining outside your house, but is it raining nearby? Is it a bit drizzly where you are but not flat-out raining? Confuse the pendulum, and see how it responds. (Just as an FYI, my pendulum goes back and forth—in any direction but always in a straight line—for yes, and around in a circle for no. For maybe, it just kind of judders and does nothing. I have a friend who gets up and down for yes, side to side for no, and around in a circle for maybe. Pay close attention!)

What Will Your Pendulum Tell You?

Now that you know how to converse with your pendulum, you're ready to start to use it as a tool. The only limitation here is the number of ideas you come up with! Your pendulum is portable, discreet, and useable nearly anywhere apart from in gale-force winds. For example, take your pendulum grocery shopping with you. Want to see how fresh that cauliflower is? Dowse over it. If the pendulum says yes, get it; if you get no or maybe as your answer, consider rethinking your purchase. Non–genetically modifed foods, non-irradiated foods, foods with pesticides, sugar-free foods, fat-free foods, additive-free foods—these are all things you can ask your pendulum to help you choose in the grocery store.

Are you looking for new romance? I've known people to dowse over photographs to tell them if that person would make a suitable partner or not. I've known people to dangle their pendulum when perusing online dating sites, asking it to indicate to whom they should send a profile and friend request. You might think it's crazy, but this particular person has now been happily married for six years!

Do you like to garden? Use your pendulum to help you plan what goes where. I've found it amusing how my pendulum chose plants that naturally make good garden companions when I used it to show me the season's layout. I'll also—rather sheepishly—admit that the one year I was in too much of a hurry to plan the garden using my spiral copper pendulum was the year that we were infested with cabbage moths and couch grass!

Not sure what cleaning products to purchase? Use your pendulum. Simply dangle it over your selections and let it tell you what's a good value for money, what's most appropriate for your use, what's going to do the best job, what's going to cause the least allergies, and more. Your pendulum will tell you whatever you want to know, as long as you ask a clear yes-or-no question when you start.

Needless to say, my pendulum goes everywhere with me. I've even dowsed over menus in cafés before to see what was best for me to eat at that particular establishment at that particular time. Oh, sure, I got some raised eyebrows and some odd looks. The point is that once you're comfortable enough to use your pendulum in public, you're not going to care. I'm fairly certain that I've avoided many an upset stomach by listening to what my pendulum told me to get and not being driven entirely by my taste buds!

Dowsing Charts

Charts are a great way to use your dowsing pendulum, and there are many available for free download online or for purchase online and in alternative shops. They're as simple or as fancy as you wish to go. Dowsing charts are very simple to make yet also very efficient to use. Simply let the pendulum swing over the chart, and it will tell you what you need to know.

To make your own dowsing chart, you'll need paper, something with which to write, a compass with which to draw a circle (or just draw around a pie plate or something similar), and a ruler or some other kind of straight edge for making a straight line. I actually make pottery dowsing plates, with the lines marked off in equal parts using a cake marker!

When you've got your chart drawn, it should look a bit like a pie chart, with all the segments of equal proportion. Assign a meaning for each of the lines. A simple chart is a very practical way of getting to know your pendulum. Mark it off into six areas and assign each line that bisects the circle either yes, no, or maybe. Then start asking it questions and see which way it swings. It's even possible to use this to double check previous queries; if the pendulum didn't give you a definite answer before, whip out the chart and ask it again.

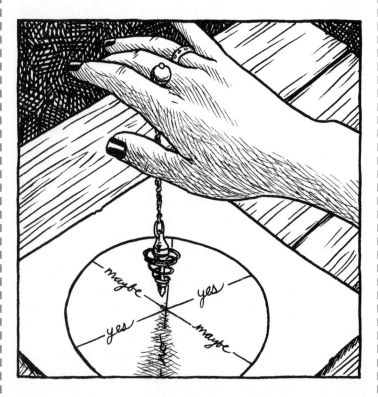

Remember that your pendulum speaks to you by swinging back and forth. It's absolutely fine to put something different in each portion of the chart, but if you're new to using your pendulum, you might want to think about placing your chosen answer along the entire length of the dividing line, so you're not trying to determine which half of the chart the pendulum is swinging in. Once you're more adept and understand your pendulum better, then you can start to use more complex charts.

Square charts and spreadsheets work just as well as pie charts when you're dowsing. This is particularly useful if you're seeking to use your dowsing pendulum to help you figure out analytics and percentages. Simply make a chart of ten lines and ten rows and put a number in each of them. The pendulum will help you to determine what your chances are.

Use square charts for making selections, too. For example, if you are unsure what crystals to purchase and want to have some insight before you get to the rock shop, put the names of the stones in the columns and rows of the grid, and then slowly dowse over them until you get a definite reaction from your pendulum. I find square charts more complicated to use than pie charts, but there's no hard and fast rule. Do what's right for you; this is an intimate journey between you and your pendulum. You'll work it out between you.

It's easy to use a pendulum with a reflexology or iridology chart to see where physical ailments or weaknesses are likely. Reflexology works with specific points on the hands and feet that are linked to every part of the body, while iridology is a study of the iris of the eye for different shapes and patterns that reveal information about your health and vitality. A reflexology foot chart is a map of the corresponding points; an iridology chart divides the iris into segments, each one pertaining to a different organ, body part, or potential ailment. Iridology and reflexology charts are available to download or purchase online or from health food stores and New Age retailers. Using the pendulum in conjunction with charts such as these can really open doors for you when it comes to getting to know your body better—I speak from experience on this one!

Of course, a pendulum should never take the place of medical advice, but it may help you follow your doctor's orders. Use your pendulum in conjunction with doctor-approved herbal supplements to choose which ones have the capability to do you the most good. Take your pendulum to your herbalist or apothecary and dowse over the items on the shelves. It could be that one brand will suit you more than another or that one dose is more appropriate for your particular needs than something else is. It's okay not to tell your doctor that you're going to go dowse for your herbs, but do seek your physician's advice before starting to take any supplements.

Conclusion

Hopefully by now you're starting to see just how useful a pendulum really is. Whether it's for pleasure, health, or profit, there's a lot of good advice available from your dangly companion. When you start regularly using your pendulum, you may just start collecting them. After all, there are so many designs, so many shapes and sizes, so many different materials and manufacturers. Like anything else, once you immerse yourself into this world, it might get enjoyably addictive!

Pagan Prayer Beads

by Elizabeth Barrette

Many different religions employ prayer beads. Hindu and Buddhist traditions use the *mala*. Islam uses the *misbaḥah*. Christianity uses the rosary. Pagan ones may go by these or other names. Just as we have many Pagan faiths, so too the prayer beads vary. A Wiccan set may look little like a Hellenic set and nothing like a Gothic Pagan set.

So how do you really make Pagan prayer beads? Ask twelve Pagans, get thirteen answers! Prayer beads differ in purpose, material, pattern, theme, and other important features. What matters is what you can get and what you want to accomplish with it. Let's explore some options for your spiritual accessories.

Uses for Prayer Beads

Prayer beads have many applications beyond counting. You may count repetitions of the same chant or lines in a longer piece of liturgy or recite different things along with the sections of your set. Pinch each bead between your fingertips as you say the prayer, and then move to the next bead and the next prayer. Beyond this, you can explore all sorts of possibilities.

Marking time: Many traditions have prayers for the morning, evening, or both. Christianity has the whole set of canonical hours; for Pagan practice, an equivalent might be astrological hours. Most faiths have sets of prayers for specific holidays. You can mark your place with prayers that aren't said all at once if your chain has a movable marker, such as a tassel on a lark's head knot.

Being present: Stone beads such as hematite or agate are good for grounding. Use them with chants designed to replenish energy or release an excess of it, making your subtle self more stable. Textured beads help you remain in the present moment; molded or lampworked glass is fantastic, and beads

83

carved from stone or wood also work. Move them through your hands as you walk or work, letting the sensations anchor your attention. Use these with prayers aimed at self-awareness.

Calming yourself: In times of stress, people naturally reach for spiritual comfort. Magic can help soothe jangled emotions too. Gentle stones such as rose quartz or howlite aid the process. Clear quartz or glass are obvious choices if you need clarity. As you pull the stones through your fingers, recite positive affirmations, steps of your safety plan, or a spell for peace. Also, some people find that fiddling with something helps them think better. If you tell curious onlookers that you're using prayer beads, they will usually leave you alone. For this, a mental stone such as lapis may help, but hard beads click if they touch each other. Wooden or plastic beads are quieter. It helps to use a thick silk cord and big knots. Amber necklaces are often made this way, and they work great as prayer beads if you simply attach a pendant or tassel to the ends.

Connecting with other people: Prayer beads make very popular gifts. When someone is ill or injured, people often pray for them. Some prayer beads are made in detachable

sections, a very long chain, or other configurations to make it easy for several people to share them.

Drawing power: Pagans often use objects to direct mystical forces. Prayer beads make a terrific place to store energy. Choose beads that match your desired goal. They build up quite a charge over time. You can also use prayer beads as a focus on your altar.

Popular Materials

The components used to create a set of prayer beads influence their performance. Use the best materials you can find and afford for magical artifacts. These work better and last longer. Inferior materials tend to burn through and break faster because they cannot sustain such a high flow of energy. For most purposes, you want natural materials like stone and silk. However, for technomagic, you need synthetic materials such as Austrian crystal and tiger tail wire instead.

Consider what you want to string your beads upon. Silk cord is a popular choice for larger beads if you plan to space them with knots. It's fairly safe with light, soft beads such as amber, but heavier or sharper ones can wear through it. Some people prefer leather cord, but it doesn't knot as easily. Leather resists fraying and has a primal look. Beading wire, like tiger tail, consists of fine metal strands twined together and protected with a synthetic coat, like nylon. Some companies make this in bright colors, and it resists wear from heavy beads or sharp edges.

Findings include things that hold the jewelry together. Clasps join the ends of a necklace or bracelet. Yokes have three or more holes to attach different sections, like the Y shape of a rosary. We can reasonably include charms in this category, which are often though not always made of metal. Yokes and charms are among the most important parts in a set of prayer beads, as they usually indicate the theme, such as the Triple Goddess.

You can make prayer beads with all or mostly the same type of bead. For instance, a *mala* customarily has 108 identical beads separated by knots and one *sumaru*, or "head bead." However, most sets use a mixture of types. One popular pattern uses large beads as counters and tiny ones as spacers. Another chooses a different style for each section. For example, the four elements might be represented by clear eggs (air), red pyramids (fire), blue spheres (water), and green cubes (earth). Some distinguish only by color or only by shape. An advantage to using shape is that it allows you to identify the beads with your eyes closed.

Beads come in many different materials. These may include gemstones, metals, wood, rose petal, glass, ceramic, plastic, polymer clay, and even paper. The type of material should suit the theme of your prayer beads. For heavy use, choose sturdy beads with smooth shapes that don't snag. For occasional use, you can consider more delicate, fancier beads.

Rosaries got their name from their construction. Originally they featured beads made from a paste of rose petals. When warmed by skin contact, these beads gave off a subtle smell of roses. While few beads are made this way today, some people still do it, and this is a terrific choice for crafty people worshipping a goddess who loves roses, such as Venus.

Wooden beads allow you to draw on the energy of their tree. Sandalwood is the most popular for spiritual beads due to its sweet fragrance. Apple, ash, birch, cedar, cherry, hickory, maple, oak, and pine are some other options. Beads made from nuts or seeds also fit here.

Metal makes up not only beads but also most findings, many charms, and yokes. Gold corresponds to masculine, Sun, and fire energy and conveys prosperity. Silver relates to feminine, Moon, and water and supports intuition, communication, and cycles. These two compose most of the high-end jewelry components. Copper corresponds to feminine, Venus, and water and the magic of love, healing, and energy manipulation. Iron matches masculine, Mars, and fire and conveys protection, strength, and grounding. Lead corresponds to masculine, Saturn, and earth and works for grounding and protection against negativity; rarely used pure, it's a common component of cheap alloys for charms. Tin relates to masculine, Jupiter, and air and bestows luck, business success, and divination. It's another popular choice for cheap components.

Gemstone beads are enormously popular for Pagan prayer beads due to their power. Common choices include agate (grounding), amber (amplification), amethyst (dreams), aquamarine (peace), carnelian (courage), cinnabar (success), citrine (communication), clear quartz (all-purpose), garnet (love), hematite (protection), howlite (cleansing), jade (longevity), leopard jasper (animal magic), malachite (healing), moss agate (plant magic), obsidian (defense), onyx (cthonic), rose quartz (friendship), rutilated quartz (inspiration), snowflake obsidian (balance), sodalite (meditation), sugilite (enlightenment), sunstone (energy), and tiger's eye (perception).

Beads of manmade materials such as glass, ceramic, plastic, polymer clay, and paper are less suited for most Pagan purposes because they lack the energy of natural materials. However, glass and ceramic remain among the most popular beads, so they are often used. Including a stone or metal charm provides a repository of power. Plastic, polymer clay, and paper are much less durable than other materials. They may serve for lightly used sets, however. For technomagic, synthetic materials tend to work better than natural ones, although you can't beat a bismuth crystal as a focus.

Patterns and Themes

Prayer beads employ a wide variety of designs. There are different patterns and shapes, along with different types of jewelry, such as a bracelet or necklace, which allow the beads to be worn for easy use. Prayer beads typically represent a particular ideal or topic as well. These features combine to make each set unique. They also divide into families based on similarities.

One useful distinction comes between branched and unbranched beads. A branched pattern has more than one part, such as a circle with a string of beads hanging down.

More complicated ones may use multiple loops or strings fastened together; these help in counting higher numbers. The shape may have special meaning; for example, a Wiccan set might use a pentacle of beads, while a Khemetic set for Hathor could use two extra strings representing her horns. An unbranched pattern may be a simple circle, which customarily has a starting point marked by a special bead or tassel. Rarely, prayer beads come in a straight line, not closed into a circle, which is followed from one end to the other. If it ends in a point, such as a crystal, a line of prayer beads may also serve as a pendulum for dowsing.

The other main distinction comes in the theme. The materials chosen help show what the prayer beads are for. Here are some popular choices:

Ancestors: Such sets may feature individual people, the branches of your family tree, different ethnicities, family religions, and so forth. These often use beads from ancestral locations, culturally significant materials, or representations of personality.

Loved ones: These prayer beads represent living people. Photographic charms are popular, but you can also use charms about their professions or anything else that reminds you of them. These are customarily used to count prayers, ensuring that you cover everyone each time you pray.

Chakras: Usually divided into seven sections, a miniature version can be made with just seven beads. Use the colors of the chakras in order: red, orange, yellow, green, blue, indigo, violet.

Elements: There are actually different sets of these. Earth, air, fire, and water (and optionally spirit) is the Western set. Wood, fire, earth, metal, and water is the Eastern set. A fey set has been proposed as earth, air, fire, water, life, light, and magic. The Celtic Three Realms fit well here: land, sea, sky. Look around and find one you like.

Goddess: The Divine Feminine may be evoked in the form of one goddess, the three faces of the Triple Goddess, or a set of goddesses who share a common interest. Look for goddess charms at a Pagan store.

God: The Divine Masculine may be evoked as one god, a pair of gods like the Oak King and the Holly King, or a set of gods, such as your personal patrons. God charms are a little harder to find than goddesses, but they exist.

Pantheon: Make a set of prayer beads representing all or a subset of the deities in a particular tradition. God or goddess sets also fall into this category. Genderqueer folks might like to make a set using all the deities of ambiguous or variable sex or gender.

Ideals: Most faiths have a set of recommended virtues or tenets of belief, such as the Nine Noble Virtues of Ásatrú. This style also lends itself well to positive affirmations.

Spellcraft: You can make prayer beads to suit any magical working. All the usual subtopics apply, such as love, home, prosperity, healing, fertility, or other magic. Use the beads to count repetitions of your incantation.

Totems: Evoke your animal power with prayer beads that mimic pawprints, teeth, claws, feathers, the animal's outline, and so forth. You may focus on a single creature or, since modern complexity means people often have multiple totems, include all of yours on a single strand.

Construction

Creating a set of prayer beads is much like creating a necklace or bracelet. At minimum you need beads and something to string them on. If you want to make your set as a circle that can be opened and closed, you will need a clasp. If you want to make a line, those customarily have an anchor at each end, which may be larger beads, metal charms, crystal points, tassels, and so on. If you want to make a branched set, you will need one or more yoke charms, typically a metal emblem with three holes to attach the string. The loose ends usually have an anchor. If you're using soft string like silk, you can just knot it. Metal won't knot, and neither will many synthetics. To fasten the ends of those, you need something called a crimp bead that clamps over the looped wire.

Check for functionality. Replace any beads that have chips or findings that don't work right. Make sure that your string fits through all of the beads and findings. Really, test this stuff before you start, because it sucks to get halfway through and *then* discover a problem.

Lay out all of your beads and findings in the order you will use them. This is easiest to do on a proper beading board, which has grooves to hold everything steady. They're affordable at a craft store, and some stores have beading nights when you can borrow their boards. Alternatively, you can find or make something else with grooves or use a piece of nappy fabric to hold everything in place.

Make sure that you have the right number of beads and that they are in the correct places. Check to see if they all reasonably fit together this way and you like the way they look. Now is the time to make changes if you're not satisfied.

Start at one end and work your way around. Either finish that end (such as by attaching an anchor), or if you're going to knot both ends later, put a craft clip there so that your beads can't slide off. String the beads in order. If you're knotting, take care to put a knot between each pair of beads. If you're using tiny spacer beads, make sure you use all of them. It's easy to miss one. When you get to the far end, either finish it or knot the two ends together. Branches are basically made in the same manner; you're just attaching one end to the main strand with a knot or finding. Trim any extra bit of string and you're done.

Consecration

Most people want to consecrate their prayer beads before putting them into use. The process includes cleansing, charging, and dedicating an artifact to its purpose. There are various ways to do this. A simple cleansing might include smudging, which uses air and fire.

One way to charge things involves laying them in sunlight and moonlight for twenty-four hours. For dedication, name the deity or other theme, and then recite the prayers that match the beads. Of course, if your tradition provides another consecration process that you prefer, you can use that instead.

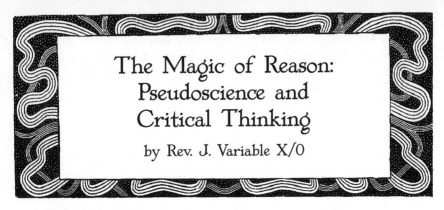

The Magic of Reason: Pseudoscience and Critical Thinking

by Rev. J. Variable X/0

Remember the good old days when everyone knew breaking a mirror meant seven years of bad luck? And your soul would escape if you didn't cover your nose when you sneezed? And left-handed folks were touched by the devil? These sound like silly superstitions to us now, but there was a time when they were passed along as common knowledge and accepted without question by many people. Some folk tales had a kernel of truth to them, of course, but others are so outlandish that we have to wonder how anyone could have ever taken them seriously.

Then again, if some of the "information" being passed around on the Internet today is any indication, humans are just as irrational and gullible as ever.

Why are we so willing, even eager, to swallow unfounded rumors and junk science? With all the conflicting stories and articles out there on the web, how can you tell the difference between good reporting and plain old claptrap?

Faith, Magic, and Skepticism

To emphasize logic and scientific method in a book about magic and spirituality may seem incongruous, but the ability to recognize nonsense, and the willingness to call it out when we see it, is an important part of the magical life. As enthusiasts of the mystical world, we're already surrounded by questionable claims, and we eagerly incorporate unscientific lore into our daily lives. We *know* our beliefs are true . . . or do we? *How* do we know? Can we prove it? Do we have to?

I'm not going to try to debunk any of our dearly held spiritual perspectives here. (That would be pointless, anyway, as you'll see.)

Belief and passion are good. Objectivity and healthy skepticism are also good. What's *not* good is when we get these approaches confused. It's a slippery slope from passion and belief to fanaticism and pseudoscience.

Consider the Source

Caitlin Dewey writes in *The Washington Post*, "Since early 2014, a series of Internet entrepreneurs have realized that not much drives traffic as effectively as stories that vindicate and/or inflame the biases of their readers."

If a hyperbolic headline gets you riled up, frantically hopeful, or feeling smug, make sure your left brain is paying attention, too. The media is supposed to be fair and unbiased, but these days, too much of it is all about "clickbait": getting viewers to click on the link and share the picture or the article. You know those headlines—"She Bought a Bag of Tomatoes, but Wait till You See What Else Was in There!" or "He Never Believed in Ghosts until He Saw *This* . . ." You just *have* to click through to find out.

Those types of sites aren't out to impress anyone with their journalistic integrity. They rely on page views to collect payment for the ad space. Some "news" sources are really nothing more than vehicles to deliver advertisements. They don't even care if you read the material they present. Every time someone clicks on their link, they get to charge their advertisers a few more pennies.

Such tactics aren't limited to silly stories about puppies or dubious spiritual manifestations. As I write this, the United States is about one month away from the next presidential election, and I don't care whose side you're on—social media is rife with half truths, blind rage, and outright lies about the candidates and the issues. The big-name news services we used to trust are bad enough, but the past few years have brought a plague of small-time news blogs of every political persuasion trying to outdo one another with stories that are little more than carefully edited material designed to get a reaction rather than to inform. These stories get posted and reposted by people whom I know should know better.

Religion and paranormal topics also make effective clickbait. If you're bored with politics, go check out the latest "evidence"

for the existence of ghosts. Or government conspiracies. Or Bigfoot. When it comes to getting your attention, it's all the same to the marketers. The more sensational the headline, the more readers will respond to it on an emotional level and share it with their friends.

Learn to recognize your own knee-jerk reactions. Start asking questions before you repost the article or meme. Out-of-context statistics, quotes, and snarky one-liners that wrap up the entire issue soundly in your favor are probably leaving something out.

Time for a little fact-checking.

Pick an issue—politics, rumors, spirituality, paranormal—and study the opinions and claims of its most fervent supporters and detractors. Doesn't it seem as though both sides are so busy yelling at each other that the real truth of the matter, whatever it is, has been lost? You want to convince others your position makes good sense, however, sharing *everything* that supports your opinion can backfire. Research the opposing views. Double-check their sources as well as your own.

The downside to fact-checking is that you're likely to discover some facts you don't like. Finding out you're wrong is discouraging but useful: it leads to a greater understanding of your subject. It's so much more satisfying to *know* you're right and be able to back up your position with sound research and objective evidence than it is to spread rumors and hope for the best.

Arguing 101: Recognize Logical Fallacies

An argument isn't necessarily a yelling match. Ideally, arguing is a process: a rational discussion of a particular claim or problem, with the goal of reaching an agreement and finding solutions. The human mind isn't always rational, though. Our passions and emotions can get in the way, twisting perspectives and preventing us from really understanding one another and working together. "Logical fallacies" are common patterns of faulty reasoning that you can learn to spot in your own and others' arguments, whether the topic is supernatural phenomena or a problem in the material world.

First, think about the original claim itself, and consider these questions:

Is it falsifiable?

Albert Einstein is supposed to have said, "No amount of experimentation can prove me right; a single experiment can prove me wrong." No matter how much the evidence supports a hypothesis, it only takes *one* time when it doesn't for the whole thing to fall to pieces.

A common example in logical philosophy is the case of the black swan. If I say, "All swans are white," it doesn't matter how many white swans we see—my statement isn't confirmed until we've taken a look at every swan in existence. Finding even one single black swan will disprove my statement.

Now, what if I say, "All humans were made in the image of a deity"? Well, we could look at every human, but there's really no way to tell if I'm wrong, since we have no physical examples of deities with which to compare them. This statement may or may not be true.

By the same token, someone who says there are no deities at all is also offering a nonfalsifiable claim: one might, some day, appear to objective observers. In other words, atheists who insist there's nothing outside of this mundane reality are relying on *faith*, not facts, much like the fanatical believers who want to argue with them about it. (No matter how strongly we believe one way or another, we all have to wait until death before we can know for sure!)

A falsifiable claim can be *proven* to be true or false. A nonfalsifiable claim might be true or false, but there's no way to tell.

Is it reproducible?

A single experiment or personal experience is not proof. A claim has to be true all the time, for everyone, in order to be valid. Given the same environmental factors, any independent researcher should be able to get the same result. If the ghost of Great Uncle Felix haunts the bell tower at midnight, then anyone (including a team of objective investigators) should be able to see him. If he only appears to his favorite niece, that doesn't automatically mean she's just imagining things, but it also gives no one else a reason to believe in ghosts.

Logical Fallacies

Next, examine the points being made and see if you can spot any of these classic logical fallacies:

Confirmation Bias: It's a natural human tendency to pay more attention to facts and ideas that support our position while ignoring or rejecting those which might contradict us. We tend to give extra weight to material that confirms what we already think. We *want* magic and souls and the afterlife to be real. We *want* the annoying politician or celebrity to be taken down a few notches. But it's important to understand and acknowledge all the facts, without cherry-picking only the ones we like, before we can make an intelligent conclusion.

Strawman: When someone counters a claim by bringing up a different problem, they divert attention from the original topic.

"Children in war-torn countries are suffering."

"Yes, but how can we worry about that when so many children in our own country are homeless?"

Both problems merit concern, but the second point doesn't really address the first.

Appeal to Emotion: This is what makes you accept a claim (or click on a link) out of pity, anger, fear, a sense of self-righteousness, or some other emotional reaction. We want to trust our intuitions so badly when something "just feels right," but no matter how strong the feelings may be, someone else is always going to have equally strong opposing feelings. Feelings are not proof.

Appeal to Authority: It's tempting to trust Dr. Smartypants, PhD, to do the thinking and the research for us (even if his or her chosen field has nothing to do with the issue in question), but everyone—including scientists, professors, and spiritual leaders—has an agenda, even if their intentions are honest. Sometimes they exaggerate to sound more impressive. Sometimes they want to win grant money or sell books. Educated professionals are subject to confirmation bias, too, and sometimes they're just plain wrong.

Ad Hominem: This is Latin for "to the person." An *ad hominem* attack is when one person tries to refute another's claim on the basis of their character, rather than addressing the claim itself. "He's a bad guy, so I know he's lying!" Well, he might be the worst guy in the world, but he might also be right about some things.

Appeal to Popular Opinion: "A million people can't be wrong!" Yes. Yes, they can.

False Cause: As magical practitioners, we've all had experiences that seem to indicate there's more to the universe beyond mundane reality. If your spell works, especially more than once, there might be something to it. One event happening after another, though, doesn't necessarily imply the first one caused the second. Is the effect consistently reproducible for any spellcaster? What else might have created the effect? The magical arts provide an excellent field for study and experimentation, and the laws of physics are probably far stranger than the naysayers realize. Take lots of notes! You just might discover something new.

False Compromise (or Middle Ground): "Well, the real truth is somewhere in between." Often it is. Sometimes it isn't. This fallacy is a good way to sidestep any further arguing and change the subject.

The Fallacy Fallacy: The most poorly crafted argument you've ever heard might still contain some truth. Just because someone commits a logical fallacy (or ten) doesn't mean their idea is automatically wrong.

～

Critical thinking is not an outright denial of faith. It doesn't invalidate your feelings. It's simply an intelligent way to process information. You can be a skeptic, a believer, an activist, and a realist and practice your Craft all at the same time—they're not mutually exclusive, as long as you don't get your objective truths mixed up with your subjective ideas. Critical thinking does more than protect you from looking foolish. It can help you convince others to agree with your position and to take up your cause: a valuable tool in any magical arsenal!

Resource

Dewey, Caitlin. "What Was Fake on the Internet This Week: Why This Is the Final Column." *The Washington Post*, December 18, 2015. https://www.washingtonpost.com/news/the-intersect/wp/2015/12/18/what-was-fake-on-the-internet-this-week-why-this-is-the-final-column/.

Creating Quintessence:
The Balancing of Elements

by Tiffany Lazic

Earth, air, fire, and water each carry their own signatures, guiding us in their own different ways. Ancient alchemists spoke of a transformative fifth element, quintessence, which was created when each of the other four elements achieved perfect balance. Using our own lives as the alchemist's crucible, we can discern those places in which we are elementally out of balance, shift ourselves to create cohesion, and experience the magic of quintessence in our lives.

Alchemy has its beginnings so far back through the reaches of time that its source has become mythic. Said to have been gifted to humankind by the Egyptian god Thoth, alchemy is best known as the esoteric science of transformation, presenting the steps for transmuting base lead into precious gold and creating the elixir of everlasting life. There have been times in history when this was approached quite literally, prompting a quest for health and wealth that made alchemists particularly popular with royalty. Perhaps if alchemy had kept to the areas of longevity and finance, it would have enjoyed a different history. But one key aspect of the alchemical process is that the work, what is being worked upon, and the one doing the work are inextricably linked. To put it more simply, if the alchemist is to successfully transmute lead into gold, the alchemist must pay attention to his or her own inner workings, transmuting anything of a base nature within as part of the process. The achievement of inner gold is not that far from the recognition that the divine resides within.

This was not a popular sentiment with the church of the Middle Ages, and thus it became quite dangerous to be an alchemist. The image of the slightly crazed old man hidden away in a dark room surrounded by books and beakers comes in large part from the fact that were he to stand in the light of day while he worked, he probably wouldn't live to see the next day.

In the twenty-first century, we are not so concerned with the creation of gold nor with the juice of immortality (lottery tickets and age-defying serums notwithstanding). But there is growing interest in the path to enlightenment, joy, and authenticity. It is exactly the potential to uncover this path that makes alchemy so exciting and relevant. The ultimate goal of alchemy is the attainment of the Philosopher's Stone, which is sometimes referred to as "the intelligence of the heart." Paulo Coelho states in his much-loved parable *The Alchemist*, "Because, wherever your heart is, that is where you'll find your treasure." The treasure of alchemy is the wealth that comes from knowing one's own nature and living from that place of truth.

What do the alchemists of ages past teach us about attaining the precious Stone? Though the stages involved in completing the alchemical process are notoriously (and intentionally) confusing, there are a few details that remain consistent. One of the main aspects of alchemy is the belief that there are four basic elemental building blocks to all of life. It was the Greek philosopher Empedocles, writing in the fifth century BCE, who implored in his book, *Tetrasomia* (The Doctrine of the Four Elements), "Now, hear the fourfold roots of everything: enlivening Hera, Hades, shining Zeus. And Nestis, moistening mortal springs with tears." Nature itself has a fourfold structure that is represented by earth (Hera), water (Nestis), air (Zeus), and fire (Hades).

These four elements are familiar to anyone with even a passing interest in magical work and the creation of sacred space, but the second key aspect in alchemical teaching is that when one has brought all four elements into perfect balance with each other, there is the revelation of a fifth element, the quintessence, which transcends them all. Another Greek philosopher, Pythagoras, referred to quintessence as "aether." It was thought to be the air breathed by the gods, purer and finer than the air of the human world. In the creation of sacred space, quintessence can be seen as the center of the ritual circle, the sitting place for the gods and goddesses, and often the place where the altar is situated.

In alchemy, quintessence and the Philosopher's Stone can be seen as interchangeable. Clearly, the key to achieving the intelligence of the heart is in bringing the four elements into balance. Brilliant men, many centuries, and hundreds of books have all grappled with the question of the attainment of the Stone. What follows here can only be, at best, a teeny morsel of all the wisdom available on this topic, but for those who are intrigued by the inner application of elemental balance, here are some basic pointers:

The Earth of Body

If we have any hope of achieving a balanced, open, and full heart, we must pay attention to the needs of the body. There can sometimes be an impulse to elevate the significance of spirit, dismissing our human needs as somehow "less than." But if the body is to be a strong vessel for the containment of spirit, it needs to be well cared for. The element of earth urges us to get adequate rest and fuel ourselves with nourishing, healthy food. It highlights the importance of safety and security. When we are balanced in earth, we enjoy our work life and our home life. We feel capable of meeting survival needs, making sure we are able to pay our bills, keep a roof over our heads, food on the table, and clothes on our backs. This is not a call to extravagance. One can create balanced earth simply by recognizing and meeting basic, simple needs.

The Water of Emotions

Emotions pulse through us as surely as does our blood. They bring color to life, even though there are many emotions we would rather not experience. We have a tendency to want to avoid emotions such as fear, sadness, anger, despair, hopelessness, and anxiety. They do not feel nice at all, and often they drop us into a dark, mucky, awful emotion called shame. We feel sad at having been left out of a group outing and almost instantly find ourselves thinking, "There must be something wrong with me, and that's why I wasn't invited."

In the blink of an eye, we move from feeling sad to feeling shame: "I'm not good enough. I'm not accepted by others. I'm unlovable." Very few of us have been introduced to the tools for working through shame. As a result, we stay as far away as possible from those emotions which may inadvertently land us there.

Challenging though it may be, in order to balance water, we must accept all our emotions. This does not mean we accept the validity of every internal emotional stance. Shame, for instance, is never informing us of an emotional truth. But it does mean that we accept that the very presence of an emotion flowing through us is giving significant information about our experience of the world in that moment. Psychologist Eugene Gendlin said that "every bad feeling is a potential energy toward a more right way of being if you give it space to move toward its rightness." The element of water gives us a place to begin that exploration.

The Air of Mind

As with our emotional life, our thoughts, beliefs, opinions, and perspectives shape our experience of the world. In some sense, this becomes a chicken-egg type of circular

interrelationship. Which came first, the thought or the emotion? One approach to this question is the sense that we come into this life as positive, trusting, and open beings but that we all have painful experiences that possibly result in negative, limiting, or even cynical beliefs. We are not born mistrustful, but, after a few heart-wrenching relationships, we may develop the belief that people can't be trusted so deeply that it feels like it has always been a part of us. Becoming balanced in air requires us to sort through our thoughts and beliefs, challenging those that close our hearts or keep us in fear or isolate us.

Balanced air allows for the differentiation of emotion and thought. This means that I may have a negative emotional experience without defaulting to a negative belief. I may have been hurt in a painful relationship, but I do not close my heart to future relationships, believing that either I am unlovable or all people are untrustworthy. I learn from that relationship, exercise discernment, and step fully into the next relationship when the opportunity presents itself.

The Fire of My Spirit

Motivation. Passion. Mojo. Chutzpah. These are all expressions of the fire within. Absence of fire results in physical lethargy, emotional depression, and mental confusion. Without fire, we are barely engaged in life. We flop through our days as "hollow men," in the evocative words of T. S. Eliot. The healthy presence of fire enlivens us to purpose. It is not necessarily that we are prompted to achieve a goal in order to draw accolades to ourselves. It is that we feel the swell of spirit move through us, and we are compelled to be the vessel through which spirit expresses itself in our lives. In other words, it doesn't really matter what it is that excites us. What is important is that we are excited by something. Fire brings a spark to our lives and ultimately, it can be argued, that our purpose in life is to nurture that spark into a gorgeous conflagration. Be the bright light of spirit on earth.

The Quintessence of My Heart

When we are strong in body, balanced in emotions, clear in mind, and impassioned in purpose, we have achieved the fifth element. The Philosopher's Stone is the inner experience of self anchored in positive self-regard, solid self-esteem, and empowerment. It allows us to gaze bravely at our limitations, knowing that we are not defined by them. We recognize the divine within and allow that to be the compass that guides us. Attaining quintessence is the ability to see that the core truth of who we are has been with us since the moment we came into this world. Certain experiences may have hampered our vision, like massive storm clouds that dim the sun. It does not mean the sun is not there. It merely means the storm clouds need dispersing. Quintessence allows for the sun to shine brightly in our lives once again. Or, as stated in *The Alchemist*, "The boy and his heart had become friends, and neither was capable now of betraying the other."

For those whose hearts are drawn to magical working, this whole process is beautiful and powerful when translated to ritual work, particularly around calling in the quarters. Dion Fortune linked magic and alchemy together when she stated that "magic is the art of changing consciousness at will." The next time you step into the sacred space of your circle, see yourself reflected in the earth of the north, the air of the east, the fire of the south, and the water of the west. Allow yourself to be consciously aware of your physical self in the north, your mental self in the east, your passion and motivation in the south, and your emotional self in the west. As clearly as you would invite an elemental, dragon, or watchtower, invite an aspect of self to be fully present and accepted as integral to your whole experience. Open to the possibility of seeing yourself reflected in the face of the divine at the center, knowing that some aspect of the spark that flames in the Mighty Ones also flames within you yourself. Let your vision be guided by that flame and experience the activation of quintessence, knowing that the intelligence of your heart creates an unshakeable foundation upon which to build a remarkable future. You have achieved the Philosopher's Stone, and from there nothing looks the same again.

Resources

Coelho, Paulo. *The Alchemist*. New York: HarperCollins, 1993.

Gendlin, Eugene T. *Focusing*. New York: Random House, 1982.

Hauck, Dennis William. *Sorcerer's Stone: A Beginner's Guide to Alchemy*. New York: Citadel, 2004.

Don't Be Afraid of the Tarot

by Deborah Blake

I have been reading tarot professionally for many years, and one of the things that surprised me the most was not how accurate it could be (although that was kind of amazing) but how many people were afraid to have their cards read.

Whenever I sat down with a new client, we would begin by chatting, and a number of times I had people say to me that they were scared of getting bad news or having negative cards turn up in a reading. These folks had genuine trepidation—enough so that some of them had put off getting a reading for years, despite a real longing to have one.

Don't get me wrong. I am not in any way belittling these fears. Some people do end up getting bad news, and negative cards show up all the time. But contrary to what you might think, none of this is scary and certainly not a reason to avoid getting a tarot reading. If anything, it is the opposite. I'll tell you why, and hopefully you'll never be afraid of the tarot again.

Bad News

One of the concerns people have voiced to me the most often over the years is the fear that a tarot reading will reveal some unanticipated upcoming disaster or catastrophe. I can honestly tell you that in all the readings I have done, that has only happened once. That's right—once.

Does this mean that only one of the tarot readings I did ever showed bad news? Of course not. What it does mean is that almost every time, the person I was doing the reading for *already knew* what that bad news was going to be. The readings showed plenty of relationships going wrong, financial situations blowing up, bad choices being made.

Sometimes they even showed death. But rarely were any of these things a surprise.

Instead, the tarot cards merely served to confirm what the querents already knew. If someone came to me to ask if a spouse was cheating or if a bad relationship was going to continue to cause pain, somewhere inside, she already knew the answer. Much of the time, a tarot reading serves to confirm the truths you already know on some level or another, acknowledged or not.

That doesn't mean that the reading is unnecessary or has no value. We often need to have confirmation from an outside source, and the tarot serves that purpose well. But hardly ever is the bad news a surprise.

In fact, I have found that, for most people, having the cards corroborate what they already knew on some gut level gives them the courage to act on that knowledge and move forward in a positive way to create changes or deal with difficult truths. Rather than being upset to discover that their worst fears were true, most people were relieved to know that they were right and could now move forward accordingly. At the very least, they have been able share their burdens, and that alone makes the reading worth it for most people.

The Scary Cards

There are certain cards that people are often afraid will turn up in their reading. Death is the one most commonly mentioned, but also the Devil, the Tower, the Hanged Man, and others are perceived as "bad" cards, and some folks are quite fearful that these cards will appear during a session. It is normal to be leery of the cards, but what most people don't realize is that there is no such thing as a "bad" tarot card. All the cards I mentioned, plus others often perceived as negative, can have a positive side as well. It is all in how you interpret them.

This isn't to say that having the Devil or Death cards show up in your reading means that everything is swell, but let's face it: few people ask for a reading when everything in their life is going smoothly. Although I do sometimes get folks who just want a general idea of what's coming next, most of my clients come for a reading during a time of crisis or when important decisions have to be made.

In these cases, the cards that people often perceive as negative or scary can serve an important purpose. Usually, they are there as a message from the universe (or whatever name you want to put on it). That message might be a warning, such as "Don't go down that path!" or "Continuing in the direction you are heading will only lead to unhappiness." Sometimes they seem like they carry bad news but actually herald the potential for positive change or new opportunities, in which case the message is more likely to be "Pay attention" or "What are you missing?"

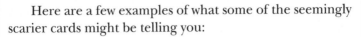

Here are a few examples of what some of the seemingly scarier cards might be telling you:

The Hanged Man

The Hanged Man is usually a card about being stuck. Obviously, no one likes that feeling, and it can be frustrating if this card comes up when you are trying to move forward in a situation. But sometimes this card is telling you that this isn't the right time for change or that you are wasting your energy banging your head against the same old wall in the same old way. If what you're doing isn't working, maybe you need to look at things differently. Can you try going around instead of through?

Or maybe you're not addressing the issues that are *really* holding you back. It's also possible that you're stuck because you're not willing to walk away from a particular person or position; in short, this card may be telling you that you have chosen to remain stuck. If so, you might need to figure out why. Is there something about the situation that makes you feel safe, even though it isn't optimum? Is it just fear of change? The Hanged Man is often a hint that you need to look closer at whatever the issue is.

Death

Death is probably the card that scares people the most. But in my experience, it rarely means *actual* death, although of course it can. Much more often, it signifies the death *of* something: the end of a dream or a relationship or the loss of a job. This almost always feels like bad news, but is it really? After all, the end of one thing is often the beginning of another. One door closing can mean another door opening in a way you might never have expected.

How many of us have suffered through the painful "death" of a relationship we thought at the time was The One, only to discover later that the loss of that person freed us up to be available to someone better? A job crisis might seem like a disaster at first, but sometimes leads us down a new path we might not have taken otherwise.

The Death card usually tells us that whatever the issue is, there is no going back. The answer is final. So the message here is often "Stop trying to fix it; it can't be saved" and "Accept this reality and move on. Mourn if you need to, but start trying to figure out what good might come of the ending of whatever it was." Don't forget—death can often lead to rebirth.

The Devil

The Devil is another scary card. But it doesn't necessarily mean what you think it does. Yes, occasionally it is a warning about a particular person, in which case you probably already knew that keeping that person in your life was a bad idea. If the Devil pops up in a spread where you are asking about someone else's intentions or affect on your life, this card is probably saying, "Run away! Run away now!"

But just as often, the Devil represents something else. Something more internal. We all have our devils that we fight—bad habits, addictions, patterns of behavior we know don't work but that we cling to anyway. If the Devil card is representing one of these, the message may be "You can choose to change this" or "Time to walk away from temptation." There is a reason for the saying "better the devil you know than the devil you don't." We are all afraid of the unknown. The Devil card might be asking, "What are you clinging to because you are comfortable with the devil you know?"

The Tower

The Tower is never good news when it shows up in a reading, but it is also rarely a surprise. It's hard not to notice when your life is blowing up all around you. On the other hand, if the Tower shows up in a future position or in reference to a relationship, the message is clear: "This way lies disaster." It can be a powerful warning, and one which you ignore at your peril.

But the Tower also has a positive side that most people might miss if they're too busy freaking out. It is never fun when things crash and burn, and the Tower doesn't signify minor destruction—it's always huge. But you can't have progress without change, and sometimes things have to fall apart before you can rebuild them into something even better.

If the disaster has already hit, the Tower may be asking, "What can you build out of the ruins?" or "How can you look at this differently? Maybe there is an upside you're missing." If the crisis is still in your future but clearly unavoidable, the Tower card can give you a chance to brace yourself before it hits. In this case, the message might be, "How can I prepare for this better or mitigate the damage?"

No Bad Cards

In truth, there are no bad cards in the tarot. Some cards are more likely than others to herald bad news or make you face tough truths you would really rather have ignored. But hey, if you weren't ready to face those things, you wouldn't have gone for a reading in the first place. Not only are these scary cards probably telling you what you already knew,

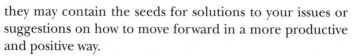

they may contain the seeds for solutions to your issues or suggestions on how to move forward in a more productive and positive way.

To a great extent, the meaning of any card is dependent on where it falls in a reading. I usually use the Celtic Cross spread, which has ten cards. The way I do it, both the sixth card and the last card are indications of future outcomes. The sixth card is either the near future, in which case you may only have time to brace yourself for whatever is coming, or it is a warning to change the path you are on. If the card in that position is one with more negative connotations, it is probably a warning that if you continue with your current behavior, the results are not going to be what you want.

If that last card, which represents the outcome of your current situation (or whatever you were asking about) ends up being one of these "scary" cards, that doesn't mean that doom is inevitable. Any given tarot reading may be accurate at the moment it is done, if the cards are read by someone with skill, but it is not written in stone. Situations shift, people change their minds and their attitudes, paths veer in unexpected directions. If you don't like the answers you get in a reading, perhaps those cards were there to give you the push you needed to make those changes in your own life.

So don't be afraid. Take the messages the cards are giving you, *especially* the uncomfortable or frightening ones, and use them to help you find the answers you came for in the first place. And then maybe try getting another reading in a little while, and don't be surprised if the "scary" cards have been replaced by happier ones because you listened and acted on what you learned.

Key Magick

by Blake Octavian Blair

I've always had an infatuation with keys. They've always seemed to possess a mystical and magickal allure to me, holding an inherent power. Keys let us access a number of things, like vehicles to take us one place to another, our homes, our diaries, or on the magickal level . . . great power and otherworlds. Even the word has gained power in our language and moves beyond even the physical item we mostly familiarly associate with the word. We have key codes, PINs, and even flat, electronic, card-style "pass keys" that have in some instances replaced the traditional key. However, I still have an affinity for the old-fashioned physical key. The mystical, magickal, enchanting key!

Keys have long-standing magickal symbolism. I can't even hazard a guess as to the point in history in which the key was first bestowed such power other than to surmise it was at the time of the invention of the key itself! Keys are synonymous with access, initiation. When one sees a key, one thinks of moving forward. One thinks of revealing the unknown and the previously obscured and locked away. However, it is important to recognize the stark duality of keys. When one holds the key, one may have the power to gain the advancement and liberation the key provides. On the flip side, one who possesses a key has the ability to lock or keep locked away things of great potential power and value. To hold or gain access to a key is to possess great responsibility. However, if you are not the key holder, quickly the key turns to a symbol of denial, obfuscation, and, in perhaps worse scenarios, imprisonment, oppression, or being held captive. Let us dive into the enchanted realm of key magick!

Keys

There is a host of spirits and deities who are associated with keys. The goddess Hecate, revered by magickal folk the world over, is deeply associated with keys. She is a guardian of the crossroads. Crossroads being a sort of gateway to new and different places in and of themselves begets an association with keys, the symbol and tool of passage into new realms. As Hecate is seen to traverse and

serve as a liaison between the realms of the living and the dead, she is said to hold the great skeleton key that that unlocks the gates to all other realms.

Not surprisingly, another spirit closely associated with keys is also a spirit of the crossroads, Papa Legba from the Vodou tradition. He is also often associated with keys, and many people include one on his altars and shrines as an offering. He, too, in this culture, serves as an intermediary between realms. Such spirits can often be seen as spiritual key holders and can be worked with to obtain the keys needed for passage along one's journey.

Keys are a sacred symbol in Christian traditions as well. I'm sure many are familiar with an old phrase that is tossed around in Abrahamic traditions: "the keys to the kingdom of heaven." It has become cultural vernacular, among Christian and non-Christian persons alike, to use the phrase "the pearly gates" to refer to the gated entrance to heaven, at which St. Peter is said to stand with the keys bestowed upon him by Christ. Crossed keys are often thus used as a papal symbol as well. The symbolism of a gate in some form dividing realms and otherworlds is a widespread concept among spiritual traditions.

As shamanic practitioners, my colleagues and I have encountered many instances of spirits (both widely and lesser known) who have prescribed various individual uses and directives for the use of keys as spiritual objects, from being a medicine bag ingredient to a charm to wear, to an offering to be made, to showing the location of lost objects or future places to visit (in both earthly and otherworldly realms). The key is certainly a magickal tool and symbol recognized cross-culturally and through all realms and realities. Keys hold inherent power!

What are good types of keys to use in magick, and where does one find them? Well, while we will get into more nontraditional forms of keys later, let's begin with the good old metal key. Both antique skeleton keys and modern keys make great magickal curios. The antique type can be culled from a variety of sources. Antique shops, thrift stores, yard sales, flea markets, online venues such as eBay, and Pagan and occult shops that carry spell components and magickal curios are all viable options. The ones, however, that have served me the best are flea markets and eBay.

Both generally have an abundance of keys available and at very low prices. Their conditions vary, but some of the wear on older ones is part of their charm. Also, most are very easy to clean up a bit if need be. Hardware stores also, believe it or not, still sell skeleton keys and the locks that go with them for the internal doors in homes.

Modern keys also hold magickal power. Most of us have a key chain we carry house keys, car keys, and other keys on. Even if you don't have a car, you likely have a key for some type of transportation, whether it's a bicycle lock key or a subway pass. Earlier I mentioned electronic pass cards. My husband and I take mass transit subway trains at least five days a week. My subway pass is one such electronic pass card; it is very much a key in its own right. Whether traditional metal keys or pass cards, where there are keys, there is opportunity for magick. You can choose a key chain with magickal symbolism or energy. Key chains with crystals on them can be bought or made. Perhaps try a red jasper for safe travel or a yellow jasper, which is said by some to assist with motion sickness. I have a skeleton-key key chain that I have

enchanted for protection. If you have a pass card key, you can always store it in your wallet with a small, trimmed index card you've inscribed with a sigil with magickal intent.

I use a very modern version of the key every time I write—the USB key. It's called by many names: thumb drive, flash drive, USB stick, etc. However, one of its many titles is in fact USB key, and some people even keep one on their key chain. I save all my writing to USB keys. So, in my authoring, I practice a bit of techno magick. The USB key is both lock and key all at once, as I can also set a password for access to the data on the drive. This leaves the opportunity for another key to be used within the key—a magickal password.

Passwords are an opportunity for enchantment in and of themselves. Since they function as the key that opens the gate to the data they guard, we are certainly in the territory of key magick. However, you have an opportunity for another layer of magick, since whatever you choose as your password is a message you'll be repeating out into the universe every time you type it. Words have power, after all. Think of your password as an affirmation you repeat. Example, if you included "HappyHome" in your password, you'd be infusing those vibes and sending that message into the universe every time you typed it, reinforcing those qualities and drawing them near to you.

Now that we have looked into a bit of the cross-cultural history and magick of keys, figured out what kind of keys you might already be using or have not thought of in day-to-day life, and considered where you might source some keys for use in magick and spellcraft, let us now look at a few simple and fun spells that we can use to dive into the realm of key magick.

Key of Knowledge Talisman

In this ritual spell you will create for yourself your very own key of knowledge to help you with a task or question. Perhaps you are a college student and perpetually studying. Perhaps you are preparing to take a specific professional exam. Maybe you have a pressing life question you've been contemplating heavily. Whichever it may be, hold that intention in mind during the ritual. You can do this ritual many times, for many purposes, and you can even cleanse and reuse the key if you desire. I prefer to use a skeleton key for this particular working. It has a lovely magickal, old-school flare to it! However, any lock- or door-type key will work.

You will need:

Key (skeleton preferred)
Cord of your choice
Candle
Bell
Incense of your choice

Begin by placing all the items on your altar space. Create sacred space and call in your helping spirits and deities according to the protocol of your tradition. Light the incense and use it to smudge all other components if you have not done so already. Place extra attention to the key and cleanse it of any prior intent and purpose.

Pick up and hold the key to your heart. Recite to the spirits,

I, (your name)*, ask you to assist me to empower this key for the growth of my knowledge and ease of learning. Please assist me in* (state your question or what you are studying for).

Now hold the key to your third eye and recite the same request again.

Light the candle, pass the key above its flame, and recite,

I ask for the illumination of wisdom on the topic at hand. Please shed light on my situation so that I can see the best possible solutions clearly and more readily.

Hold your intention in your heart and mind. Hold the key cupped in your hands and blow your intention into it three times.

Tie the cord to the key, and then place it around your neck. Take the bell and ring it around the key and around yourself, calling forth the wisdom and power of your spirits and the universe, further awakening and empowering the key.

Release the sacred space, your helping spirits, and deities as your tradition calls for.

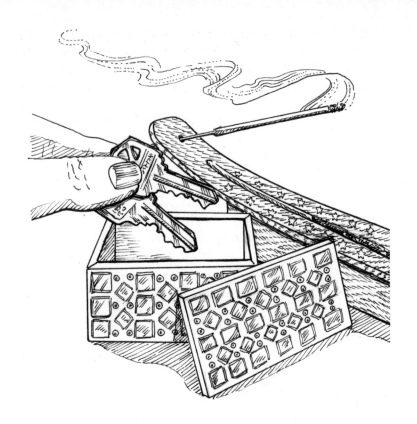

Spell for Home Protection

I particularly like this next spell for when I may be out of town for a couple of days and just want to put that extra boost of energetic protection on my home. The principle of what we are doing magickally in this spell is casting an energetic invisibility cloak around your home. Of course, your home won't literally turn invisible, but the intent is to divert the attention of less-than-noble eyes and minds from your home, simply making your dwelling not of noticeable interest to them.

You will need:

Copies of all the keys to the entrances of your home

A small, externally mirrored box

A protective incense of your choice (optional)

Gather the listed supplies in your working space. If you do not have an externally mirrored box, a simple one can be made with supplies found at your local craft store. Create sacred space and call in your deities and helping spirits in accordance with the methods of your tradition. If you have chosen to use an incense, light it now and use it to smudge all spell components.

Hold the mirrored box in your hands and recite,

Spirit of the mirror, I call to thee!
Surface so shiny, affecting what we see!
I call upon you to please assist me!

Set the box down, with the lid open, and pick up the keys and hold them in your hand and up to your heart. Recite,

Keys to my home, a place so dear,
I ask to boost your protection while I am not here!

Place keys in box.

Spirit of the mirror, I ask of you:
All ignoble eyes and intentions please deflect,
By your powers to reflect!
Blessed be; so mote it be!

Store the box in a secret location inside your home until your return, at which time you may remove the keys from the box, automatically ending the spell.

～

The fun part about key magick is you can use a physical key as a magickal object: even when in plain sight, it does not necessarily have to draw attention. As a common, everyday object, it provides an opportunity for clandestine magick. Because of its varied symbolism both in an artistic, mundane way and in various cultures and religions, people won't think much of seeing a key. Even when it's a skeleton key mundanely dangling around your neck or hanging from an extra hook on your key rack at home, it can work its magick in plain sight without so much as a second thought by those who casually see it. Of course, your fellow magick workers will probably have the idea you're up to something!

As you can see, keys come in a variety of forms, shapes, sizes, and purposes that are both magickal and mundane. However, a mundane key seems in my eye to be simply a blank canvas begging for a splash of magick. The key is an object of power, whether tangible like the house key or transit pass or intangible or philosophical, such as a computer password or a piece of knowledge that makes everything "click" and allows us to move forward. I hope this introduction to the realm of the mystical and magickal key has in fact served as a key in and of itself to help unlock the world of key magick for you. May you traverse forward and unlock your own gateways!

Resources

Illes, Judika. *Encyclopedia of 5,000 Spells: The Ultimate Reference Book for the Magical Arts.* New York: Harper One, 2008.

Illes, Judika. *Encyclopedia of Spirits: The Ultimate Guide to the Magic of Fairies, Genies, Demons, Ghosts, Gods & Goddesses.* New York: Harper One, 2009.

Mueller, Mickie. *The Witch's Mirror: The Lore & Magick of the Looking Glass.* Woodbury, MN: Llewellyn Publications, 2016.

Tresidder, Jack, ed. *The Complete Dictionary of Symbols.* San Francisco: Chronicle Books, 2004.

Almanac Section

Calendar

Time Zones

Lunar Phases

Moon Signs

Full Moons

Sabbats

World Holidays

Incense of the Day

Color of the Day

Almanac Listings

In these listings you will find the date, day, lunar phase, Moon sign, color, and incense for the day, as well as festivals from around the world.

The Date

The date is used in numerological calculations that govern magical rites.

The Day

Each day is ruled by a planet that possesses specific magical influences:

MONDAY (MOON): Peace, sleep, healing, compassion, friends, psychic awareness, purification, and fertility.

TUESDAY (MARS): Passion, sex, courage, aggression, and protection.

WEDNESDAY (MERCURY): The conscious mind, study, travel, divination, and wisdom.

THURSDAY (JUPITER): Expansion, money, prosperity, and generosity.

FRIDAY (VENUS): Love, friendship, reconciliation, and beauty.

SATURDAY (SATURN): Longevity, exorcism, endings, homes, and houses.

SUNDAY (SUN): Healing, spirituality, success, strength, and protection.

The Lunar Phase

The lunar phase is important in determining the best times for magic.

THE WAXING MOON (from the New Moon to the Full) is the ideal time for magic to draw things toward you.

THE FULL MOON is the time of greatest power.

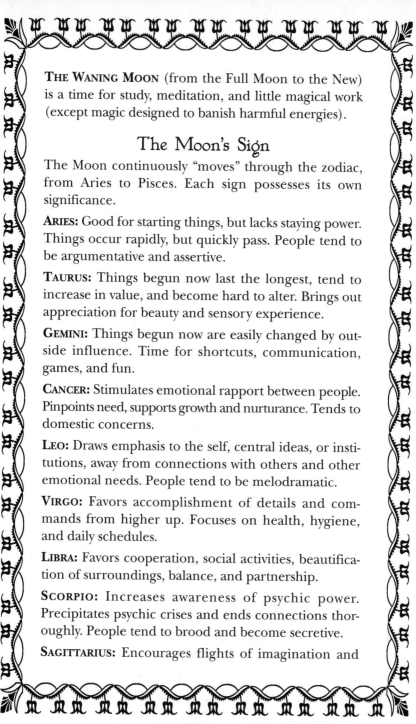

THE WANING MOON (from the Full Moon to the New) is a time for study, meditation, and little magical work (except magic designed to banish harmful energies).

The Moon's Sign

The Moon continuously "moves" through the zodiac, from Aries to Pisces. Each sign possesses its own significance.

ARIES: Good for starting things, but lacks staying power. Things occur rapidly, but quickly pass. People tend to be argumentative and assertive.

TAURUS: Things begun now last the longest, tend to increase in value, and become hard to alter. Brings out appreciation for beauty and sensory experience.

GEMINI: Things begun now are easily changed by outside influence. Time for shortcuts, communication, games, and fun.

CANCER: Stimulates emotional rapport between people. Pinpoints need, supports growth and nurturance. Tends to domestic concerns.

LEO: Draws emphasis to the self, central ideas, or institutions, away from connections with others and other emotional needs. People tend to be melodramatic.

VIRGO: Favors accomplishment of details and commands from higher up. Focuses on health, hygiene, and daily schedules.

LIBRA: Favors cooperation, social activities, beautification of surroundings, balance, and partnership.

SCORPIO: Increases awareness of psychic power. Precipitates psychic crises and ends connections thoroughly. People tend to brood and become secretive.

SAGITTARIUS: Encourages flights of imagination and

confidence. This is an adventurous, philosophical, and athletic Moon sign. Favors expansion and growth.

Capricorn: Develops strong structure. Focus on traditions, responsibilities, and obligations. A good time to set boundaries and rules.

Aquarius: Rebellious energy. Time to break habits and make abrupt changes. Personal freedom and individuality is the focus.

Pisces: The focus is on dreaming, nostalgia, intuition, and psychic impressions. A good time for spiritual or philanthropic activities.

Color and Incense

The color and incense for the day are based on information from *Personal Alchemy* by Amber Wolfe, and relate to the planet that rules each day. This information can be taken into consideration along with other factors when planning works of magic or when blending magic into mundane life. Please note that the incense selections listed are not hard and fast. If you cannot find or do not like the incense listed for the day, choose a similar scent that appeals to you.

Festivals and Holidays

Festivals and holidays of many cultures and nations are listed throughout the year. The exact dates of many ancient festivals are difficult to determine; prevailing data has been used.

Time Zones

The times and dates of all astrological phenomena in this almanac are based on **Eastern Standard Time (EST)**. If you live outside of the Eastern time zone, you will need to make the following adjustments:

PACIFIC STANDARD TIME: Subtract three hours.

MOUNTAIN STANDARD TIME: Subtract two hours.

CENTRAL STANDARD TIME: Subtract one hour.

ALASKA: Subtract four hours.

HAWAII: Subtract five hours.

DAYLIGHT SAVING TIME (ALL ZONES): Add one hour.

Daylight Saving Time begins at 2 am on March 11, 2018, and ends at 2 am on November 4, 2018.

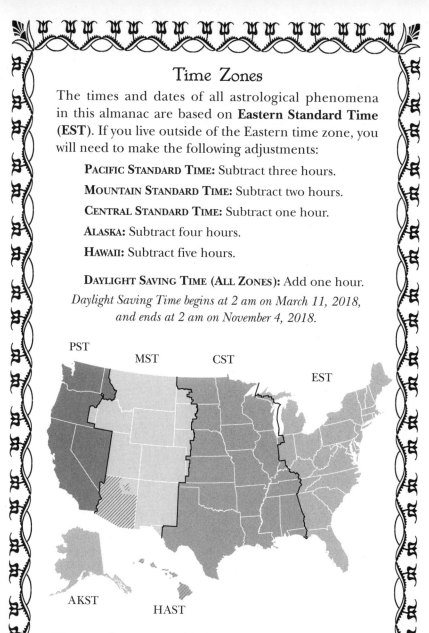

Please refer to a world time zone resource for time adjustments for locations outside the United States.

2018 Sabbats
and Full Moons

January 1	Cancer Full Moon 9:24 pm
January 31	Leo Full Moon 8:27 am
February 2	Imbolc
March 1	Virgo Full Moon 7:51 pm
March 20	Ostara (Spring Equinox)
March 31	Libra Full Moon 8:37 am
April 29	Scorpio Full Moon 8:58 pm
May 1	Beltane
May 29	Sagittarius Full Moon 10:20 am
June 21	Midsummer (Summer Solstice)
June 28	Capricorn Full Moon 12:53 am
July 27	Aquarius Full Moon 4:20 pm
August 1	Lammas
August 26	Pisces Full Moon 7:56 am
September 22	Mabon (Fall Equinox)
September 24	Aries Full Moon 10:52 pm
October 24	Taurus Full Moon 12:45 pm
October 31	Samhain
November 23	Gemini Full Moon 12:39 am
December 21	Yule (Winter Solstice)
December 22	Cancer Full Moon 12:49 pm

All times are Eastern Standard Time (EST)
or Eastern Daylight Time (EDT)

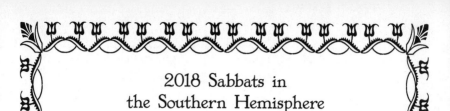

2018 Sabbats in
the Southern Hemisphere

Because Earth's Northern and Southern Hemispheres experience opposite seasons at any given time, the season-based sabbats listed on the previous page and in this almanac section are not correct for those residing south of the equator. Listed here are the Southern Hemisphere sabbat dates for 2018:

February 1	Lammas
March 20	Mabon (Fall Equinox)
May 1	Samhain
June 21	Yule (Winter Solstice)
August 1	Imbolc
September 22	Ostara (Spring Equinox)
November 1	Beltane
December 21	Midsummer (Summer Solstice)

Birthstone poetry reprinted from
The Occult and Curative Powers of Precious Stones
by William T. Fernie, M.D.
Harper & Row (1981)

Originally printed in 1907 as
Precious Stones:
For Curative Wear; and Other Remedial Uses;
Likewise the Nobler Metals

January

☺ **Monday**
New Year's Day • Kwanzaa ends
Waxing Moon
Full Moon 9:24 pm
Color: Gray

Moon Sign: Gemini
Moon enters Cancer 3:10 am
Incense: Rosemary

---

2 **Tuesday**
First Writing Day (Japanese)
Waning Moon
Moon phase: Third Quarter
Color: Black

Moon Sign: Cancer
Incense: Ginger

---

3 **Wednesday**
St. Genevieve's Day
Waning Moon
Moon phase: Third Quarter
Color: White

Moon Sign: Cancer
Moon enters Leo 2:23 am
Incense: Lilac

---

4 **Thursday**
Kamakura Workers' Festival (Japanese)
Waning Moon
Moon phase: Third Quarter
Color: Crimson

Moon Sign: Leo
Incense: Clove

---

5 **Friday**
Bird Day
Waning Moon
Moon phase: Third Quarter
Color: Purple

Moon Sign: Leo
Moon enters Virgo 3:12 am
Incense: Vanilla

---

6 **Saturday**
Epiphany
Waning Moon
Moon phase: Third Quarter
Color: Blue

Moon Sign: Virgo
Incense: Ivy

---

7 **Sunday**
Tricolor Day (Italian)
Waning Moon
Moon phase: Third Quarter
Color: Yellow

Moon Sign: Virgo
Moon enters Libra 7:15 am
Incense: Marigold

January

○ **Monday**
Midwives' Day (Bulgarian)
Waning Moon
Fourth Quarter 5:25 pm
Color: Lavender

Moon Sign: Libra
Incense: Hyssop

9 **Tuesday**
Feast of the Black Nazarene (Filipino)
Waning Moon
Moon phase: Fourth Quarter
Color: White

Moon Sign: Libra
Moon enters Scorpio 3:05 pm
Incense: Bayberry

10 **Wednesday**
Feast of St. Leonie Aviat
Waning Moon
Moon phase: Fourth Quarter
Color: Brown

Moon Sign: Scorpio
Incense: Honeysuckle

11 **Thursday**
Carmentalia (Roman)
Waning Moon
Moon phase: Fourth Quarter
Color: Green

Moon Sign: Scorpio
Incense: Jasmine

12 **Friday**
Revolution Day (Tanzanian)
Waning Moon
Moon phase: Fourth Quarter
Color: Pink

Moon Sign: Scorpio
Moon enters Sagittarius 2:04 am
Incense: Thyme

13 **Saturday**
Twentieth Day (Norwegian)
Waning Moon
Moon phase: Fourth Quarter
Color: Black

Moon Sign: Sagittarius
Incense: Sandalwood

14 **Sunday**
Feast of the Ass (French)
Waning Moon
Moon phase: Fourth Quarter
Color: Gold

Moon Sign: Sagittarius
Moon enters Capricorn 2:42 pm
Incense: Frankincense

15 Monday
Martin Luther King Jr. Day   Moon Sign: Capricorn
Waning Moon   Incense: Lily
Moon phase: Fourth Quarter
Color: Silver

☽ Tuesday
Teachers' Day (Thai)   Moon Sign: Capricorn
Waning Moon   Incense: Geranium
New Moon 9:17 pm
Color: Maroon

17 Wednesday
St. Anthony's Day (Mexican)   Moon Sign: Capricorn
Waxing Moon   Moon enters Aquarius 3:32 am
Moon phase: First Quarter   Incense: Lavender
Color: Yellow

18 Thursday
Feast of St. Athanasius   Moon Sign: Aquarius
Waxing Moon   Incense: Nutmeg
Moon phase: First Quarter
Color: Turquoise

19 Friday
Edgar Allen Poe's birthday   Moon Sign: Aquarius
Waxing Moon   Moon enters Pisces 3:26 pm
Moon phase: First Quarter   Sun enters Aquarius 10:09 pm
Color: Rose   Incense: Rose

20 Saturday
Vogel Gryff (Swiss)   Moon Sign: Pisces
Waxing Moon   Incense: Pine
Moon phase: First Quarter
Color: Indigo

21 Sunday
St. Agnes's Day   Moon Sign: Pisces
Waxing Moon   Incense: Heliotrope
Moon phase: First Quarter
Color: Yellow

January

22 Monday

St. Vincent's Day (French)
Waxing Moon
Moon phase: First Quarter
Color: Ivory

Moon Sign: Pisces
Moon enters Aries 1:27 am
Incense: Neroli

23 Tuesday

Feast of St. Ildefonsus
Waxing Moon
Moon phase: First Quarter
Color: Red

Moon Sign: Aries
Incense: Cedar

◖ Wednesday

Alasitas Fair (Bolivian)
Waxing Moon
Second Quarter 5:20 pm
Color: Topaz

Moon Sign: Aries
Moon enters Taurus 8:39 am
Incense: Bay laurel

25 Thursday

Burns Night (Scottish)
Waxing Moon
Moon phase: Second Quarter
Color: Purple

Moon Sign: Taurus
Incense: Balsam

26 Friday

Australia Day
Waxing Moon
Moon phase: Second Quarter
Color: Coral

Moon Sign: Taurus
Moon enters Gemini 12:40 am
Incense: Violet

27 Saturday

Holocaust Remembrance Day
Waxing Moon
Moon phase: Second Quarter
Color: Gray

Moon Sign: Gemini
Incense: Sage

28 Sunday

St. Charlemagne's Day
Waxing Moon
Moon phase: Second Quarter
Color: Amber

Moon Sign: Gemini
Moon enters Cancer 1:57 pm
Incense: Eucalyptus

29 Monday
Feast of St. Gildas
Waxing Moon
Moon phase: Second Quarter
Color: White

Moon Sign: Cancer
Incense: Narcissus

---

30 Tuesday
Up Helly Aa (Scottish)
Waxing Moon
Moon phase: Second Quarter
Color: Scarlet

Moon Sign: Cancer
Moon enters Leo 1:53 pm
Incense: Cinnamon

 Wednesday
Independence Day (Nauru)
Waxing Moon
Full Moon 8:27 am
Color: Brown

Moon Sign: Leo
Incense: Marjoram

January Birthstones

*By her in January born
No gem save Garnets should be worn;
They will ensure her constancy,
True friendship, and fidelity.*

Modern: Garnet   Zodiac (Capricorn): Ruby

February Birthstones

*The February-born shall find
Sincerity, and peace of mind,
Freedom from passion and from care,
If they the Amethyst will wear.*

Modern: Amethyst   Zodiac (Aquarius): Garnet

February

1 **Thursday**
St. Brigid's Day (Irish) .
Waning Moon
Moon phase: Third Quarter
Color: Green

Moon Sign: Leo
Moon enters Virgo 2:13 pm
Incense: Apricot

---

2 **Friday**
Imbolc • Groundhog Day
Waning Moon
Moon phase: Third Quarter
Color: White

Moon Sign: Virgo
Incense: Orchid

---

3 **Saturday**
St. Blaise's Day
Waning Moon
Moon phase: Third Quarter
Color: Brown

Moon Sign: Virgo
Moon enters Libra 4:47 pm
Incense: Patchouli

---

4 **Sunday**
Independence Day (Sri Lankan)
Waning Moon
Moon phase: Third Quarter
Color: Gold

Moon Sign: Libra
Incense: Almond

---

5 **Monday**
Constitution Day (Mexican)
Waning Moon
Moon phase: Third Quarter
Color: Silver .

Moon Sign: Libra
Moon enters Scorpio 10:56 pm
Incense: Clary sage

---

6 **Tuesday**
Bob Marley's birthday (Jamaican)
Waning Moon
Moon phase: Third Quarter
Color: Gray

Moon Sign: Scorpio
Incense: Bayberry

◐ **Wednesday**
Feast of St. Richard the Pilgrim
Waning Moon
Fourth Quarter 10:54 am
Color: Topaz

Moon Sign: Scorpio
Incense: Honeysuckle

February

8 Thursday
Prešeren Day (Slovenian)
Waning Moon
Moon phase: Fourth Quarter
Color: White

Moon Sign: Scorpio
Moon enters Sagittarius 8:53 am
Incense: Carnation

9 Friday
St. Maron's Day (Lebanese)
Waning Moon
Moon phase: Fourth Quarter
Color: Rose

Moon Sign: Sagittarius
Incense: Yarrow

10 Saturday
Feast of St. Scholastica
Waning Moon
Moon phase: Fourth Quarter
Color: Blue

Moon Sign: Sagittarius
Moon enters Capricorn 9:21 pm
Incense: Magnolia

11 Sunday
National Foundation Day (Japanese)
Waning Moon
Moon phase: Fourth Quarter
Color: Orange

Moon Sign: Capricorn
Incense: Juniper

12 Monday
Abraham Lincoln's birthday
Waning Moon
Moon phase: Fourth Quarter
Color: Gray

Moon Sign: Capricorn
Incense: Hyssop

13 Tuesday
Mardi Gras (Fat Tuesday)
Waning Moon
Moon phase: Fourth Quarter
Color: Maroon

Moon Sign: Capricorn
Moon enters Aquarius 10:11 am
Incense: Basil

14 Wednesday
Valentine's Day • Ash Wednesday
Waning Moon
Moon phase: Fourth Quarter
Color: White

Moon Sign: Aquarius
Incense: Bay laurel

February

Thursday
Susan B. Anthony Day
Waning Moon
New Moon 4:05 pm
Color: Crimson

Moon Sign: Aquarius
Moon enters Pisces 9:42 pm
Incense: Mulberry

16 Friday
Lunar New Year (Dog)
Waxing Moon
Moon phase: First Quarter
Color: Pink

Moon Sign: Pisces
Incense: Mint

17 Saturday
Quirinalia (Roman)
Waxing Moon
Moon phase: First Quarter
Color: Indigo

Moon Sign: Pisces
Incense: Rue

18 Sunday
St. Bernadette's Third Vision
Waxing Moon
Moon phase: First Quarter
Color: Yellow

Moon Sign: Pisces
Moon enters Aries 7:05 am
Sun enters Pisces 12:18 pm
Incense: Heliotrope

19 Monday
Presidents' Day
Waxing Moon
Moon phase: First Quarter
Color: Ivory

Moon Sign: Aries
Incense: Rosemary

20 Tuesday
World Day of Social Justice
Waxing Moon
Moon phase: First Quarter
Color: Red

Moon Sign: Aries
Moon enters Taurus 2:12 pm
Incense: Ylang-ylang

21 Wednesday
Feralia (Roman)
Waxing Moon
Moon phase: First Quarter
Color: Brown

Moon Sign: Taurus
Incense: Lilac

February

22 Thursday
Caristia (Roman)
Waxing Moon
Moon phase: First Quarter
Color: Turquoise

Moon Sign: Taurus
Moon enters Gemini 7:07 pm
Incense: Jasmine

◑ Friday
Mashramani Festival (Guyana)
Waxing Moon
Second Quarter 3:09 am
Color: Purple

Moon Sign: Gemini
Incense: Rose

24 Saturday
Regifugium (Roman)
Waxing Moon
Moon phase: Second Quarter
Color: Black

Moon Sign: Gemini
Moon enters Cancer 10:06 pm
Incense: Sandalwood

25 Sunday
St. Walburga's Day (German)
Waxing Moon
Moon phase: Second Quarter
Color: Amber

Moon Sign: Cancer
Incense: Marigold

26 Monday
Zamboanga Day (Filipino)
Waxing Moon
Moon phase: Second Quarter
Color: Lavender

Moon Sign: Cancer
Moon enters Leo 11:42 pm
Incense: Neroli

27 Tuesday
Independence Day (Dominican)
Waxing Moon
Moon phase: Second Quarter
Color: White

Moon Sign: Leo
Incense: Ginger

28 Wednesday
Kelevala Day (Finnish)
Waxing Moon
Moon phase: Second Quarter
Color: Yellow

Moon Sign: Leo
Incense: Lavender

March

Thursday
Purim
Waxing Moon
Full Moon 7:51 pm
Color: Green

Moon Sign: Leo
Moon enters Virgo 12:57 am
Incense: Clove

---

2 Friday
Lantern Festival (Chinese)
Waning Moon
Moon phase: Third Quarter
Color: White

Moon Sign: Virgo
Incense: Cypress

---

3 Saturday
Doll Festival (Japanese)
Waning Moon
Moon phase: Third Quarter
Color: Gray

Moon Sign: Virgo
Moon enters Libra 3:20 am
Incense: Ivy

---

4 Sunday
St. Casimir's Fair (Polish and Lithuanian)
Waning Moon
Moon phase: Third Quarter
Color: Gold

Moon Sign: Libra
Incense: Hyacinth

---

5 Monday
Navigium Isidis Festival (Roman)
Waning Moon
Moon phase: Third Quarter
Color: Silver

Moon Sign: Libra
Moon enters Scorpio 8:23 am
Incense: Lily

---

6 Tuesday
Alamo Day (Texan)
Waning Moon
Moon phase: Third Quarter
Color: Scarlet

Moon Sign: Scorpio
Incense: Geranium

---

7 Wednesday
Vejovis Festival (Roman)
Waning Moon
Moon phase: Third Quarter
Color: Topaz

Moon Sign: Scorpio
Moon enters Sagittarius 5:03 pm
Incense: Bay laurel

8   Thursday

International Women's Day   Moon Sign: Sagittarius

Waning Moon   Incense: Myrrh

Moon phase: Third Quarter

Color: Purple

◐   Friday

Teachers' Day (Lebanese)   Moon Sign: Sagittarius

Waning Moon   Incense: Violet

Fourth Quarter 6:20 am

Color: Coral

---

10   Saturday

Tibet Uprising Day   Moon Sign: Sagittarius

Waning Moon   Moon enters Capricorn 4:52 am

Moon phase: Fourth Quarter   Incense: Sage

Color: Blue

---

11   Sunday

Johnny Appleseed Day   Moon Sign: Capricorn

Waning Moon   Incense: Eucalyptus

Moon phase: Fourth Quarter   *Daylight Saving Time begins at 2 am*

Color: Amber

---

12   Monday

Girl Scouts' birthday   Moon Sign: Capricorn

Waning Moon   Moon enters Aquarius 6:44 pm

Moon phase: Fourth Quarter   Incense: Narcissus

Color: White

---

13   Tuesday

Feast of St. Leander of Seville   Moon Sign: Aquarius

Waning Moon   Incense: Cedar

Moon phase: Fourth Quarter

Color: Red

---

14   Wednesday

Pi Day   Moon Sign: Aquarius

Waning Moon   Incense: Marjoram

Moon phase: Fourth Quarter

Color: Yellow

15 Thursday
Fertility Festival (Japanese)
Waning Moon
Moon phase: Fourth Quarter
Color: Turquoise

Moon Sign: Aquarius
Moon enters Pisces 6:12 am
Incense: Balsam

16 Friday
St. Urho's Day (Finnish-American)
Waning Moon
Moon phase: Fourth Quarter
Color: Pink

Moon Sign: Pisces
Incense: Thyme

Saturday
St. Patrick's Day
Waning Moon
New Moon 9:12 am
Color: Black

Moon Sign: Pisces
Moon enters Aries 2:57 pm
Incense: Magnolia

18 Sunday
Blue Dragon Festival (Chinese)
Waxing Moon
Moon phase: First Quarter
Color: Orange

Moon Sign: Aries
Incense: Juniper

19 Monday
Minna Canth's birthday (Finnish)
Waxing Moon
Moon phase: First Quarter
Color: Gray

Moon Sign: Aries
Moon enters Taurus 9:07 pm
Incense: Hyssop

20 Tuesday
Ostara • Spring Equinox
Waxing Moon
Moon phase: First Quarter
Color: Maroon

Moon Sign: Taurus
Sun enters Aries 12:15 pm
Incense: Cinnamon

21 Wednesday
Harmony Day (Australian)
Waxing Moon
Moon phase: First Quarter
Color: Brown

Moon Sign: Taurus
Incense: Honeysuckle

22 Thursday
World Water Day
Waxing Moon
Moon phase: First Quarter
Color: Green

Moon Sign: Taurus
Moon enters Gemini 1:30 am
Incense: Jasmine

---

23 Friday
Denver March Powwow (ends Mar. 25)
Waxing Moon
Moon phase: First Quarter
Color: White

Moon Sign: Gemini
Incense: Vanilla

** Saturday**
Day of Blood (Roman)
Waxing Moon
Second Quarter 11:35 am
Color: Indigo

Moon Sign: Gemini
Moon enters Cancer 4:53 am
Incense: Pine

---

25 Sunday
Palm Sunday
Waxing Moon
Moon phase: Second Quarter
Color: Gold

Moon Sign: Cancer
Incense: Frankincense

---

26 Monday
Prince Kuhio Day (Hawaiian)
Waxing Moon
Moon phase: Second Quarter
Color: Lavender

Moon Sign: Cancer
Moon enters Leo 7:45 am
Incense: Clary sage

---

27 Tuesday
World Theatre Day
Waxing Moon
Moon phase: Second Quarter
Color: Black

Moon Sign: Leo
Incense: Basil

---

28 Wednesday
Weed Appreciation Day
Waxing Moon
Moon phase: Second Quarter
Color: Yellow

Moon Sign: Leo
Moon enters Virgo 10:30 am
Incense: Lilac

March

29   Thursday

Feast of St. Eustace of Luxeuil   Moon Sign: Virgo
Waxing Moon   Incense: Nutmeg
Moon phase: Second Quarter
Color: Crimson

---

30   Friday

Good Friday   Moon Sign: Virgo
Waxing Moon   Moon enters Libra 1:52 pm
Moon phase: Second Quarter   Incense: Orchid
Color: Rose

☺   Saturday

Passover begins   Moon Sign: Libra
Waxing Moon   Incense: Patchouli
Full Moon 8:37 am
Color: Blue

March Birthstones

Who in this world of ours, her eyes
In March first opens, shall be wise.
In days of peril, firm and brave,
And wear a Bloodstone to her grave.

Modern: Aquamarine
Zodiac (Pisces): Amethyst

April

♈

1 Sunday
All Fools' Day • April Fools' Day • Easter   Moon Sign: Libra
Waning Moon   Moon enters Scorpio 6:57 pm
Moon phase: Third Quarter   Incense: Almond
Color: Amber

2 Monday
The Battle of Flowers (French)   Moon Sign: Scorpio
Waning Moon   Incense: Rosemary
Moon phase: Third Quarter
Color: Ivory

3 Tuesday
Feast of St. Mary of Egypt   Moon Sign: Scorpio
Waning Moon   Incense: Ylang-ylang
Moon phase: Third Quarter
Color: White

4 Wednesday
Megalesia (Roman)   Moon Sign: Scorpio
Waning Moon   Moon enters Sagittarius 2:55 am
Moon phase: Third Quarter   Incense: Marjoram
Color: Topaz

5 Thursday
Tomb-Sweeping Day (Chinese)   Moon Sign: Sagittarius
Waning Moon   Incense: Apricot
Moon phase: Third Quarter
Color: Purple

6 Friday
Orthodox Good Friday   Moon Sign: Sagittarius
Waning Moon   Moon enters Capricorn 2:01 pm
Moon phase: Third Quarter   Incense: Alder
Color: Pink

7 Saturday
Passover ends   Moon Sign: Capricorn
Waning Moon   Incense: Sandalwood
Moon Phase: Third Quarter
Color: Gray

April

○ **Sunday**
Orthodox Easter
Waning Moon
Fourth Quarter 3:18 am
Color: Yellow

Moon Sign: Capricorn
Incense: Heliotrope

9 Monday
Valour Day (Filipino)
Waning Moon
Moon phase: Fourth Quarter
Color: Gray

Moon Sign: Capricorn
Moon enters Aquarius 2:50 am
Incense: Neroli

10 Tuesday
Siblings Day
Waning Moon
Moon phase: Fourth Quarter
Color: Maroon

Moon Sign: Aquarius
Incense: Bayberry

11 Wednesday
Juan Santamaría Day (Costa Rican)
Waning Moon
Moon phase: Fourth Quarter
Color: White

Moon Sign: Aquarius
Moon enters Pisces 2:40 pm
Incense: Lavender

12 Thursday
Children's Day (Bolivian and Haitian)
Waning Moon
Moon phase: Fourth Quarter
Color: Green

Moon Sign: Pisces
Incense: Carnation

13 Friday
Thai New Year (ends April 15)
Waning Moon
Moon phase: Fourth Quarter
Color: Coral

Moon Sign: Pisces
Moon enters Aries 11:25 pm
Incense: Mint

14 Saturday
Black Day (South Korean)
Waning Moon
Moon phase: Fourth Quarter
Color: Brown

Moon Sign: Aries
Incense: Rue

April ♈

🌙 Sunday
Fordicidia (Roman)　　　　　　　Moon Sign: Aries
Waning Moon　　　　　　　　　　Incense: Hyacinth
First Quarter 9:57 pm
Color: Orange

---

16 Monday
Sechseläuten (Swiss)　　　　　　Moon Sign: Aries
Waxing Moon　　　　　Moon enters Taurus 4:51 pm
Moon phase: First Quarter　　　　Incense: Narcissus
Color: White

---

17 Tuesday
Yayoi Matsuri (Japanese)　　　　Moon Sign: Taurus
Waxing Moon　　　　　　　　　　Incense: Ginger
Moon phase: First Quarter
Color: Scarlet

---

18 Wednesday
International Day for Monuments and Sites　Moon Sign: Taurus
Waxing Moon　　　　Moon enters Gemini 8:02 am
Moon phase: First Quarter　　　　Incense: Bay laurel
Color: Brown

---

19 Thursday
Primrose Day (British)　　　　　Moon Sign: Gemini
Waxing Moon　　　　Sun enters Taurus 11:13 pm
Moon phase: First Quarter　　　　Incense: Myrrh
Color: Crimson

---

20 Friday
Drum Festival (Japanese)　　　　Moon Sign: Gemini
Waxing Moon　　　　Moon enters Cancer 10:26 am
Moon phase: First Quarter　　　　Incense: Orchid
Color: Rose

---

21 Saturday
Tiradentes Day (Brazilian)　　　Moon Sign: Cancer
Waxing Moon　　　　　　　　　　Incense: Ivy
Moon phase: First Quarter
Color: Blue

( ) Sunday
Earth Day
Waxing Moon
Second Quarter 5:46 pm
Color: Gold

Moon Sign: Cancer
Moon enters Leo 1:09 pm
Incense: Marigold

---

23 Monday
St. George's Day
Waxing Moon
Moon phase: Second Quarter
Color: Silver

Moon Sign: Leo
Incense: Hyssop

---

24 Tuesday
St. Mark's Eve
Waxing Moon
Moon phase: Second Quarter
Color: Red

Moon Sign: Leo
Moon enters Virgo 4:40 pm
Incense: Cedar

---

25 Wednesday
Robigalia (Roman)
Waxing Moon
Moon phase: Second Quarter
Color: Yellow

Moon Sign: Virgo
Incense: Lilac

---

26 Thursday
Chernobyl Remembrance Day (Belarusian)
Waxing Moon
Moon phase: Second Quarter
Color: Turquoise

Moon Sign: Virgo
Moon enters Libra 9:13 pm
Incense: Mulberry

---

27 Friday
Arbor Day
Waxing Moon
Moon phase: Second Quarter
Color: White

Moon Sign: Libra
Incense: Rose

---

28 Saturday
Floralia (Roman)
Waxing Moon
Moon phase: Second Quarter
Color: Indigo

Moon Sign: Libra
Incense: Magnolia

April

☺ **Sunday**
Showa Day (Japanese)
Waxing Moon
Full Moon 8:58 pm
Color: Orange

Moon Sign: Libra
Moon enters Scorpio 3:11 am
Incense: Eucalyptus

---

30 **Monday**
Walpurgis Night • May Eve
Waning Moon
Moon phase: Third Quarter
Color: Gray

Moon Sign: Scorpio
Incense: Lily

April Birthstones

She who from April dates her years,
Diamonds shall wear, lest bitter tears
For vain repentance flow; this stone
Emblem for innocence is known.

Modern: Diamond
Zodiac (Aries): Bloodstone

May

1   Tuesday
Beltane • May Day
Waning Moon
Moon phase: Third Quarter
Color: Maroon

Moon Sign: Scorpio
Moon enters Sagittarius 11:20 am
Incense: Geranium

---

2   Wednesday
National Education Day (Indonesian)
Waning Moon
Moon phase: Third Quarter
Color: Brown

Moon Sign: Sagittarius
Incense: Honeysuckle

---

3   Thursday
Roodmas
Waning Moon
Moon phase: Third Quarter
Color: White

Moon Sign: Sagittarius
Moon enters Capricorn 10:06 pm
Incense: Nutmeg

---

4   Friday
Bona Dea (Roman)
Waning Moon
Moon phase: Third Quarter
Color: Purple

Moon Sign: Capricorn
Incense: Violet

---

5   Saturday
Cinco de Mayo (Mexican)
Waning Moon
Moon phase: Third Quarter
Color: Black

Moon Sign: Capricorn
Incense: Pine

---

6   Sunday
Martyrs' Day (Lebanese and Syrian)
Waning Moon
Moon phase: Third Quarter
Color: Yellow

Moon Sign: Capricorn
Moon enters Aquarius 10:48 am
Incense: Juniper

○   Monday
Pilgrimage of St. Nicholas (Italian)
Waning Moon
Fourth Quarter 10:09 pm
Color: Ivory

Moon Sign: Aquarius
Incense: Neroli

May

8 Tuesday
White Lotus Day (Theosophical)
Waning Moon
Moon phase: Fourth Quarter
Color: Gray

Moon Sign: Aquarius
Moon enters Pisces 11:11 pm
Incense: Basil

---

9 Wednesday
Lemuria (Roman)
Waning Moon
Moon phase: Fourth Quarter
Color: Topaz

Moon Sign: Pisces
Incense: Lavender

---

10 Thursday
Independence Day (Romanian)
Waning Moon
Moon phase: Fourth Quarter
Color: Green

Moon Sign: Pisces
Incense: Jasmine

---

11 Friday
Ukai season opens (Japanese)
Waning Moon
Moon phase: Fourth Quarter
Color: Rose

Moon Sign: Pisces
Moon enters Aries 8:40 am
Incense: Yarrow

---

12 Saturday
Florence Nightingale's birthday
Waning Moon
Moon phase: Fourth Quarter
Color: Blue

Moon Sign: Aries
Incense: Patchouli

---

13 Sunday
Mother's Day
Waning Moon
Moon phase: Fourth Quarter
Color: Gold

Moon Sign: Aries
Moon enters Taurus 2:15 pm
Incense: Frankincense

---

14 Monday
Carabao Festival (Spanish)
Waning Moon
Moon phase: Fourth Quarter
Color: Lavender

Moon Sign: Taurus
Incense: Clary sage

May

☽ **Tuesday**
Festival of St. Dymphna
Waning Moon
New Moon 7:48 am
Color: White

Moon Sign: Taurus
Moon enters Gemini 4:43 pm
Incense: Bayberry

---

16 **Wednesday**
Ramadan begins
Waxing Moon
Moon phase: First Quarter
Color: Yellow

Moon Sign: Gemini
Incense: Marjoram

---

17 **Thursday**
Norwegian Constitution Day
Waxing Moon
Moon phase: First Quarter
Color: Purple

Moon Sign: Gemini
Moon enters Cancer 5:47 pm
Incense: Balsam

---

18 **Friday**
Battle of Las Piedras Day (Uruguayan)
Waxing Moon
Moon phase: First Quarter
Color: Coral

Moon Sign: Cancer
Incense: Vanilla

---

19 **Saturday**
Mother's Day (Kyrgyzstani)
Waxing Moon
Moon phase: First Quarter
Color: Indigo

Moon Sign: Cancer
Moon enters Leo 7:11 pm
Incense: Sage

---

20 **Sunday**
Shavuot
Waxing Moon
Moon phase: First Quarter
Color: Amber

Moon Sign: Leo
Sun enters Gemini 10:15 pm
Incense: Almond

○ **Monday**
Victoria Day (Canadian)
Waxing Moon
Second Quarter 11:49 pm
Color: Gray

Moon Sign: Leo
Moon enters Virgo 10:03 pm
Incense: Rosemary

May

22 Tuesday
Harvey Milk Day (Californian)
Waxing Moon
Moon phase: Second Quarter
Color: Red

Moon Sign: Virgo
Incense: Cedar

23 Wednesday
Tubilustrium (Roman)
Waxing Moon
Moon phase: Second Quarter
Color: Topaz

Moon Sign: Virgo
Incense: Bay laurel

24 Thursday
Education and Culture Day (Bulgarian)
Waxing Moon
Moon phase: Second Quarter
Color: Turquoise

Moon Sign: Virgo
Moon enters Libra 2:52 am
Incense: Clove

25 Friday
Missing Children's Day
Waxing Moon
Moon phase: Second Quarter
Color: Pink

Moon Sign: Libra
Incense: Cypress

26 Saturday
Pepys's Commemoration (English)
Waxing Moon
Moon phase: Second Quarter
Color: Black

Moon Sign: Libra
Moon enters Scorpio 9:39 am
Incense: Sandalwood

27 Sunday
Feast of St. Bede the Venerable
Waxing Moon
Moon phase: Second Quarter
Color: Orange

Moon Sign: Scorpio
Incense: Hyacinth

28 Monday
Memorial Day
Waxing Moon
Moon phase: Second Quarter
Color: Silver

Moon Sign: Scorpio
Moon enters Sagittarius 6:29 pm
Incense: Hyssop

May

Tuesday
Oak Apple Day (English)
Waxing Moon
Full Moon 10:20 am
Color: Scarlet

Moon Sign: Sagittarius
Incense: Cinnamon

30 Wednesday
Canary Islands Day
Waning Moon
Moon phase: Third Quarter
Color: White

Moon Sign: Sagittarius
Incense: Honeysuckle

31 Thursday
Visitation of Mary
Waning Moon
Moon phase: Third Quarter
Color: Green

Moon Sign: Sagittarius
Moon enters Capricorn 5:27 am
Incense: Apricot

May Birthstones

Who first beholds the light of day,
In spring's sweet flowery month of May,
And wears an Emerald all her life,
Shall be a loved, and happy wife.

Modern: Emerald
Zodiac (Taurus): Sapphire

June ♊

1 Friday
Dayak Harvest Festival (Malaysian)
Waning Moon
Moon phase: Third Quarter
Color: Rose

Moon Sign: Capricorn
Incense: Thyme

2 Saturday
Republic Day (Italian)
Waning Moon
Moon phase: Third Quarter
Color: Gray

Moon Sign: Capricorn
Moon enters Aquarius 6:06 pm
Incense: Ivy

3 Sunday
Feast of St. Clotilde
Waning Moon
Moon phase: Third Quarter
Color: Yellow

Moon Sign: Aquarius
Incense: Heliotrope

4 Monday
Flag Day (Estonian)
Waning Moon
Moon phase: Third Quarter
Color: Lavender

Moon Sign: Aquarius
Incense: Lily

5 Tuesday
Constitution Day (Danish)
Waning Moon
Moon phase: Third Quarter
Color: Red

Moon Sign: Aquarius
Moon enters Pisces 6:53 am
Incense: Ginger

☽ Wednesday
National Day of Sweden
Waning Moon
Fourth Quarter 2:32 pm
Color: Topaz

Moon Sign: Pisces
Incense: Lavender

7 Thursday
Vestalia begins (Roman)
Waning Moon
Moon phase: Fourth Quarter
Color: Crimson

Moon Sign: Pisces
Moon enters Aries 5:26 pm
Incense: Balsam

June ♊

8 Friday
World Oceans Day
Waning Moon
Moon phase: Fourth Quarter
Color: Purple

Moon Sign: Aries
Incense: Rose

---

9 Saturday
Heroes' Day (Ugandan)
Waning Moon
Moon phase: Fourth Quarter
Color: Blue

Moon Sign: Aries
Incense: Rue

---

10 Sunday
Portugal Day
Waning Moon
Moon phase: Fourth Quarter
Color: Orange

Moon Sign: Aries
Moon enters Taurus 12:04 am
Incense: Marigold

---

11 Monday
Kamehameha Day (Hawaiian)
Waning Moon
Moon phase: Fourth Quarter
Color: White

Moon Sign: Taurus
Incense: Narcissus

---

12 Tuesday
Independence Day (Filipino)
Waning Moon
Moon phase: Fourth Quarter
Color: Scarlet

Moon Sign: Taurus
Moon enters Gemini 2:53 am
Incense: Ylang-ylang

☽ Wednesday
St. Anthony of Padua's Day
Waning Moon
New Moon 3:43 pm
Color: Yellow

Moon Sign: Gemini
Incense: Lilac

---

14 Thursday
Ramadan ends • Flag Day
Waxing Moon
Moon phase: First Quarter
Color: Green

Moon Sign: Gemini
Moon enters Cancer 3:20 am
Incense: Mulberry

June

♊

15 Friday
Vestalia ends (Roman)
Waxing Moon
Moon phase: First Quarter
Color: Coral

Moon Sign: Cancer
Incense: Mint

16 Saturday
Bloomsday (Irish)
Waxing Moon
Moon phase: First Quarter
Color: Brown

Moon Sign: Cancer
Moon enters Leo 3:21 am
Incense: Magnolia

17 Sunday
Father's Day
Waxing Moon
Moon phase: First Quarter
Color: Gold

Moon Sign: Leo
Incense: Eucalyptus

18 Monday
Waterloo Day (British)
Waxing Moon
Moon phase: First Quarter
Color: Silver

Moon Sign: Leo
Moon enters Virgo 4:41 am
Incense: Clary sage

19 Tuesday
Juneteenth
Waxing Moon
Moon phase: First Quarter
Color: Gray

Moon Sign: Virgo
Incense: Basil

☾ Wednesday
Flag Day (Argentinian)
Waxing Moon
Second Quarter 6:51 am
Color: White

Moon Sign: Virgo
Moon enters Libra 8:29 am
Incense: Bay laurel

21 Thursday
Litha • Summer Solstice
Waxing Moon
Moon phase: Second Quarter
Color: Turquoise

Moon Sign: Libra
Sun enters Cancer 6:07 am
Incense: Myrrh

June

22 Friday
Teachers' Day (El Salvadoran)
Waxing Moon
Moon phase: Second Quarter
Color: Rose

Moon Sign: Libra
Moon enters Scorpio 3:11 pm
Incense: Alder

23 Saturday
St. John's Eve
Waxing Moon
Moon phase: Second Quarter
Color: Indigo

Moon Sign: Scorpio
Incense: Sage

24 Sunday
St. John's Day
Waxing Moon
Moon phase: Second Quarter
Color: Yellow

Moon Sign: Scorpio
Incense: Frankincense

25 Monday
Fiesta de Santa Orosia (Spanish)
Waxing Moon
Moon phase: Second Quarter
Color: Gray

Moon Sign: Scorpio
Moon enters Sagittarius 12:29 am
Incense: Hyssop

26 Tuesday
Pied Piper Day (German)
Waxing Moon
Moon phase: Second Quarter
Color: Maroon

Moon Sign: Sagittarius
Incense: Geranium

27 Wednesday
Seven Sleepers' Day (German)
Waxing Moon
Moon phase: Second Quarter
Color: Brown

Moon Sign: Sagittarius
Moon enters Capricorn 11:52 am
Incense: Honeysuckle

☻ Thursday
Paul Bunyan Day
Waxing Moon
Full Moon 12:53 am
Color: Purple

Moon Sign: Capricorn
Incense: Carnation

June

29 Friday

Haro Wine Battle (Spain)
Waning Moon
Moon phase: Third Quarter
Color: Pink

Moon Sign: Capricorn
Incense: Yarrow

30 Saturday

The Burning of the Three Firs (French)
Waning Moon
Moon phase: Third Quarter
Color: Blue

Moon Sign: Capricorn
Moon enters Aquarius 12:37 am
Incense: Patchouli

June Birthstones

Who comes with summer to this earth,
And owes to June her hour of birth,
With ring of Agate on her hand,
Can health, wealth, and long life command.

Modern: Moonstone or Pearl
Zodiac (Gemini): Agate

July

1 Sunday
Mt. Fuji climbing season opens
Waning Moon
Moon phase: Third Quarter
Color: Gold

Moon Sign: Aquarius
Incense: Almond

---

2 Monday
World UFO Day
Waning Moon
Moon phase: Third Quarter
Color: White

Moon Sign: Aquarius
Moon enters Pisces 1:31 pm
Incense: Rosemary

---

3 Tuesday
Dog Days of Summer begin
Waning Moon
Moon phase: Third Quarter
Color: Scarlet

Moon Sign: Pisces
Incense: Bayberry

---

4 Wednesday
Independence Day
Waning Moon
Moon phase: Third Quarter
Color: Yellow

Moon Sign: Pisces
Incense: Marjoram

---

5 Thursday
Tynwald Day (Manx)
Waning Moon
Moon phase: Third Quarter
Color: Green

Moon Sign: Pisces
Moon enters Aries 12:50 am
Incense: Nutmeg

◗ Friday
San Fermín begins (Spanish)
Waning Moon
Fourth Quarter 3:51 am
Color: Purple

Moon Sign: Aries
Incense: Orchid

---

7 Saturday
Star Festival (Japanese)
Waning Moon
Moon phase: Fourth Quarter
Color: Gray

Moon Sign: Aries
Moon enters Taurus 8:51 am
Incense: Pine

July
♋

8 Sunday
Feast of St. Sunniva
Waning Moon
Moon phase: Fourth Quarter
Color: Amber

Moon Sign: Taurus
Incense: Juniper

---

9 Monday
Battle of Sempach Day (Swiss)
Waning Moon
Moon phase: Fourth Quarter
Color: Ivory

Moon Sign: Taurus
Moon enters Gemini 12:58 pm
Incense: Neroli

---

10 Tuesday
Nicola Tesla Day
Waning Moon
Moon phase: Fourth Quarter
Color: Red

Moon Sign: Gemini
Incense: Cedar

---

11 Wednesday
Mongolian Naadam Festival (ends July 13)
Waning Moon
Moon phase: Fourth Quarter
Color: Topaz

Moon Sign: Gemini
Moon enters Cancer 1:59 pm
Incense: Lilac

☽ **Thursday**
Malala Day
Waning Moon
New Moon 10:48 pm
Color: White

Moon Sign: Cancer
Incense: Jasmine

---

13 Friday
Feast of St. Mildrith
Waxing Moon
Moon phase: First Quarter
Color: Pink

Moon Sign: Cancer
Moon enters Leo 1:31 pm
Incense: Vanilla

---

14 Saturday
Bastille Day (French)
Waxing Moon
Moon phase: First Quarter
Color: Black

Moon Sign: Leo
Incense: Sandalwood

July ♋

15 Sunday
St. Swithin's Day
Waxing Moon
Moon phase: First Quarter
Color: Yellow

Moon Sign: Leo
Moon enters Virgo 1:31 pm
Incense: Hyacinth

16 Monday
Fiesta de la Tirana (Chilean)
Waxing Moon
Moon phase: First Quarter
Color: Gray

Moon Sign: Virgo
Incense: Lily

17 Tuesday
Gion Festival first Yamaboko parade (Japanese)
Waxing Moon
Moon phase: First Quarter
Color: Maroon

Moon Sign: Virgo
Moon enters Libra 3:42 pm
Incense: Ylang-ylang

18 Wednesday
Nelson Mandela International Day
Waxing Moon
Moon phase: First Quarter
Color: Brown

Moon Sign: Libra
Incense: Lavender

☽ Thursday
Flitch Day (English)
Waxing Moon
Second Quarter 3:52 pm
Color: Purple

Moon Sign: Libra
Moon enters Scorpio 9:13 pm
Incense: Clove

20 Friday
Binding of Wreaths (Lithuanian)
Waxing Moon
Moon phase: Second Quarter
Color: Rose

Moon Sign: Scorpio
Incense: Cypress

21 Saturday
National Day (Belgian)
Waxing Moon
Moon phase: Second Quarter
Color: Blue

Moon Sign: Scorpio
Incense: Rue

July

22 Sunday
St. Mary Magdalene's Day
Waxing Moon
Moon phase: Second Quarter
Color: Orange

Moon Sign: Scorpio
Moon enters Sagittarius 6:12 am
Sun enters Leo 5:00 pm
Incense: Marigold

23 Monday
Mysteries of St. Cristina (Italian)
Waxing Moon
Moon phase: Second Quarter
Color: Lavender

Moon Sign: Sagittarius
Incense: Hyssop

24 Tuesday
Gion Festival second Yamaboko parade (Japanese)
Waxing Moon
Moon phase: Second Quarter
Color: Gray

Moon Sign: Sagittarius
Moon enters Capricorn 5:49 pm
Incense: Ginger

25 Wednesday
Illapa Festival (Incan)
Waxing Moon
Moon phase: Second Quarter
Color: White

Moon Sign: Capricorn
Incense: Bay laurel

26 Thursday
St. Anne's Day
Waxing Moon
Moon phase: Second Quarter
Color: Crimson

Moon Sign: Capricorn
Incense: Apricot

☉ Friday
Sleepyhead Day (Finnish)
Waxing Moon
Full Moon 4:20 pm
Color: Coral

Moon Sign: Capricorn
Moon enters Aquarius 6:41 am
Incense: Rose

28 Saturday
Independence Day (Peruvian)
Waning Moon
Moon phase: Third Quarter
Color: Indigo

Moon Sign: Aquarius
Incense: Ivy

July

29 Sunday
St. Olaf Festival (Faroese)
Waning Moon
Moon phase: Third Quarter
Color: Amber

Moon Sign: Aquarius
Moon enters Pisces 7:28 pm
Incense: Heliotrope

---

30 Monday
Micman Festival of St. Ann
Waning Moon
Moon phase: Third Quarter
Color: Silver

Moon Sign: Pisces
Incense: Narcissus

---

31 Tuesday
Feast of St. Ignatius
Waning Moon
Moon phase: Third Quarter
Color: Red

Moon Sign: Pisces
Incense: Cinnamon

July Birthstones

The glowing Ruby shall adorn
Those who in warm July are born;
Then will they be exempt and free
From love's doubt, and anxiety.

Modern: Ruby
Zodiac (Cancer): Emerald

August

1 Wednesday
Lammas
Waning Moon
Moon phase: Third Quarter
Color: Topaz

Moon Sign: Pisces
Moon enters Aries 6:54 am
Incense: Honeysuckle

---

2 Thursday
Porcingula (Pecos)
Waning Moon
Moon phase: Third Quarter
Color: Turquoise

Moon Sign: Aries
Incense: Myrrh

---

3 Friday
Flag Day (Venezuelan)
Waning Moon
Moon phase: Third Quarter
Color: White

Moon Sign: Aries
Moon enters Taurus 3:51 pm
Incense: Thyme

○ Saturday
Constitution Day (Cook Islands)
Waning Moon Waxing
Fourth Quarter 2:18 pm
Color: Indigo

Moon Sign: Taurus
Incense: Magnolia

---

5 Sunday
Carnival of Bogotá
Waning Moon
Moon phase: Fourth Quarter
Color: Yellow

Moon Sign: Taurus
Moon enters Gemini 9:32 pm
Incense: Eucalyptus

---

6 Monday
Hiroshima Peace Memorial Ceremony
Waning Moon
Moon phase: Fourth Quarter
Color: Ivory

Moon Sign: Gemini
Incense: Clary sage

---

7 Tuesday
Republic Day (Ivorian)
Waning Moon
Moon phase: Fourth Quarter
Color: White

Moon Sign: Gemini
Incense: Basil

8 **Wednesday**
Farmers' Day (Tanzanian)
Waning Moon
Moon phase: Fourth Quarter
Color: Brown

Moon Sign: Gemini
Moon enters Cancer 12:01 am
Incense: Lilac

9 **Thursday**
Nagasaki Peace Memorial Ceremony
Waning Moon
Moon phase: Fourth Quarter
Color: Purple

Moon Sign: Cancer
Incense: Carnation

10 **Friday**
Puck Fair (ends Aug. 12; Irish)
Waning Moon
Moon phase: Fourth Quarter
Color: Pink

Moon Sign: Cancer
Moon enters Leo 12:18 am
Incense: Violet

☽ **Saturday**
Mountain Day (Japanese)
Waning Moon
New Moon 5:58 am
Color: Blue

Moon Sign: Leo
Moon enters Virgo 11:59 pm
Incense: Patchouli

12 **Sunday**
World Elephant Day
Waxing Moon
Moon phase: First Quarter
Color: Gold

Moon Sign: Virgo
Incense: Juniper

13 **Monday**
Glorious Twelfth (United Kingdom)
Waxing Moon
Moon phase: First Quarter
Color: Lavender

Moon Sign: Virgo
Incense: Lily

14 **Tuesday**
Independence Day (Pakistani)
Waxing Moon
Moon phase: First Quarter
Color: Scarlet

Moon Sign: Virgo
Moon enters Libra 12:57 am
Incense: Cedar

August

15 Wednesday
Bon Festival (Japanese)
Waxing Moon
Moon phase: First Quarter
Color: White

Moon Sign: Libra
Incense: Marjoram

---

16 Thursday
Xicolatada (French)
Waxing Moon
Moon phase: First Quarter
Color: Turquoise

Moon Sign: Libra
Moon enters Scorpio 4:54 am
Incense: Mulberry

---

17 Friday
Black Cat Appreciation Day
Waxing Moon
Moon phase: First Quarter
Color: Coral

Moon Sign: Scorpio
Incense: Vanilla

☽ **Saturday**
St. Helen's Day
Waxing Moon
Second Quarter 3:49 am
Color: Brown

Moon Sign: Scorpio
Moon enters Sagittarius 12:45 pm
Incense: Sage

---

19 Sunday
Vinalia Rustica (Roman)
Waxing Moon
Moon phase: Second Quarter
Color: Amber

Moon Sign: Sagittarius
Incense: Almond

---

20 Monday
St. Stephen's Day (Hungarian)
Waxing Moon
Moon phase: Second Quarter
Color: Silver

Moon Sign: Sagittarius
Incense: Rosemary

---

21 Tuesday
Consualia (Roman)
Waxing Moon
Moon phase: Second Quarter
Color: Maroon

Moon Sign: Sagittarius
Moon enters Capricorn 12:00 am
Incense: Geranium

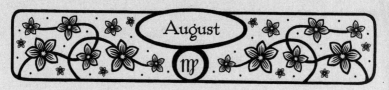

22 Wednesday

Feast of the Queenship of Mary (English)
Waxing Moon
Moon phase: Second Quarter
Color: Yellow

Moon Sign: Capricorn
Incense: Bay laurel

23 Thursday

National Day (Romanian)
Waxing Moon
Moon phase: Second Quarter
Color: Green

Moon Sign: Capricorn
Moon enters Aquarius 12:56 pm
Sun enters Virgo 12:09 am
Incense: Balsam

24 Friday

St. Bartholomew's Day
Waxing Moon
Moon phase: Second Quarter
Color: Purple

Moon Sign: Aquarius
Incense: Yarrow

25 Saturday

Ghost Festival (Chinese)
Waxing Moon
Moon phase: Second Quarter
Color: Black

Moon Sign: Aquarius
Incense: Pine

☺ Sunday

Heroes' Day (Namibian)
Waxing Moon
Full Moon 7:56 am
Color: Orange

Moon Sign: Aquarius
Moon enters Pisces 1:32 am
Incense: Frankincense

27 Monday

Independence Day (Moldovan)
Waning Moon
Moon phase: Third Quarter
Color: White

Moon Sign: Pisces
Incense: Narcissus

28 Tuesday

St. Augustine's Day
Waning Moon
Moon phase: Third Quarter
Color: Gray

Moon Sign: Pisces
Moon enters Aries 12:35 pm
Incense: Bayberry

August

29 Wednesday

St. John's Beheading

Waning Moon

Moon phase: Third Quarter

Color: Brown

Moon Sign: Aries

Incense: Lilac

---

30 Thursday

St. Rose of Lima Day (Peruvian)

Waning Moon

Moon phase: Third Quarter

Color: Crimson

Moon Sign: Aries

Moon enters Taurus 9:30 pm

Incense: Clove

---

31 Friday

La Tomatina (Valencian)

Waning Moon

Moon phase: Third Quarter

Color: Rose

Moon Sign: Taurus

Incense: Alder

August Birthstones

Wear Sardonyx, or for thee
No conjugal felicity;
The August-born without this stone,
'Tis said, must live unloved, and lone.

Modern: Peridot

Zodiac (Leo): Onyx

September ♍

1 Saturday
Wattle Day (Australian)
Waning Moon
Moon phase: Third Quarter
Color: Gray

Moon Sign: Taurus
Incense: Sandalwood

Sunday
St. Mammes's Day
Waning Moon
Fourth Quarter 10:37 pm
Color: Gold

Moon Sign: Taurus
Moon enters Gemini 4:02 am
Incense: Hyacinth

---

3 Monday
Labor Day
Waning Moon
Moon phase: Fourth Quarter
Color: Gray

Moon Sign: Gemini
Incense: Neroli

---

4 Tuesday
Feast of St. Rosalia
Waning Moon
Moon phase: Fourth Quarter
Color: Black

Moon Sign: Gemini
Moon enters Cancer 8:03 am
Incense: Cinnamon

---

5 Wednesday
International Day of Charity
Waning Moon
Moon phase: Fourth Quarter
Color: White

Moon Sign: Cancer
Incense: Marjoram

---

6 Thursday
Unification Day (Bulgaria)
Waning Moon
Moon phase: Fourth Quarter
Color: Turquoise

Moon Sign: Cancer
Moon enters Leo 9:54 am
Incense: Nutmeg

---

7 Friday
Independence Day (Brazilian)
Waning Moon
Moon phase: Fourth Quarter
Color: Pink

Moon Sign: Leo
Incense: Rose

8 Saturday
International Literacy Day
Waning Moon
Moon phase: Fourth Quarter
Color: Blue

Moon Sign: Leo
Moon enters Virgo 10:29 am
Incense: Rue

☽ Sunday
Grandparents' Day
Waning Moon
New Moon 2:01 pm
Color: Amber

Moon Sign: Virgo
Incense: Marigold

---

10 Monday
Rosh Hashanah
Waxing Moon
Moon phase: First Quarter
Color: Lavender

Moon Sign: Virgo
Moon enters Libra 11:20 am
Incense: Hyssop

---

11 Tuesday
Islamic New Year
Waxing Moon
Moon phase: First Quarter
Color: Scarlet

Moon Sign: Libra
Incense: Ylang-ylang

---

12 Wednesday
Mindfulness Day
Waxing Moon
Moon phase: First Quarter
Color: Topaz

Moon Sign: Libra
Moon enters Scorpio 2:15 pm
Incense: Lavender

---

13 Thursday
The Gods' Banquet (Roman)
Waxing Moon
Moon phase: First Quarter
Color: White

Moon Sign: Scorpio
Incense: Apricot

---

14 Friday
Holy Cross Day
Waxing Moon
Moon phase: First Quarter
Color: Coral

Moon Sign: Scorpio
Moon enters Sagittarius 8:45 pm
Incense: Mint

15 Saturday
International Day of Democracy
Waxing Moon
Moon phase: First Quarter
Color: Black

Moon Sign: Sagittarius
Incense: Ivy

○ Sunday
Independence Day (Mexican)
Waxing Moon
Second Quarter 7:15 pm
Color: Gold

Moon Sign: Sagittarius
Incense: Heliotrope

17 Monday
Constitution Day
Waxing Moon
Moon phase: Second Quarter
Color: Ivory

Moon Sign: Sagittarius
Moon enters Capricorn 7:07 am
Incense: Clary sage

18 Tuesday
World Water Monitoring Day
Waxing Moon
Moon phase: Second Quarter
Color: Red

Moon Sign: Capricorn
Incense: Ginger

19 Wednesday
Yom Kippur
Waxing Moon
Moon phase: Second Quarter
Color: Brown

Moon Sign: Capricorn
Moon enters Aquarius 7:52 pm
Incense: Honeysuckle

20 Thursday
St. Eustace's Day
Waxing Moon
Moon phase: Second Quarter
Color: Crimson

Moon Sign: Aquarius
Incense: Carnation

21 Friday
UN International Day of Peace
Waxing Moon
Moon phase: Second Quarter
Color: White

Moon Sign: Aquarius
Incense: Thyme

September

22 Saturday

Mabon • Fall Equinox
Waxing Moon
Moon phase: Second Quarter
Color: Indigo

Moon Sign: Aquarius
Moon enters Pisces 8:27 am
Sun enters Libra 9:54 pm
Incense: Sage

23 Sunday

Feast of St. Padre Pio
Waxing Moon
Moon phase: Second Quarter
Color: Gold

Moon Sign: Pisces
Incense: Eucalyptus

Monday

Sukkot begins
Waxing Moon
Full Moon 10:52 pm
Color: Silver

Moon Sign: Pisces
Moon enters Aries 7:04 pm
Incense: Lily

25 Tuesday

Doll Memorial Service (Japanese)
Waning Moon
Moon phase: Third Quarter
Color: Maroon

Moon Sign: Aries
Incense: Cedar

26 Wednesday

Feast of Santa Justina (Mexican)
Waning Moon
Moon phase: Third Quarter
Color: Yellow

Moon Sign: Aries
Incense: Bay laurel

27 Thursday

Meskel (Ethiopian and Eritrean)
Waning Moon
Moon phase: Third Quarter
Color: Purple

Moon Sign: Aries
Moon enters Taurus 3:16 am
Incense: Mulberry

28 Friday

Confucius's birthday
Waning Moon
Moon phase: Third Quarter
Color: Pink

Moon Sign: Taurus
Incense: Orchid

September

29 Saturday
Michaelmas
Waning Moon
Moon phase: Third Quarter
Color: Brown

Moon Sign: Taurus
Moon enters Gemini 9:26 am
Incense: Magnolia

---

30 Sunday
Sukkot ends
Waning Moon
Moon phase: Third Quarter
Color: Orange

Moon Sign: Gemini
Incense: Juniper

September Birthstones

A maiden born when autumn leaves
Are rustling in September's breeze,
A Sapphire on her brow should bind;
'Twill cure diseases of the mind.

Modern: Sapphire
Zodiac (Virgo): Carnelian

October

1 Monday
Armed Forces Day (South Korean)
Waning Moon
Moon phase: Third Quarter
Color: White

Moon Sign: Gemini
Moon enters Cancer 2:00 pm
Incense: Rosemary

◖ Tuesday
Gandhi's birthday
Waning Moon
Fourth Quarter 5:45 am
Color: Scarlet

Moon Sign: Cancer
Incense: Basil

3 Wednesday
German Unity Day
Waning Moon
Moon phase: Fourth Quarter
Color: Topaz

Moon Sign: Cancer
Moon enters Leo 5:12 pm
Incense: Marjoram

4 Thursday
St. Francis's Day
Waning Moon
Moon phase: Fourth Quarter
Color: Green

Moon Sign: Leo
Incense: Clove

5 Friday
Republic Day (Portuguese)
Waning Moon
Moon phase: Fourth Quarter
Color: Coral

Moon Sign: Leo
Moon enters Virgo 7:19 pm
Incense: Yarrow

6 Saturday
German-American Day
Waning Moon
Moon phase: Fourth Quarter
Color: Blue

Moon Sign: Virgo
Incense: Pine

7 Sunday
Nagasaki Kunchi Festival (ends Oct. 9)
Waning Moon
Moon phase: Fourth Quarter
Color: Yellow

Moon Sign: Virgo
Moon enters Libra 9:10 pm
Incense: Marigold

October ♎

☽ **Monday**
Columbus Day • Indigenous Peoples' Day
Waning Moon
New Moon 11:47 pm
Color: Ivory

Moon Sign: Libra
Incense: Neroli

9 **Tuesday**
Leif Erikson Day
Waxing Moon
Moon phase: First Quarter
Color: Gray

Moon Sign: Libra
Incense: Bayberry

10 **Wednesday**
Finnish Literature Day
Waxing Moon
Moon phase: First Quarter
Color: White

Moon Sign: Libra
Moon enters Scorpio 12:09 am
Incense: Lilac

11 **Thursday**
Medetrinalia (Roman)
Waxing Moon
Moon phase: First Quarter
Color: Crimson

Moon Sign: Scorpio
Incense: Jasmine

12 **Friday**
National Festival of Spain
Waxing Moon
Moon phase: First Quarter
Color: Rose

Moon Sign: Scorpio
Moon enters Sagittarius 5:53 am
Incense: Violet

13 **Saturday**
Fontinalia (Roman)
Waxing Moon
Moon phase: First Quarter
Color: Gray

Moon Sign: Sagittarius
Incense: Rue

14 **Sunday**
National Education Day (Polish)
Waxing Moon
Moon phase: First Quarter
Color: Amber

Moon Sign: Sagittarius
Moon enters Capricorn 3:17 pm
Incense: Frankincense

October ♎

15 Monday
The October Horse (Roman)
Waxing Moon
Moon phase: First Quarter
Color: Lavender

Moon Sign: Capricorn
Incense: Hyssop

☾ Tuesday
The Lion Sermon (British)
Waxing Moon
Second Quarter 2:02 pm
Color: Maroon

Moon Sign: Capricorn
Incense: Geranium

17 Wednesday
Double Ninth Festival (Chinese)
Waxing Moon
Moon phase: Second Quarter
Color: Topaz

Moon Sign: Capricorn
Moon enters Aquarius 3:36 am
Incense: Lavender

18 Thursday
Feast of St. Luke
Waxing Moon
Moon phase: Second Quarter
Color: Purple

Moon Sign: Aquarius
Incense: Balsam

19 Friday
Mother Teresa Day (Albanian)
Waxing Moon
Moon phase: Second Quarter
Color: Pink

Moon Sign: Aquarius
Moon enters Pisces 4:20 pm
Incense: Cypress

20 Saturday
Feast of St. Acca
Waxing Moon
Moon phase: Second Quarter
Color: Black

Moon Sign: Pisces
Incense: Patchouli

21 Sunday
Apple Day (United Kingdom)
Waxing Moon
Moon phase: Second Quarter
Color: Orange

Moon Sign: Pisces
Incense: Almond

October ♏

22 Monday
Jidai Festival (Japanese)
Waxing Moon
Moon phase: Second Quarter
Color: Gray

Moon Sign: Pisces
Moon enters Aries 2:58 am
Incense: Narcissus

23 Tuesday
Revolution Day (Hungarian)
Waxing Moon
Moon phase: Second Quarter
Color: White

Moon Sign: Aries
Sun enters Scorpio 7:22 am
Incense: Ylang-ylang

☺ Wednesday
United Nations Day
Waxing Moon
Full Moon 12:45 pm
Color: Yellow

Moon Sign: Aries
Moon enters Taurus 10:33 am
Incense: Marjoram

25 Thursday
St. Crispin's Day
Waning Moon
Moon phase: Third Quarter
Color: Turquoise

Moon Sign: Taurus
Incense: Myrrh

26 Friday
Death of Alfred the Great
Waning Moon
Moon phase: Third Quarter
Color: Purple

Moon Sign: Taurus
Moon enters Gemini 3:41 pm
Incense: Rose

27 Saturday
Feast of St. Abbán
Waning Moon
Moon phase: Third Quarter
Color: Indigo

Moon Sign: Gemini
Incense: Sage

28 Sunday
Ohi Day (Greek)
Waning Moon
Moon phase: Third Quarter
Color: Gold

Moon Sign: Gemini
Moon enters Cancer 7:27 pm
Incense: Hyacinth

October

29 Monday
National Cat Day
Waning Moon
Moon phase: Third Quarter
Color: White

Moon Sign: Cancer
Incense: Clary sage

---

30 Tuesday
John Adams's birthday
Waning Moon
Moon phase: Third Quarter
Color: Red

Moon Sign: Cancer
Moon enters Leo 10:42 pm
Incense: Cedar

Wednesday
Halloween • Samhain
Waning Moon
Fourth Quarter 12:40 pm
Color: Brown

Moon Sign: Leo
Incense: Honeysuckle

October Birthstones

October's child is born for woe,
And life's vicissitudes must know;
But lay an Opal on her breast,
And hope will lull those foes to rest.

Modern: Opal or Tourmaline
Zodiac (Libra): Peridot

November ♏

1 Thursday
All Saints' Day • Día de los Muertos
Waning Moon
Moon phase: Fourth Quarter
Color: White

Moon Sign: Leo
Incense: Carnation

---

2 Friday
All Souls' Day
Waning Moon
Moon phase: Fourth Quarter
Color: Rose

Moon Sign: Leo
Moon enters Virgo 1:48 am
Incense: Alder

---

3 Saturday
St. Hubert's Day (Belgian)
Waning Moon
Moon phase: Fourth Quarter
Color: Brown

Moon Sign: Virgo
Incense: Magnolia

---

4 Sunday
Mischief Night (British)
Waning Moon
Moon phase: Fourth Quarter
Color: Amber

Moon Sign: Virgo
Moon enters Libra 4:01 am
Incense: Juniper
Daylight Saving Time ends at 2 am

---

5 Monday
Guy Fawkes Night (British)
Waning Moon
Moon phase: Fourth Quarter
Color: Silver

Moon Sign: Libra
Incense: Neroli

---

6 Tuesday
Election Day (general)
Waning Moon
Moon phase: Fourth Quarter
Color: Black

Moon Sign: Libra
Moon enters Scorpio 8:02 am
Incense: Ginger

☽ Wednesday
Diwali
Waning Moon
New Moon 11:02 am
Color: Yellow

Moon Sign: Scorpio
Incense: Bay laurel

8 Thursday
World Urbanism Day   Moon Sign: Scorpio
Waxing Moon   Moon enters Sagittarius 1:59 pm
Moon phase: First Quarter   Incense: Apricot
Color: Green

---

9 Friday
Fateful Day (German)   Moon Sign: Sagittarius
Waxing Moon   Incense: Vanilla
Moon phase: First Quarter
Color: Purple

---

10 Saturday
Martin Luther's Birthday   Moon Sign: Sagittarius
Waxing Moon   Moon enters Capricorn 10:55 pm
Moon phase: First Quarter   Incense: Ivy
Color: Blue

---

11 Sunday
Veterans Day   Moon Sign: Capricorn
Waxing Moon   Incense: Heliotrope
Moon phase: First Quarter
Color: Orange

---

12 Monday
Feast Day of San Diego (Tesuque Puebloan)   Moon Sign: Capricorn
Waxing Moon   Incense: Lily
Moon phase: First Quarter
Color: Ivory

---

13 Tuesday
Festival of Jupiter (Roman)   Moon Sign: Capricorn
Waxing Moon   Moon enters Aquarius 10:45 am
Moon phase: First Quarter   Incense: Basil
Color: Maroon

---

14 Wednesday
Feast of St. Lawrence O'Toole   Moon Sign: Aquarius
Waxing Moon   Incense: Lavender
Moon phase: First Quarter
Color: White

○ **Thursday**
Seven-Five-Three Festival (Japanese)
Waxing Moon
Second Quarter 9:54 am
Color: Turquoise

Moon Sign: Aquarius
Moon enters Pisces 11:41 pm
Incense: Jasmine

---

16 Friday
St. Margaret of Scotland's Day
Waxing Moon
Moon phase: Second Quarter
Color: Rose

Moon Sign: Pisces
Incense: Thyme

---

17 Saturday
National Adoption Day
Waxing Moon
Moon phase: Second Quarter
Color: Indigo

Moon Sign: Pisces
Incense: Sandalwood

---

18 Sunday
Independence Day (Moroccan)
Waxing Moon
Moon phase: Second Quarter
Color: Gold

Moon Sign: Pisces
Moon enters Aries 10:56 am
Incense: Eucalyptus

---

19 Monday
Garifuna Settlement Day (Belizean)
Waxing Moon
Moon phase: Second Quarter
Color: Gray

Moon Sign: Aries
Incense: Hyssop

---

20 Tuesday
Revolution Day (Mexican)
Waxing Moon
Moon phase: Second Quarter
Color: Red

Moon Sign: Aries
Moon enters Taurus 6:43 pm
Incense: Cinnamon

---

21 Wednesday
Feast of the Presentation of Mary
Waxing Moon
Moon phase: Second Quarter
Color: Brown

Moon Sign: Taurus
Incense: Lilac

November

22 Thursday
Thanksgiving Day   Moon Sign: Taurus
Waxing Moon   Sun enters Sagittarius 4:01 am
Moon phase: Second Quarter   Moon enters Gemini 11:10 pm
Color: Purple   Incense: Nutmeg

☺ **Friday**
Native American Heritage Day   Moon Sign: Gemini
Waxing Moon   Incense: Yarrow
Full Moon 12:39 am
Color: Coral

---

24 Saturday
Evolution Day   Moon Sign: Gemini
Waning Moon   Incense: Rue
Moon phase: Third Quarter
Color: Gray

---

25 Sunday
Feast of St. Catherine of Alexandria   Moon Sign: Gemini
Waning Moon   Moon enters Cancer 1:38 am
Moon phase: Third Quarter   Incense: Frankincense
Color: Yellow

---

26 Monday
Constitution Day (Indian)   Moon Sign: Cancer
Waning Moon   Incense: Rosemary
Moon phase: Third Quarter
Color: White

---

27 Tuesday
Feast of St. Virgilius   Moon Sign: Cancer
Waning Moon   Moon enters Leo 3:35 am
Moon phase: Third Quarter   Incense: Bayberry
Color: Scarlet

---

28 Wednesday
Republic Day (Chadian)   Moon Sign: Leo
Waning Moon   Incense: Marjoram
Moon phase: Third Quarter
Color: Topaz

November

◖ **Thursday**
William Tubman's birthday (Liberian)
Waning Moon
Fourth Quarter 7:19 pm
Color: Crimson

Moon Sign: Leo
Moon enters Virgo 6:08 am
Incense: Mulberry

---

30 Friday
St. Andrew's Day (Scottish)
Waning Moon
Moon phase: Fourth Quarter
Color: Pink

Moon Sign: Virgo
Incense: Mint

November Birthstones

Who first come to this world below,
With drear November's fog, and snow,
Should prize the Topaz's amber hue,
Emblem of friends, and lovers true.

Modern: Topaz or Citrine
Zodiac (Scorpio): Beryl

December

1 Saturday
Feast for Death of Aleister Crowley (Thelemic)
Waning Moon
Moon phase: Fourth Quarter
Color: Blue

Moon Sign: Virgo
Moon enters Libra 9:49 am
Incense: Sage

2 Sunday
Republic Day (Laotian)
Waning Moon
Moon phase: Fourth Quarter
Color: Orange

Moon Sign: Libra
Incense: Marigold

3 Monday
Hanukkah begins
Waning Moon
Moon phase: Fourth Quarter
Color: Ivory

Moon Sign: Libra
Moon enters Scorpio 2:55 pm
Incense: Narcissus

4 Tuesday
Feasts of Shango and St. Barbara
Waning Moon
Moon phase: Fourth Quarter
Color: Maroon

Moon Sign: Scorpio
Incense: Geranium

5 Wednesday
Krampus Night (European)
Waning Moon
Moon phase: Fourth Quarter
Color: White

Moon Sign: Scorpio
Moon enters Sagittarius 9:49 pm
Incense: Lavender

6 Thursday
St. Nicholas's Day
Waning Moon
Moon phase: Fourth Quarter
Color: Turquoise

Moon Sign: Sagittarius
Incense: Balsam

☽ Friday
Burning the Devil (Guatemalan)
Waning Moon
New Moon 2:20 am
Color: Purple

Moon Sign: Sagittarius
Incense: Violet

December

8 Saturday
Bodhi Day (Japanese)
Waxing Moon
Moon phase: First Quarter
Color: Black

Moon Sign: Sagittarius
Moon enters Capricorn 7:01 am
Incense: Pine

---

9 Sunday
Anna's Day (Sweden)
Waxing Moon
Moon phase: First Quarter
Color: Gold

Moon Sign: Capricorn
Incense: Juniper

---

10 Monday
Hanukkah ends
Waxing Moon
Moon phase: First Quarter
Color: Lavender

Moon Sign: Capricorn
Moon enters Aquarius 6:39 pm
Incense: Clary sage

---

11 Tuesday
Pilgrimage at Tortugas
Waxing Moon
Moon phase: First Quarter
Color: Gray

Moon Sign: Aquarius
Incense: Ylang-ylang

---

12 Wednesday
Fiesta of Our Lady of Guadalupe (Mexican)
Waxing Moon
Moon phase: First Quarter
Color: Brown

Moon Sign: Aquarius
Incense: Honeysuckle

---

13 Thursday
St. Lucy's Day (Scandanavian and Italian)
Waxing Moon
Moon phase: First Quarter
Color: Crimson

Moon Sign: Aquarius
Moon enters Pisces 7:40 am
Incense: Clove

---

14 Friday
Forty-Seven Ronin Memorial (Japanese)
Waxing Moon
Moon phase: First Quarter
Color: Rose

Moon Sign: Pisces
Incense: Orchid

December

○ Saturday
Consualia (Roman)
Waxing Moon
Second Quarter 6:49 am
Color: Indigo

Moon Sign: Pisces
Moon enters Aries 7:44 pm
Incense: Patchouli

---

16 Sunday
Las Posadas begin (end Dec. 24)
Waxing Moon
Moon phase: Second Quarter
Color: Yellow

Moon Sign: Aries
Incense: Almond

---

17 Monday
Saturnalia (Roman)
Waxing Waning Moon
Moon phase: Second Quarter
Color: Silver

Moon Sign: Aries
Incense: Lily

---

18 Tuesday
Feast of the Virgin of Solitude
Waxing Moon
Moon phase: Second Quarter
Color: Maroon

Moon Sign: Aries
Moon enters Taurus 4:37 am
Incense: Cedar

---

19 Wednesday
Opalia (Roman)
Waxing Moon
Moon phase: Second Quarter
Color: Topaz

Moon Sign: Taurus
Incense: Marjoram

---

20 Thursday
Feast of St. Dominic of Silos
Waxing Moon
Moon phase: Second Quarter
Color: Green

Moon Sign: Taurus
Moon enters Gemini 9:34 am
Incense: Apricot

---

21 Friday
Yule • Winter Solstice
Waxing Moon
Moon phase: Second Quarter
Color: White

Moon Sign: Gemini
Sun enters Capricorn 5:23 pm
Incense: Alder

December ♄

☺ Saturday
Feasts of SS. Chaeremon and Ischyrion
Waxing Moon
Full Moon 12:49 pm
Color: Blue

Moon Sign: Gemini
Moon enters Cancer 11:28 am
Incense: Ivy

---

23 Sunday
Larentalia (Roman)
Waning Moon
Moon phase: Third Quarter
Color: Orange

Moon Sign: Cancer
Incense: Hyacinth

---

24 Monday
Christmas Eve
Waning Moon
Moon phase: Third Quarter
Color: Gray

Moon Sign: Cancer
Moon enters Leo 11:59 am
Incense: Neroli

---

25 Tuesday
Christmas Day
Waning Moon
Moon phase: Third Quarter
Color: Red

Moon Sign: Leo
Incense: Ginger

---

26 Wednesday
Kwanzaa begins (ends Jan. 1)
Waning Moon
Moon phase: Third Quarter
Color: Yellow

Moon Sign: Leo
Moon enters Virgo 12:50 pm
Incense: Lilac

---

27 Thursday
St. Stephen's Day
Waning Moon
Moon phase: Third Quarter
Color: Purple

Moon Sign: Virgo
Incense: Myrrh

---

28 Friday
Feast of the Holy Innocents
Waning Moon
Moon phase: Third Quarter
Color: Pink

Moon Sign: Virgo
Moon enters Libra 3:23 pm
Incense: Rose

December

○ **Saturday**
Feast of St. Thomas à Becket
Waning Moon
Fourth Quarter 4:34 am
Color: Gray

Moon Sign: Libra
Incense: Sandalwood

---

30 Sunday
Republic Day (Madagascan)
Waning Moon
Moon phase: Fourth Quarter
Color: Amber

Moon Sign: Libra
Moon enters Scorpio 8:23 pm
Incense: Eucalyptus

---

31 Monday
New Year's Eve
Waning Moon
Moon phase: Fourth Quarter
Color: White

Moon Sign: Scorpio
Incense: Hyssop

December Birthstones

If cold December gives you birth,
The month of snow, and ice, and mirth,
Place in your hand a Turquoise blue;
Success will bless whate'er you do.

Modern: Turquoise or Blue Topaz
Zodiac (Sagittarius): Topaz

Fire Magic

Metalsmith Magic

by Suzanne Ress

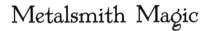

Like many people, I've long been attracted to gleaming metal jewelry. It's difficult for me to walk by a jeweler's display window without stopping for a closer look. I love the smooth and permanent shininess of gold, silver, and copper earrings, rings, and other "trinkets," but not only because they are pretty. I believe that carefully chosen pieces of jewelry become much more than just body decoration. They are usually worn as expressions of one's deeper identity, often hold important sentimental value, and are frequently employed as magical amulets for luck, protection, love, strength, or some other purpose.

Some years ago I picked up a small pamphlet in an art jewelry shop. There I read about an introductory metal smithing course offered by a master jewelry artist in Milan, Italy, about forty-five minutes by train from where I live. I called the phone number and found that the course was held weekday mornings, that I could afford it, and that I could fit it into my schedule, so I signed up and started the following week.

Everything was new to me—the saw blades as fine as hairs, the files finer and smaller than fingernail files, the drill bits like pins, the tiny ball-peen hammer. The tools were fascinating, but when the master demonstrated how to make a simple band ring using nothing but a short length of silver half-round wire and a tiny speck of solder under the blue flame of a gas torch, I was mesmerized! That a substance hard enough to hold a precious carved stone in place for millennia with only a few miniscule prongs could turn malleable and then liquid under the heat of a flame seemed magic.

Metalsmith Myth and History

In most spellcasting and magic work a knife or athame is used to cast the circle, to open it, and to close it again. The athame is also often used for drawing down the power of the elements, gods, or energy in general. It is a important tool in magic work, usually handmade and often very beautiful. Its blade is forged of metal—steel or sometimes brass, copper, or silver.

Metal, a great conductor of heat and hence of fire and Sun energy, was found by our long-ago ancestors in rocks and stones. From these stones skilled metalsmiths were able to extract the metal and harden it for use in making weapons and tools that were far more effective and precise than the previous tools and weapons made of stone or wood.

From the start, metalsmiths were regarded with awe, and the tools, weapons, implements, jewelry, and chain mail they produced were considered to be imbued with natural magic and power. In ancient times they were considered to be akin to magicians. Their powers were believed to be godlike.

Many ancient pagan societies had a metalsmith god. One of the most well known to English-speaking people was Wayland the Smith. He was an Anglo-Saxon god, and his workshop was believed to be located at the huge Neolithic barrow in the mysterious Vale of the White Horse in Oxfordshire County, England, long known as Wayland's Smithy. Iron Age metal money bars were found there at its excavation about a hundred years ago.

Preceding Wayland was the Nordic smith god, Volund. Wayland's (or Volund's) father had a magic boat,

and Wayland's grandmother was a sea witch. One day, when they were young men, Wayland and his two brothers were walking by a lake when three swans landed there. They transformed into three lovely young ladies, and everyone fell in love. Wayland married Allwise, and all three couples lived happily for nine years. Then the women grew homesick and disappeared. Wayland's brothers went in search of their wives, but Wayland stayed home, working in his smithy.

The king of the Niars sent thieves to steal Wayland's sword and a golden ring he'd made, and then they bound Wayland and brought him to the king. The king had Wayland lamed and imprisoned him on an island, where he was only allowed to work for the king. After some years, the king's sons came to see Wayland, and Wayland took revenge by cutting off their heads. He then flew away on gold wings he had made.

Other metalsmith gods were the Greek Haphaestus, his sons, and the Dactyls, female goddesses who invented smithcraft; the Irish bronze weapons makers, Credne and Gavida, and the celestial smith, Luno; the Roman smith god Vulcan; the Finnish magical smith Ilmarinen; the Lithuanian and Latvian smith god Kalvelis; and the Slavic smith god Svarog.

Amulets have been an important part of every human culture forever. People have always believed that the magic act of transforming an object from a stone to a sword or body ornament imbued that object with magic. Because body ornaments or jewelry were powerfully magical, they could protect the wearer, guide her, and heal her. As ritual tools, these magic-imbued items were able to draw down the powers of nature and the gods from which they came.

By the beginning of the Iron Age (about 1200 BCE), the skills of the metalsmith in bronze and gold were already long established. Casting, sheet-working, hammer work, chasing, inscribing, repoussé—these techniques were done in the same way 5,000 years ago as they are today. These early metalsmiths made bridle buttons, breast plates, mouth bits, and harness mounts for their horses; swords, chain mail tunics, helmets, shields, and scabbards for their warriors; brooches, necklaces and torcs, and rings to decorate themselves; and firedogs, cauldrons, knives, and tools for everyday living.

Hephaestus, son of Zeus and Hera, was the ancient Greeks' smith god. He was born lame and ugly. Ashamed, Hera threw him into the sea. He was adopted by two sea goddesses, who raised him for nine years, to young manhood. During his time with the sea goddesses, he forged for them many beautiful and ingenious tools and jewels. Although Hera had treated him unkindly, Hephaestus had not lost his love for his mother. He made for her a lovely coral and golden belt. Hera was so delighted with this gift that she asked Zeus to give Hephaestus anything he wanted. Hephaestus asked to marry the gorgeous goddess of sexual love, Aphrodite, and this desire was granted. From then on, Hephaestus was known as the smith of the gods, and he made many wonderful things for them, including Zeus's throne, scepter, and thunderbolts. Although Aphrodite bore him two sons, who also became metalsmiths to the gods, she was often unfaithful to Hephaestus. When he learned that she was having an affair with Ares, the god of war, Hephaestus made an unbreakable net and trapped the lovers in it for the other gods to mock.

Metals and Their Uses

More than seventy pure metals are known to exist, but, of these, only about twenty are used in jewelry and

implement making. These twenty can be divided into ferrous and nonferrous; the second group is further divided into base metals and noble metals. Base metals are abundant and are not considered precious. Some of these are copper, tin, nickel, and zinc. Noble metals, less abundant and most sought after, are gold, silver, and the platinum group. The noble metals are more chemically stable than base metals, and gold and silver are also the easiest to work with because they become quite malleable when heated. Ferrous metals are iron and any alloy containing iron, such as steel.

Alloys are two or more metals joined together to make a compound that suits its purpose better than a single metal. Gold, in its pure state, is too soft to be used alone in jewelry; it would get nicked and bent out of shape with normal wear. Eighteen-karat gold is the alloy with the highest percentage of gold normally used in jewelry. This contains about one-quarter fine silver and copper, in different proportions according the shade of gold desired, such as light yellow, deep yellow, rose, greenish, or white. Silver used for jewelry, coins, and in implements must also be alloyed with small amounts of copper to render it reasonably hard enough to be useful.

To extract metals from their naturally found places, in rocks or mines, high heat is applied. This is called smelting and causes the metal to liquefy and leave the other minerals behind. After the original smelting, the metal is heated and refined several more times until it is nearly pure. It is then cast into rectangular chunks, or ingots. The ingots can then be reheated, alloyed with other metals, and formed into any desired shape. If metal is properly heated and cooled it can be reworked indefinitely without suffering fractures.

We think of the Bronze Age following the Stone Age and may not realize that gold was probably the first metal noticed and used as body ornament and talisman by humans. Gold, with its bright yellow color, was easy to notice, and 10,000 years ago as now, it could be found in waterways and in rocks much more easily than other metal ores, as it required no digging, mining or smelting.

Because gold retains its shine and does not oxidize due to its chemical inactivity and because of its unique color, it was thought of as being symbolic of the Sun, God, and immortality. Alchemists, whose early work eventually led to modern pharmaceutical chemistry, were searching for a way to transform base metal, such as tin, into gold. Gold was god, the Holy Grail, the ultimate measure of things.

Wearing gold ornaments against one's skin mystically charges the body with the object's power. Because gold is immutable, heavy, and a symbol of immortality, it also came to be the base of trade or money. Even now, many people all over the world invest in gold, considering its worth to be untouchable.

By transforming ore from rock, with the use of fire, into metal weapons or body ornaments, the smith reveals to us the magical truth that all manifestations are one— an element can change from rock to liquid to hardened immortal metal, but it is always the same energy. The smith frees the metal imprisoned in rock just as a sculptor frees the figure within a block of marble.

It is likely that early humans discovered the magical properties of metal by accident—perhaps a hammered copper knife fell into the fire, and, when taken out, had melted and changed form. Perhaps meteoric stone beads fell into the fire and the metal ore contained in

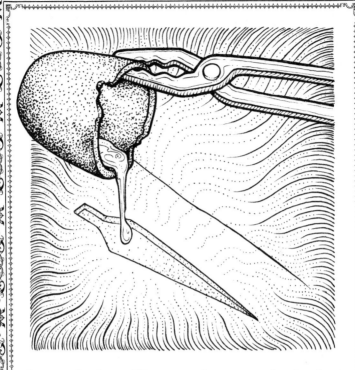

them melted out. We cannot know exactly what happened, but we do know that, by perhaps as long ago as 8700 BCE, metal had become such an important part of our lives that humans began to systematically mine for copper. Smelting was carried out in large clay or stone crucibles.

The alloying of two metals was probably another accidental discovery—perhaps, along with the copper ore, some tin was mixed in. Melting these two together made bronze, which is much more durable for weapons and household implements than copper alone. This was the start of the Bronze Age, around 2800 BCE.

About a thousand years after this, the Hittites began working extensively in iron, and, four hundred years later, iron was annealed in very hot charcoal-fired ovens to form steel. The much harder steel quickly replaced bronze in weaponry.

A metalsmith's techniques include hammering and rolling ingots to make metal sheet, which can then be sawed, pierced, cold bent, filed, hammered into domes, and stamped. Metal can be drawn through ever-smaller holes in a plate to form any shape of wire, which can then be hammered with a mallet around a mandrel to form rings. Wire can be bent with pliers into filigree designs or made into chain links for chains or chain mail. Metal pieces can be heated and soldered together or pierced and riveted together.

Metal ingots can also be melted down to liquid state and cast into cuttlebone. Stones can be set and secured into metal, and metal can be treated with acids to form patinas, fused for multilayered effects, reticulated to change its texture, or granulated for ornamentation.

Smithing in Personal Practice

All of these ancient techniques are still taught today in much the same way they were thousands of years ago.

After that first introductory jewelry making course, I set up a small laboratory in our basement, and, little by little, purchased the necessary tools. At first not much was needed: a packet of saw blades, a hand saw, some squares of copper sheet metal, a handheld gas torch, sandpaper, needle-nose pliers. I subscribed to a couple of jewelry makers' magazines and bought several books. As I discovered new techniques, I bought more tools. I met other jewelers, and one of these allowed me to assist in his shop for a few months, where I learned new techniques hands on. Another jeweler I met was moving and no longer needed his bench or his stone

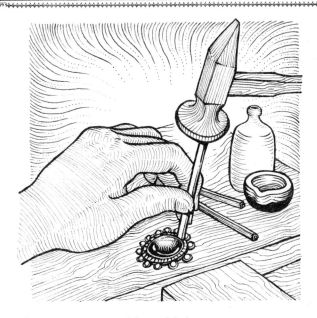

and prong setter, and he sold these to me at a very reasonable price. These jewelers told me where to go to buy precious and semiprecious stones and where there was a foundry for having rubber molds made and pieces cast. I invested in a polishing wheel and a wire draw plate; I bought gold and silver maker's marks and had another one made with my initials. I made many pieces of jewelry, some more successfully than others. Among these were some pieces of magic jewelry, pentagrams, and athames for myself and for like-minded friends. I was invited to show my jewelry in galleries and small art jewelry shops, and people bought my work.

I still cannot resist stopping and looking at jewelry shop showcases when I come to them, and I love frequenting arts and crafts fairs, where many jewelers start out selling their work, and museum displays of ancient jewelry really turn me on. Like all knowledge, the knowledge of how jewelry is made has turned me into a connoisseur, easily able to distinguish what is handmade from what is machine made or called handmade but really made up of machine-made components.

If your magical tools and jewelry are handmade by yourself they will be especially powerful, but if you have neither the time nor inclination to learn at least basic metal smithing, it is well worthwhile to seek out someone who can hand make what you require. Perhaps you have a friend or an acquaintance with metal smithing skills. If not, arts and crafts fairs and small gallery-type shops are good places to start looking. Most metalsmiths are delighted to fulfill special orders. You can design what you want, describe what you have in mind, and let her design it, or you can ask the metalsmith for suggestions. In any case, what you will end up with will have been uniquely created for you and your magic work, and you will surely notice the difference in effectiveness!

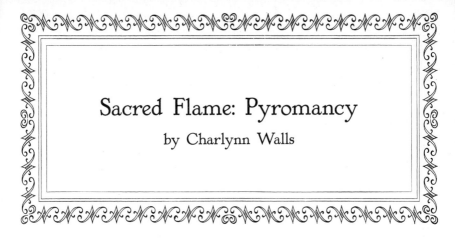

Sacred Flame: Pyromancy
by Charlynn Walls

Fire has played a pivotal role in the evolution of humanity. It has provided us light, heat, and a way to cook our food. Therefore, it is little wonder that we have sought to utilize the sacred flame in its various forms as a divinatory tool to shed light on our lives and our individual pathways.

There are many different ways to interpret the various components of flames, smoke, ash, and items placed into the pyre. The diviner may look at factors such as the interpretation of color, shape, intensity, and movement to aid in understanding the question posed. Each variation offers its own unique insight into the question that a practitioner asks.

Types of Pyromancy

The form of pyromancy that most may be familiar with would be the flames of a fire in which a sorceress sees a visage take shape. Once the image dissipates and she has had time to ponder what she has seen, she makes her proclamation about the viability of a future endeavor or event. Whether she sees the image as a good or a bad omen, it is heeded by those who seek her council.

This form of divination could take place around a hearth fire, campfire, or ritual fire. However, there are many other forms of pyromancy that are equally viable. The following are just a few that I have personally experienced.

Capnomancy

Capnomancy is the divination based on the rising smoke from a ritual fire or candle. Typically, the more direct and straight the plume of smoke is the better the omen. Smoke that sank or began to waft around the room was thought to be an indicator that the gods did not have a favorable response to the question or matter at hand.

I have lit candles before that smoked excessively while I tried to do a spell. Those were the spells that never really seemed to work out in retrospect. I have since taken it as an omen that the spell is not meant to be and that there is a block to this work. So I will cancel and clear my spellwork when a candle begins to emit a large amount of smoke. I will try the spell again at a later time after I have attempted to remove the block.

Causimomancy

Causimomancy occurs when the diviner casts an item such as incense, grain, or something of personal interest into the flames. They then make an interpretation based on if the item burns or not. The more quickly the item ignites, the more favorable the omen. Items that burn slowly or do not burn at all are thought to be particularly bad signs.

There was a time when I was attempting to start over after a particularly bad breakup. I created a blend of herbs that were designed to bring clarity, focus, and openness. I tossed the blend into a campfire at a festival late at night after the majority of the people had wandered to their beds. The herbs ignited almost before they touched the flames. The fire burned bright and then returned to normal. I took this as a good sign that I was on the right path.

Lampadomancy

Lampadomancy divines the message provided by the flickering flame of a candle or oil lamp. This encompasses how the flame moves, its color, or if it is particularly loud. If the flame lists to one side or another, crackles, or is any color besides a bright yellow flame, it is not a favorable portent.

My coven interpreted a flickering flame at Samhain a few years ago. We had been working with our ancestors and the ritual had been particularly exhausting. We were resting around the fire and a log started to spew a blue flame out its side. It was very loud and would have been difficult to ignore. It was up to us, the practitioners, to determine what the message was. In this case we felt we still had spirits among us that needed to be released from the prior ritual.

Lychnomancy

Lychnomancy, though traditionally conducted by interpreting the flames of three candles, is often interpreted by modern diviners through the use of one candle. The color, size, movement, and quality of the flame are considered. A good reading is established by a bright flame that is devoid of flickering or popping.

I have often used this type of pyromancy for personal and group work. I am reminded of a time during another coven meeting when we were dealing with several different deities during a Samhain ritual. We had finished a part where we had petitioned Papa Legba. The candle flames in the circle grew strong and bright for a moment and then extinguished. The ritual was outside, and only a few of our participants saw this. We had to interpret what the meaning was. We were certain that our petition had been heard and that he had left immediately after hearing what was said.

Spodomancy

Spodomancy examines the ashes, cinders, or soot left by a ritual fire. The diviner writes a message in the ashes, and the result is discerned based upon what is left the next morning. Alternately, the shapes and designs left naturally in the remaining ashes from a ritual fire can be interpreted in a similar manner. Parallels can be drawn between the shapes left in the ashes and one's own life. This was a popular divination to use in order to determine aspects of the past, present, or future.

At a women's retreat I attended one year, I had retired early. A good friend was still up when I emerged from my tent much later in the evening, and I asked her what she was still doing up. We sat and talked a while as we were staring into the remaining coals of the fire. One coal looked particularly like a phoenix to us both. We took it as a sign that our group was heading for a rebirth, and a short time later things changed. Several people left, and we had a few new members come into the group.

Pyromancy in Fire Festivals

We are able to utilize and benefit from pyromancy during the Greater Sabbats, which are also traditionally known as fire festivals. Each festival has the potential to utilize pyromancy in its celebration and connect with the spirits to obtain insight.

Samhain

Samhain (October 31) is a time to honor and connect with those that have passed into the otherworld. One way we can honor and

connect with our ancestors is by creating a symbolic pyre. The ritual fire is to be constructed in a similar way to a funeral pyre.

The wood can be systematically built and prepared several days prior to the rite. This will give the participants a chance to focus on the rite to come. A symbolic body can then be created to represent the loved ones that you are trying to reach in order to obtain a sign or warning. The representation can be a poppet constructed of simple materials like cloth and straw. Questions from each member can also be incorporated into the stuffing materials, should that be desired.

Once lit, the flames will start to rise from the funeral pyre. How they rise can be noted by the group, and each member can provide their own interpretation or ask what other group members think regarding the question that they posed.

Imbolc

Imbolc (February 2) is a celebration of the returning light to the earth along with new beginnings. This day is also sometimes referred to as Candlemas. It is the perfect time to practice the divinatory arts.

Candles are traditionally incorporated into this festival, and it is the perfect time to practice lychnomancy. The diviners should take three large pillar candles of the same size, shape, and color and place them on the altar. They should be arranged in a triangle. One candle represents the present, one represents the past, and one represents the future. These should be clearly identified to all parties prior to the start of the ritual.

Once the ritual is underway, the diviner or diviners are given paper to write down their question, and then they should place it in the space that is left open on the altar between the candles. They should then clear their minds and stare toward the center of all the candles. When one candle begins to burn brighter, flicker, or pop, it will catch the petitioners' attention. They should then note why it caught their attention and write down if that candle represented the past, present, or future. They should also note everything they notice about that candle.

Beltane

Beltane (May 1) represents the emergence of the light half of the year. The veil between the worlds is as thin during this time of year as it is at Samhain. It is an excellent time of the year to make contact with otherworldly beings such as the Fae and to perform divination.

The balefire should be lit and allowed to burn throughout the night. It will provide a beacon to spirits and the Fae who may want to provide insight into the diviner's life. This provides an excellent opportunity to explore spodomancy more directly.

Each individual wishing to participate should toss a paper with a question into the balefire. This will signal the spirits or Fae to offer their assistance in answering the questions. Once the revelry and festivities are over, the fire should be allowed to extinguish on its own.

Once extinguished, the ashes and remnants of the fire can be examined. Those performing the divination should note what shapes are present within the ashes. Sometimes drawing on paper what is seen can help provide further interpretation and avoid any missing information. Also, any odd occurrences such as reigniting of coals or having ashes blow out of the pit at the time of interpretation should be noted as significant to the question at hand.

Lammas

Lammas (August 2) marks the beginning of the harvest festivals. It is a time to recognize the abundance of the harvest and the prosperity that it brings to a community. A hearth fire would be best to harness the harvest energies.

Causimomancy would be a good type of pyromancy to use during this time of year. One could take harvest grains or loaves of bread made from the grain and toss them into the fire. Not only is this an offering to the gods, but the reaction of the fire to it and the question of the diviner can then be deciphered.

The diviner should look at what item was thrown into the hearth fire and assess how long it took to ignite along with what happened once it did. Did the grain or bread take a long time to ignite? Was there an abundance of smoke or loud popping noises? This scenario would not be favorable to the question at hand. Did the flames get larger and brighter with very little smoke? This would indicate a much more favorable response.

The possibilities for the use of pyromancy during ritual are only as limited as our imaginations. These are only a few options that can be expanded upon for further customization for your particular path or practice. These can be adapted for solitary or coven use as well.

Conclusions

The practice of pyromancy likely developed soon after the first fire was created because we as humans seek answers to the world around us. Fire is transforming and sacred to many cultures as both life giving and destructive. It offers various ways for us to work with it, whether through the flame, smoke, or remnants of the fire once it has been extinguished.

One must be open to the potential offered through this form of divination and be willing to explore its myriad of possibilities. Pyromancy, in its varied forms, allows the practitioner to highly personalize their divinatory practice.

Resources

Digitalis, Raven. *Shadow Magick Compendium: Exploring Darker Aspects of Magickal Spirituality.* Woodbury, MN: Llewellyn Publications, 2008.

Dunwich, Gerina. *A Wiccan's Guide to Prophecy and Divination.* New York: Citadel Press, 1997.

Morwyn. *The Complete Book of Psychic Arts: Divination Practices from Around the World.* St. Paul, MN: Llewellyn Publications, 1999.

Charming Chickens

by Natalie Zaman

I have a thing about chickens. Maybe it's because I was born in a Rooster year. (For the record, Rooster people are observant, hardworking, and perseverant—not unlike our avian counterparts.) I'm into my second decade of keeping hens (and the occasional rooster), during which time I've come to know them as magical creatures. Chickens miss nothing; they're fastidious and good at finding things. Intruders? They'll warn you. And, they're organized. Together a flock will protect home and garden and rule the roost—fiercely if necessary.

Sun Birds

Hens and roosters are, of course, practical, birds. For thousands of years they've been a source of protein, a means of natural pest control—and an alarm clock (although I've had roosters who crowed at all hours of the day and night). Perhaps it's this last trait that hints at their divine qualities. In many Asian cultures roosters and hens are the original "Sun birds." Once a wild bird in mountainous Asia, *Gallus gallus* was eventually domesticated around 3000–2000 BCE and then spread across continents to become an indispensible and sacred animal.

Most folks already associate the rooster and his crow with the sunrise, but in Korea it was believed that the sacrifice of a hen in the morning (most likely to be eaten later) ensured a good day and that her cry (cluck) chased away negativity. Hens and roosters are also Sun symbols in India. In the state of Rajasthan the hen goddess Murga Mata presides over wandering flocks. Like many other such little-known deities, she is an expression of the divinity and importance of everyday things. Familiar figures on tombs in Japan, roosters and hens are guides to the afterlife. They also act as messengers.

Several Greek gods held chickens in high esteem. Along with her beloved owls, chickens (also intelligent birds) were sacred to Athena. Chickens were fertility talismans for Persephone and emblems of love and desire to Eros. Ever practical, Hermes appreciated chickens as living symbols of commerce and productivity.

Chicken is matriarch and manifestress of change. Rooster is a light in the darkness and courage incarnate. Tap into the energy of these extraordinary birds and bring their magic into your life.

A Sylvan Sewel for Clear Communication

Feathers are associated with the element of air and so are ideal for use in communication magic. Finding a feather can be a token from a totem animal or guardian angel or a message from someone who has passed on. Different colors carry distinct energies: white feathers purify, black protects, brown grounds, and gray balances. Red or orange feathers embody creativity and passion. The birds from which they come also bring their unique energies to workings in which feathers are used. In Hoodoo and Conjure practices, feathers from black or speckled hens—bundled into a kind of esoteric feather duster and used in conjunction with incenses and powders—break jinxes and hexes. If you've ever used a feather duster for mundane cleaning, you've seen a feather's drawing powers.

In 1878 the discovery of a knotted cord woven with feathers tucked into the rafters of a cottage in Somerset, England, pricked the interest of Charles Godfrey Leland. He'd written about similar practices he'd seen in Italy, where such talismans were called "witches' garlands." Made with feathers woven into a rope, the charm was a curse, but one that could be broken by tossing the garland into running water. Leland called the charm a "sewel," or "wishing rope," although it has become more commonly known as a "witch's ladder." Simply, a witch's ladder is a knotting spell, one that can be personalized with specific intentions that are bound in the feathers as they're tied into the cord that forms the ladder.

Create a witch's ladder with black yarn and white feathers to bless your home with honest communication. Openness and honesty prevent permanent and damaging rifts and ultimately strengthen relationships. Spend enough time around chickens and you'll notice that they're always chattering; our ladder will draw on this aspect of hen energy. The black wool adds an element of protection, while the white feathers represent purity of thought. Together, the juxtaposition of black and white promotes balance and harmony.

You will need:

A pair of scissors
About 4 yards of black wool
9 white chicken feathers

Before you begin, smudge the wool and feathers with sage to cleanse them of any lingering energy, particularly any trauma that the animals from which they came may have experienced. Make a loop at one end of the length of wool and knot it closed; you'll use this to hang your ladder. Nine inches from the knot at the base of the loop, tie on your first feather with three knots. As you tie the feather into the wool, speak the first line of the spell:

We speak our truth.

When you're finished, go down another nine inches, tie on the next feather in the same manner, and speak the next line:

We listen.

Continue tying on feathers every nine inches until the spell is complete. Recite a line for each remaining feather:

We heal.
And understanding is revealed.
Facts and feeling.
And honest dealing.
In harmony congealing.
Under this roof.
So mote it be.

When the last feather is attached, trim the remaining wool so that a small tassel dangles from the bottom. Hang the ladder in a room where your family gathers. It does not

have to be in a conspicuous place. If it's possible, have each person living in the house bless the ladder with a puff of breath, adding his or her own energy to it. May your home be blessed with balance and harmony.

A Rooster Meditation to Find Your Courage

Calling someone "chicken" implies cowardice, but don't tell this to the hens and roosters of Key West, Florida—they rule the streets, literally! *Gallus gallus* of old was a fighter with sharp beak and claws that he wasn't afraid to use. Perhaps the soldiers of the Roman legions were aware of this. They took chickens into battle with them, not as food supplies but as totem animals and good luck charms.

If you've ever observed a rooster, you can see that he's a proud animal. His plumage is perfect and his legs are strong. He stands erect and puffs out his chest to crow. And of course, he struts with confidence, clearly in charge (as long as the hens allow it!). Even the most confident person has days where he or she feels less than adequate. Tap into

Rooster's energy to revive your heart and restore your courage. All you'll need is a quiet space with room to walk and about fifteen minutes.

Stand tall. *Kukkutasana,* or rooster pose, is a very advanced yoga stance. The body imitates the fullness of rooster's plumage, emphasized as the practitioner balances on his hands. It's much easier to stand tall, like Rooster: plant your feet firmly on the ground, and then pop out your rear. Straighten your back, shoulders, and head. Take a deep breath, letting your chest expand.

Plump out your plumage. A rooster's feathers encompass many colors—brown, red, green, and iridescent blue-black. Continue to take deep breaths, filling your lungs and expanding your chest. As you do so, envision waves of light around you in rooster colors. Brown grounds you, green nurtures you, red emboldens you, black protects you, and blue imparts a sense of calm.

Feel your spurs. Roosters and hens have three toes with a fourth "spur" as a heel that helps for scratching, defense, and in the case of the rooster, a means of hanging on while mating. Scarily (for the hens, anyway), some roosters can have thick spurs that are several inches long. (There was a documented case of a rooster's spur piercing the belly of a python after it had been eaten!) These are fierce birds! Know that you have the armor you need for whatever challenge you're facing. What is your spur? Think about what you need to develop and nurture to feel empowered. Visualize it and make a commitment to follow it.

Strut. Movement activates thought. Walk and see the colors of Rooster move with you. Feel—or find—your spurs. Use words to add power to your strut:

> *I am crowned with color.*
> *I walk with weapons of confidence and care.*
> *Like Rooster, I do. I dare!*
> *I am powerful!*

Use this meditation to feel your power or to inspire you to take the steps you need to do so. Be like Hen and scratch deeply to discover what you need. Repeat the meditation whenever you need a confidence boost.

A Chicken-Foot Charm for Protection

A rabbit's foot may be lucky, but a chicken foot is a multi-tasking charm—and a common tool in Hoodoo, Conjure, and Voodoo practice. Chicken feet can be used to "scratch away" negativity, expose the truth, and protect and defend. Get a group of chickens together and their talk is cease-less, hence their link to gossip. It's not surprising then that chicken feet can also be used to promote silence when war-ranted. Like any charm, the magic is in the making.

To create a chicken foot amulet to keep negativity at bay you'll need:

Chicken feet (Many grocery stores carry them—they're also good for making broth!)

2–5 pound bag of salt, depending on how many feet you'll be curing

Oven-proof dish that will accommodate the feet and allow them to be completely covered in salt

Deep dish or bowl that will accommodate the feet and allow them to be completely covered in salt

Herbs and stones to charge the feet once they are dried (Because this is a protective charm for the home, use herbs and stones with related qualities: dragon's blood banishes negativity and is also sacred to the planet Mars, for defense; sandalwood is protective; mugwort promotes strength; black stones such as tourmaline and obsidian are protective; rose quartz and turquoise pro-mote love and health, respectively.)

Black spray paint, glitter, chicken feathers, and other embellishments of your choice

Ribbon or yarn

Dry it. A food dehydrator will dry out chicken feet in three to five days, but part of the magic of creating these amulets is the time it takes for the feet to preserve—which can take months. Begin drying the feet at the New Moon so that as they lose their fat, they gain in the intensity of your intention. Fill the oven-proof dish with enough salt to nestle the feet in so that they don't touch the bottom. Cover the feet completely in salt, and then put the dish in the oven on the lowest setting and leave it for 10–12 hours.

Allow the feet to cool before taking them out and breaking off the crust of salt that will form around them. Next, pour some salt in your bowl, nestle in the chicken feet, and then cover them with more salt. Set the bowl aside, preferably in a cool, dry place where it won't be disturbed. Now, patience is key. Change the salt every week until all of the fat and moisture have been drained from the feet. There should be no seepage or funky odors. (See Resources for Madame May's excellent tutorial.)

As you're working with animal parts, it's important that you talk to Chicken through each step of the process. Thank her for her sacrifice, tell her your intentions, ask for her help; she is still a living spirit.

Charge it. Once your chicken feet are completely dry, lay them in a bed of herbs, stones, and resins to charge them with your intention. Since this is a talisman for home protection, I've suggested herbs and stones with those qualities (see supply list). While you shouldn't get the feet wet, you can also dress them with oil. Use your favorite references to choose which elements to include. Just as you did while you were in the drying stage, tell Chicken about your intentions as you cover the feet with the herbs and stones. Again, begin at the New Moon and leave them to charge for at least a full cycle.

Embellish it. I've suggested black for its traditional protective associations, but you can decorate your chicken feet charms with colors that are protective to you. You can also ask Chicken for color guidance. Take some time to meditate and see what manifests.

Painting the feet will also help to seal them. Some folks use nail polish to paint the claws in a complimentary color. When they're completely dry, brush the cut ends with glue and dip them in glitter until they're completely covered. You can seal the glitter so that it doesn't flake with a thin layer of clear glue.

Wind the ribbon or yarn near the top of the cut end. (This is also a good place to attach the feathers if you're using them. Try to use three, a magical number of completeness.) Then tie it off with enough length to make a loop to hang it.

Hang the foot by a door or window to ward away negativity. Remember to thank Chicken again for her part in this work.

Witch Came First?

Chicken, hen, and rooster magic are inevitably linked to egg magic. Even if the age-old riddle is solved, eggs are mysterious objects. (Science has pretty much determined that chickens didn't simply appear on the planet, but, like all living beings, developed from tiny cells. So eggs, not as we know them, came first, theoretically.) They have been—and still are—used for divination and spellwork.

In the sixteenth century it was widely believed that as wholesome as an egg could be, the shells had to be thoroughly destroyed lest witches could use them as houses or boats. Once afloat they could go out to sea and wreck havoc with the weather. Double-yolk eggs were a sign of marriage (two yolks, two souls) or pregnancy—possibly twins. Most folks took the discovery of a double-yolk egg to be a sign of good (doubled!) fortune—unless you were Norse, in which case it purported the death of a family member.

The Canton (Ohio) Historical Society revealed some interesting beliefs about eggs in their bicentennial activity book: Have a headache? Get hold of an egg laid by a white hen in a new nest on Easter Day. This egg (if you own it) would also help you see witches. Break that same egg in a vineyard and it'll protect it from hail, or break it in a field to protect it from frost.

May Hen and Rooster bring order and peace to your home and courage and sunshine to your life. Bright blessings!

Resources

"An Ancient and Noble Beast." Omlet. Accessed on October 10, 2016. https://www.omlet.us/guide/chickens/about_chickens/history/.

"All about Eggs." The Canton Girl Scouts Canton Bicentennial Historical Activity Book. Canton Historical Society. Accessed on October 10, 2016. http://www.canton.org/history/eggs.htm.

Heritageofjapan. "Rooster symbolism." *Japanese Mythology & Folklore*. Accessed on October 10, 2016. https://japanesemythology.wordpress.com/rooster-symbolism/.

Madame May. "How to Make Chicken Feet Protection Charms . . . Part One." YouTube video, 4:13. February 26, 2015. https://www.youtube.com/watch?v=0swu4uw37kQ.

Madame May. "How to Make Chicken Feet Protection Charms . . . Part Two." YouTube video, 7:07. February 27, 2015. https://www.youtube.com/watch?v=xkdsh1ylRf8.

Springfield, Emma. "Strange Superstitions about Feathers." *Nature Center Magazine*. May 21, 2012. http://www.nc-mag.com/2012/05/strange-superstitions-about-feathers.html.

Pande, Mrinal. "Meet Rajasthan's Goddesses of Small Things—Garbage, Sneezing Fits, Hens and Lunar Calendar Days." *Scroll.in*. July 13, 2016. http://scroll.in/article/806034/meet-rajasthans-goddesses-of-small-things-garbage-sneezing-fits-hens-and-lunar-calendar-days.

Virata, John. "Australian Vet Removes Rooster Foot That Punctured Python's Belly." *Reptiles*. November 6, 2015. http://www.reptilesmagazine.com/australian-vet-removes-rooster-foot-that-punctured-pythons-belly-trending/.

Weiss, Kirsten. "History and Mystery: The Witches' Ladder." *Parayournormal*. August 25, 2015. https://parayournormal.wordpress.com/2015/08/25/5-things-you-should-know-about-the-witches-ladder/.

When Invasive Spirits Come Around

by Raven Digitalis

A wide variety of people from virtually all cultural backgrounds believe that there is more to life than meets the eye. Civilizations from the dawn of humankind through the present day have long held on to beliefs in nonphysical entities of one variety or another. Still, others disbelieve in these forces altogether, feeling as though strict scientific evidence supersedes experiential data. Mystics and magicians, however, understand the value of experience alongside scientific theory and are more likely to consider alternate dimensions of existence if their own personal experience leads them to such conclusions.

Gods, spirit guides, ascended masters, guardian ancestors, angels, and similar forces are often considered "upper level" astral beings, while others such as ghosts, faeries, and elementals are believed to exist in a plane that is lower and closer to our own world.

Nonphysical beings each have their own personalities and motivations. Just like humans and animals, the personalities of astral beings can be greatly varied and often depend on the "type" of being they are. Many nonphysical entities are harmless and benign. Others, however, most certainly are not.

Ancient pagans and animists from a variety of cultures have long attributed physical and mental ailments to demonic spirits and astral invaders. While modern science brilliantly explains these ailments on a physiological level, mystics understand that the physical and nonphysical realms interact and that the physical dimension is but one of many possibilities. This is not to say that all physical imbalances are caused by spiritual entities, but that it's worth consideration that the body works in conjunction with energetic planes. It is wise to be aware that the physical and nonphysical worlds are not always as separate as they may seem.

Trust Your Instincts

Because the physical body itself is connected with various energetic planes, it's important to pay attention to our body's responses and reactions. When it comes to sensing spirits, or even sensing energy in general, it's valuable to pay attention to our first instincts. If we sense the presence of a spirit or foreign entity, which emotions or sensations do we immediately experience? As magickal folks, we tend to trust our instincts when interacting with fellow humans, so why would it be any different with the spirit world?

Whether or not we rationally understand or can accurately categorize the entities we encounter, it's of utmost importance to pay attention to our instincts. From there, we are more apt to make sense of an encounter, even if it's a momentary experience.

I'm not gonna lie: it can be difficult to make sense of spiritual dimensions and astral dynamics. There are no solid answers because these realms are not solid structures. Metaphysicians of all varieties promote the belief that the mind, intellect, and even

the imagination are explicitly linked with unseen realms of existence. It is reasonable to assume that many of these worlds and realms are continually changing and being molded by human minds—and this may even hold true for the gods themselves. It's also worth mentioning that many nonphysical entities have the ability to change their appearance depending on who they are interacting with, serving to convolute things even further!

When you sense an external spiritual entity, pay attention to what your body and mind tell you. Do you get "good" or "bad" goosebumps? Do you feel a fight-or-flight sensation or heart palpitations, or do you feel at ease? Do you feel a shift in temperature? It's wise to pay attention to the instincts of the mind and body; after all, you don't want perform banishing exercises if you are receiving a friendly visitation from a spirit guide or a dearly departed loved one.

The Art of Discernment

As I mentioned, the intuitive and creative dimensions intermingle with unseen planes of existence, making it a challenge to understand where objective experience ends and mental projection begins. It's vitally important to question every experience with nonphysical entities, but it's equally important to understand the validity of each experience, even if it's only on a symbolic level. For example, if I happen to randomly see a moose in my peripheral vision, it doesn't necessarily mean that it's a spirit animal, an animal oversoul, or the ghost of a moose, but it could be any of these things. If nothing else, my subconscious mind is communicating "moose energy" to me for some reason, so either way it warrants some metaphysical contemplation. If the moose were to repeatedly appear, the question could be investigated further: What is its origin and what is the purpose of the communication? Every experience with unseen forces has its own importance, whether it's actually otherworldly or is simply psychologically symbolic.

Allow me to be up front here: I have interacted with countless people who have been in the midst of experiencing inconsolable "supernatural trauma." A spirit of some type is haunting them for one reason or another; the entity is unaffected by spellcraft, magick, prayer, and everything else; it's wreaking havoc in every aspect of the person's life; and so on. Rarely are these claims legitimate; in my experience a vast number of these cases are occurrences of psychological disturbance and delusion, not spiritual activity.

A person's psychological constitution, past experiences (perhaps causing PTSD), and coping patterns must be taken into consideration when approaching the concept of metaphysical intrusion. In many cases, medical assistance can be much more beneficial than metaphysical assistance. Therapy, psychiatry, and medical treatment are not signs of weakness but signs of empowerment. We all deserve to take control of our mental and emotional constitutions, and by doing so we can more accurately examine issues such as invasive spirits and astral entities. As magickal and metaphysical practitioners, we have the responsibility to objectively determine the nature of our experiences to the best of our abilities. When it comes to invasive spirits, some apparent entities are nothing more than thought forms: projections of the subconscious mind. Others, however, quite obviously have their own distinct agendas and personalities.

A Strange Encounter

Back in 2008 I had an experience with a spirit that still sticks out quite heavily in my memory because of its insidious intensity. While I do sometimes sense earthbound disincarnates (ghosts) and other astral entities, I've never had one become attached to such an extent. This encounter began when I visited a city in Oregon as part of my book tour for *Shadow Magick Compendium*. After doing book signings and tarot readings at a local metaphysical store, the original plan was to explore the city with a tour guide. Unfortunately, this tour guide had to cancel, and I was on my own. Because it was a weeknight, there wasn't too much going on around town. I found myself wandering downtown and throughout quieter areas of the city. I recall feeling a particularly depressed or desperate sensation in one dark, empty street that I traversed on my way back to the motel. At the time I brushed off this feeling, but for some reason the sensation didn't really seem to leave, even weeks after returning home. This is not to say that I was especially depressed, but there was a subtle draining sensation that seemed to be increasing with time. Eerily, the sensation felt similar to the feeling I experienced on that empty Oregon street. My instincts told me that something was off.

Over the next week, these sensations were palpably present on the upper right side of my body—I didn't sense the presence anywhere else. During quiet moments of the day, it almost felt as if someone was sitting on my aura and watching my every movement. It was an uncomfortable sensation that only seemed to increase in strength, coupled with the fact that my general level of energy seemed lower than normal. I decided to meditate on the situation.

It didn't take long to discover that a conscious being with an independent personality was clinging to my energetic body and thus also my physical body. In deep meditation, the spirit clearly felt female. I could feel her astral hair and even feel her breath—slightly creepy! But it didn't stop there; I sensed myself empathetically affected by this spirit's desperate sorrow. I could feel her astral body attempting to draw closer and attach to my deeper levels of energy, such as through the chakra points. I even felt sexually aroused, which was a clear indication that she was attempting to merge with my body through sexual energy. It was clear that she attached to me on that dark and empty street; the feelings were just too uncannily similar to dismiss. This entity was most likely a ghost who, for all intents and purposes, became a parasitic and vampiric succubus.

By continually repeating protective exercises, such as those mentioned toward the end of this article, I was eventually able to shake her off my aura. The whole process took a couple of weeks and involved a lot of trial and error. Because the spirit was slowly and subtly feeding off my own emotional and sexual energy, I had to be extremely mindful and self-aware of both of those realms. I had the responsibility of understanding which emotions and energies were my own and which were "other." Luckily, as an empath, I had already grown familiar with the practice of emotional discernment.

While all of the protective exercises and procedures I enacted were certainly helpful in relieving the situation, the most effective form of banishing was also the most difficult: I had to verbally command her, repeatedly and regularly, to go away. Because she had attached to my emotions and was attempting to merge with my energetic body, a feeling of rejection and sorrow would continually follow any statement of "go away and leave me alone." This, of course, was not my own sadness; it belonged to the spirit. Still, I felt like a cruel and heartless person for telling this astral stalker to disappear—incidentally, in an attempt to stay attached, this is exactly how she wanted me to feel. As difficult as it was, I built up the courage to forcibly evict the spirit and demand that she "go to the light." Eventually, it worked.

Understanding an Encounter

If you are experiencing a strange spiritual encounter that you feel is invasive toward the self, the home, or another person, try analyzing the experience for yourself by following these steps. This meditation is but one suggestion for how to identify the being or beings you may be encountering. As always, use a healthy amount of discretion to understand what may be a mental projection and what is more likely to be an objective observation.

Analytical Meditation

Situate yourself near the environment or person who has been experiencing a perceived spiritual invasion. If you are the person who is experiencing the invasive spirit, get comfortable in your own sacred space.

Close your eyes and use your subtle senses to locate the entity or energy in question. If fear arises, try to overcome it. If it feels genuinely and immediately threatening, skip to the last paragraph of this section.

First, determine whether this is an energy or an entity: Is it simply a body of energy, or does it seem to have a distinct personality? If it feels like a negative body of energy, consider using some of the suggestions in the next section. If it feels like an individual conscious entity, move on to the next step.

Try to sense the general energy of the entity. Feel it out. Does it appear to be a kind or curious spirit, or does it legitimately intend harm? Could it have been sent by another person, consciously or unconsciously, or is it simply a passerby? Does it wish to communicate with you? If you determine that the spirit "feels okay," try verbally and psychically communicating, noting the impressions you receive; the spirit might actually be there to help or might simply need a gentle "push" to move on.

If you have determined that the entity you've encountering is in fact malicious and invasive, do your best to summon the courage to fight against it. Demand that it leave; explain that it is not welcome here and must depart. Claim your power and make your needs known without hesitation. Tell it how it is! Next, proceed to follow some of the following suggestions and use your best judgment in dealing with the situation. You have a lot more influence and ability than you may think!

Spirit Cleansing

Regardless of its origins, if you feel the presence of a maliciously invasive spirit, these suggestions can help deflect its energy from your sphere. Experiment with different methods and see what works best for you personally.

- Smudge yourself with sage, using locally sourced sage if possible.

- Asperge your aura with salt water or water from a sacred location.
- Light matches: the sulfur/brimstone exorcises negative forces.
- Use a magick wand, athame, or your pointer finger to draw a large earth banishing pentagram (a star beginning in the lower left-hand corner) toward the direction of the entity. See this pentagram glowing in a bright blue flame.
- Perform protective rituals such as the Lesser Banishing Ritual of the Pentagram.
- Wear high-energy stones such as selenite and moldavite.
- Forcibly declare the Greek phrase *Apo pantos kakodaimonos*. This roughly translates to "Away, evil spirits!" The phrase is also incorporated in a basic ritual of Thelema called the Star Ruby.
- Hang protective herbs around the house, such as bulbs of garlic, sliced onions, and cloves.
- Utilize symbols such as pentagrams, the eye of the dragon, Xs, and anti–evil eye symbols. These can be put onto items, clothing, candles, artwork, and charms or drawn on the body.

- Call upon upper-level beings, such as gods, spirit guides, and angels; they are often believed to have the ability to intercede with lower-level affairs, such as hauntings, possessions, and restless spirits.
- Make it a daily practice to visualize and reinforce your energetic shields.
- Recite prayers, affirmations, and inspirational readings of holy texts. Project positive and upbeat energy toward the entity or energy in order to help avert its influence.
- Most importantly, choose to remain as optimistically positive as possible: your mood changes your energy, which in and of itself is profoundly protective.

Kindling Fire:
A Practical Discussion

by Susan Pesznecker

Fire . . . As magic users, we've all worked with fire, whether lighting candles for ritual, dancing around a magical balefire, sitting a night-long vigil next to smoldering flames, or scrying into a flickering hearth. We adore fire and wax metaphorical . . . Our spirits blaze. Our blood burns. Our passions are ignited.

Indeed, fire is both loved and feared by humans. There's nothing it can't destroy, converting matter into so much unrecognizable ash. On the other hand, it keeps us alive. Our Sun—fire incarnate—provides the warmth and light we take for granted and without it, life on earth would quickly end. Fire even seems alive in its own way. We personify it, talking about how it leaps, dances, runs wild, and consumes materials whole and even how the crackling flames "speak."

The gods revered—and feared—fire as much as as we do today. Consider the story of Prometheus bringing the gift of fire to humans and paying a horrible price for angering the gods. Or the story of Raven, risking everything to capture the Sun and give light to a once-dark world.

In magical terms, fire embodies the four classical elements: smoke becomes air, the flame's visual liquidity echoes water, ash embodies earth, and the flame is fire itself. But there's a practical side, too. Understanding fire and knowing how to work with it safely and effectively are valuable additions to our magical tool boxes. Do you know how to build a fire in the outdoors? How to choose the correct type of fire and materials, matching purpose and function?

Read on . . .

Types of Wood

Firewood can be categorized as "soft" or "hard." Most softwoods come from coniferous trees. This type of wood is rich in pitch and resins; it ignites easily, burns quickly, doesn't generate much heat, and is easy to split. Some common softwoods include pine, fir, and spruce.

Hardwoods come from deciduous, broadleaf trees. The wood is heavier (hard to split) and denser than that of softwood; it is harder to ignite but burns for a long time and produces significant heat. Hardwood trees include oak, maple, birch, and walnut.

Before You Begin: Consider Safety

Use an existing fire pit. If one isn't available, remove sticks, twigs, and other ground covers to expose bare earth. Clear a circle for eight to ten feet around the fire, and don't build under overhanging branches.

Always keep your fire as small as possible, and never leave it unintended—not even for a moment. Keep a shovel and a bucket of water near the fire for safety. Don't bury hot coals—they can ignite tree roots and start forest fires.

Before leaving a fire, make sure it's "cold out," meaning you can put your hand into the extinguished fire and feel no heat.

What Does Fire Need?

A fire needs three components to ignite and burn:

Fuel: Fire must have material to consume. The fuel should be dry and in the right size and amount to encourage ignition.

Oxygen: Fire needs oxygen in order to burn. If fuel is packed too tightly into the fire space, air can't move through the fire, and the fire will be smothered.

Heat: To start a fire burning, the combustible materials must be hot enough to ignite. If you can't ratchet up the heat, the fire won't succeed.

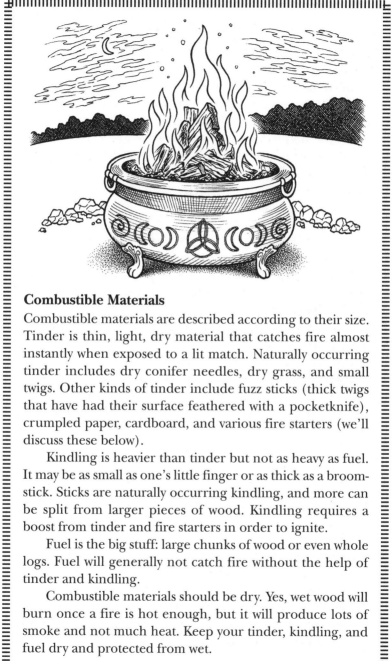

Combustible Materials

Combustible materials are described according to their size. Tinder is thin, light, dry material that catches fire almost instantly when exposed to a lit match. Naturally occurring tinder includes dry conifer needles, dry grass, and small twigs. Other kinds of tinder include fuzz sticks (thick twigs that have had their surface feathered with a pocketknife), crumpled paper, cardboard, and various fire starters (we'll discuss these below).

Kindling is heavier than tinder but not as heavy as fuel. It may be as small as one's little finger or as thick as a broomstick. Sticks are naturally occurring kindling, and more can be split from larger pieces of wood. Kindling requires a boost from tinder and fire starters in order to ignite.

Fuel is the big stuff: large chunks of wood or even whole logs. Fuel will generally not catch fire without the help of tinder and kindling.

Combustible materials should be dry. Yes, wet wood will burn once a fire is hot enough, but it will produce lots of smoke and not much heat. Keep your tinder, kindling, and fuel dry and protected from wet.

Laying a Fire

First, decide which type of fire is needed. For example, a cooking fire is typically a small-to-medium-blaze that burns hot and fast and then settles to create a nice bed of coals. Create a small tepee fire by arranging a tepee of softwood kindling over a fire starter and a big handful of tinder. Leave an opening for lighting the fire. As the fire ignites, add more kindling and then hardwood fuel. Allow it to burn down to form coals.

A ritual or ceremonial campfire catches easily, builds to a crescendo, and then slowly subsides—mimicking the way a ritual raises energy and then releases it. Begin with a tepee (see the cooking fire instructions above), placing one or two fire starters in its center. Next, use pieces of softwood fuel to build a "log cabin" around the tepee. Light the fire when the event begins—it should burn steadily throughout the ritual.

Vigil fires tend to be small and stable, burning steadily through several hours. Start the fire with a softwood tepee, then feed it with small to medium pieces of hardwood fuel to keep it going.

Fires built as heat sources work best as "reflectors." Set up a vertical barricade one to two feet tall made of wood, stone, or brick. Build a softwood tepee in front of it, adding hardwood kindling and then hardwood fuel against it. The barricade will reflect the heat back out, providing warmth.

Bonfires, also called balefires, are big and wild. Safety is a main concern with these—i.e., keeping the fire spectacular but under control. Clear an extra-large area around the bonfire. The type of wood used doesn't matter much: you just need lots of it!

Kindling Fire

Fire starters are materials that help ignite tinder and kindling. Here are three of my favorites:

1. Using a cardboard egg carton, fill each of the egg compartments with lint from the clothes dryer screen.

(Cotton balls, sawdust, and wood shavings will work, too.) Melt paraffin or bits of old candles and pour the hot wax over the stuffed egg carton compartments. Allow to cool, and then break apart. To use, place one or two fire starters on a base of wood and top with a handful of tinder. The wax and cardboard will ignite the tinder quickly, and the wax will melt over the wood base, encouraging it to burn, too.

2. Pull 100-percent cotton balls apart with your fingers, forming a flat oval. Massage plain petroleum jelly into the cotton until it is saturated, then roll the cotton back into a ball. Store these in a small container (a metal mints container works well). To use your "jelly balls," place one or two on a wooden base, pull up a few cotton strands (as wicks), and light. Each one will burn for several minutes, and the petroleum will melt, spreading flames across the wood.

3. Charcoal briquets saturated with lighter fluid can be lit with matches. Placing these on a wooden base and topping with tinder will get your fire going in no time.

Char cloth—charred cotton—is a traditional fire starter, as is fatwood—a resin-rich wood taken from certain pine trees. Blobs of pitch, picked off conifers, work brilliantly as starters, too. I like to light fires with plain old "strike anywhere" wooden matches. They're sturdy, and the matches themselves become additional pieces of tinder. Keep your matches dry by storing them in a ziplock bag; waterproof individual matches by dipping them in melted wax or clear nail polish.

Always start any fire with a large handful of tinder (and a fire starter or two!). Arrange a tepee of kindling around it and light the tinder. As it ignites and burns, add more kindling and then begin to add fuel. When adding wood to the fire, remember that the flames need air: maintain spaces between combustibles to let air move through the fire. The tepee is an ideal shape for starting a fire because it encourages the material to heat quickly, pulling air up through its base.

Cool Tools and Special Effects

Starting fires with flint and steel or magnesium and steel is both fun and showy. If you have ample sunshine, you can also experiment with fire starting via magnifying lenses.

Hand bellows or bellows tubes (which look like long steel straws) blow air into the fire's center, encouraging it to ignite.

Tongs or pokers are useful for moving pieces of wood, and heavy gloves will protect your hands from the heat.

Commonly available chemicals can add color to your campfire. Throw in handfuls of salts or soak small pieces of wood in chemical solutions and allow them to dry before burning. Examples:

- Borax: yellow-green flames
- Copper sulfate: blue-green flames
- Potassium chloride: purple flames
- Sodium chloride (table salt): yellow flames

And, of course, you can add bits of herbs, essential oils, salt, or other magical substances that suit your purposes.

Extinguishing the Flames

To extinguish the fire, allow it to burn down, then use tongs or a stick to stir and spread out the remaining coals. Scatter water over the coals and wood until there is no more steaming or hissing. Smother any remaining heat with dirt or sand. Wait a minute, stir again, and then (cautiously) examine the area for any signs of heat. It should be cool enough that your bare hand could touch the wet area safely. Repeat the process as necessary.

Behold the practical magic of fire.

Vesta: Goddess of the Eternal Flame

Estha K. V. McNevin

The Roman goddess Vesta is a magical Latin namesake of mine. Hers were among the first ceremonial fires that I lit as a priestess. As the patroness of all bakers, she is conjured into every loaf of bread, each cake, cookie, bonbon, and laddu that our temple handcrafts. Her sacred animal is the stubborn and hardworking donkey. Full of passion and purpose, the ass is agriculturally linked to wheat cultivation and millstone grinding throughout the Mediterranean.

From astrology and from the natural elements, ancient Romans derived a primitive domestic order to paganism. By using deities like Vesta to align domestic and civil routines to the seasons, months, and the days of the week, they structured society around the rulership of the planetary gods. Learning this extraordinary method of Old World magic, which is still inherent in modern ceremonialism, has led me to keep a light in prayer for the ageless, living goddess of fire in her innumerable forms. As Vesta, the matron of hearth and home, she is the keeper of the sacred temple fires. To her mighty rhythm of the earth, the radiant heart of Rome synchronized its beat.

A Roman by Any Other Genetic Marker

The patroness of fire is central to the temple, hearth, and home. Vesta is a Latin reflection of an even older Greek goddess, Hestia. Her cults were first established alongside our Stone Age mastery of domestic fire, somewhere in the Levant region: the fertile crescent of Mesopotamia. The Levant region is from where she also imports her sacred flower *Vitex agnus-castus,* or chasteberry, a medicinal treatment for menstruation cramps and labor pains. Along with her cut blossoms, the antediluvian custom of veiling was adopted as a mark of chaste modesty and devout civil service.

Vesta's eternal flame politically picks up right where Homer tells us that cultural clashes of Greek civilization left off. Along with Etruscan and Minoan myths, the Gods of antiquity legitimized the political ambitions of fledgling Roman nationalism. In linking Vesta to Rome, the allegory of orphaned children served as a metaphor for natural survivalism, relating our reliance on a populous society to our need for civic duty to understand justice and urban subsistence. According to Roman historian Titus Livius (59 BCE– 17 CE), it was from within the cave of Lupercal on Palatine Hill that the orphaned Romulus and Remus suckled from Lupa, the wild she-wolf who adopted the two as her little lost-and-foundlings.

According to the legend, Romulus and Remus's birth mother, Reha Silva, was a victim of circumstance who was forced to serve as a priestess and virgin amongst the vestals of Laurentes Lavinates. She broke her vows for the amorous advances of the god Mars, conceiving the brothers at grave risk to herself. When her uncle Amulius ordered the twins to be killed, a twist of fate led to their narrow escape down the Tiber River from Lavinium. For this reason, Vesta's oldest temple in the area was consecrated as the "mother fire" of the Roman state hearth and was a site where high-ranking officials poured their libations into the fires of Vesta on behalf of Rome.

Feed the Fire to Further the Future

The Latin word for "hearth" is *focus,* quite simply because fire played a key role in the lives of our ancient pagan ancestors. It was beneath the hearth that the first prehistoric European tribes buried their dead, giving the hearth an important role in European culture as the epicenter of community and family, both in this world and the next. Fire also made the hearth a type of magical altar with its otherworldly transmutation of wood into life-sustaining energy, transforming raw food into nourishing cuisine. Fire has long been a central focus of daily domestic routines. Ancient Romans also saw fire as a sacred life-giving and life-taking portal, leading to other worlds and alternate timelines.

Giving offerings of food, grains, wine, and other libations was a requirement of lighting a fire because it was seen as akin to evoking Vesta into the room. Offerings feed all the souls and spirits who are around a person working in their favor. The warm kettle and the *patera* (libation platter) were filled with water, wine, oil, or grains and were tipped to spill the offerings at the feet of a statue or on the base of the fire grate. Many devotees also made vows to Vesta annually. Veiling and chastity were required of both men and women in temple service for a duration of thirty years. More commonly, giving domestic offerings to seek Vesta's blessings on March 1 was part of observing the return of the warmth and light of spring. Her feasting days on June 7 through 15 celebrated betrothals amid her warmth and seasonal generosity.

Invoke Vesta

This ritual is a modern Eastern Hellenist invocation. It falls within the realm of Indo-European magic in that it is a fusion of many prayers to fire and Vesta. Here I have brazenly borrowed from Ovid's call to Vesta and a Syrian divination prayer found in the Greek Magical Papyri. It is an attempt to restore, in English, a more complete concept of Latin Hellenistic magic as truly adaptive and an unabashedly universal system. Don't be afraid, dear reader, to butcher the Latin with all the wild abandon of a modern barbarian. Google the correct brogue if you will, or simply stick to the English; it is your choice.

Ritual

On a Tuesday, begin by bathing thoroughly in a saltwater bath to cleanse yourself before the ritual. Wear a long, red veil and appear skyclad before your home fireplace, gas range, electric fire, or central heating furnace.

In a large bowl, combine the following and wash down the mantle using this mixture:

12 bay leaves
1 cup distilled white vinegar
6 cups hot soapy water (using all-natural soap)
8 drops chasteberry oil

Install the family mantel by placing the following items on and around it with loving care:

3 small lamps fitted with tea lights
1 glass vase filled with fresh-cut flowers
3 family photos
7 springs of fresh thyme strung with red string and hung as a
    garland from the left to the right side of the mantel

On the floor just before the hearth, mix the following resins to create a seven sacred woods fire meze or offering. As you grind the resins into smaller, more uniform pieces and unite them, speak aloud the listed qualities that you would like to evoke in around your hearth:

1 tablespoon frankincense resin for protection, purification,
    and antidepression
1 tablespoon dragon's blood resin for protection and clearing
1 tablespoon myrrh resin for dispersing hope, spiritual con-
    nection, and healing

1 tablespoon piñon resin for protection, healing, and nurturing new growth

1 tablespoon cedar resin for healing, spiritual strength, and nurturing courage

1 tablespoon benzoin resin (loban) for purification, blessing, and prosperity

1 tablespoon amber resin for prophecy, fortification, and antiseptic restoration

Light a charcoal patty (one designed for incense) inside a hanging brass censer and offer incense smoke to bless the hearth with the strengths, qualities, and wisdom of the great trees of the earth. Hang this from a hook in the wall or ceiling near to your hearth for regular use as needed.

When everything is in place, it's time to invite Vesta. If you have a wood-buring fireplace then begin by placing a tablespoon of seven sacred woods resin onto your stack of kindling when lighting Vesta's sacred fire. If your amenities are more modernized, begin by turning up the furnace

or otherwise dialing up the heat on the gas range to reveal a steady flame or heat source for you to work magic with. Allow the warmth to wash over you until a cozy and fulfilling energy of security emerges from deep within.

Speak the following Latin and/or English prayer aloud seven times to draw Vesta forth.

Latin:

O Domina Vesta, dare nobis fortuna!
Inflammet penates flamma foco.
Benedic omnia cum tua luce.
Dea Vesta, vivat en bonitas nostris fermentum receperint.

English:

O Lady Vesta, give us a chance.
Kindle the flame of hearth and home here.
Bless us all with your light.
Goddess Vesta, live in the goodness of our warm welcome.

Asperge the edges of the hearth and any furniture nearby with rosewater to invite Vesta's warm and loving blessing into the room.

Give the following call to Vesta with your palms facing the fire. Draw the warmth and light of the goddess as you ask her to fill your hearth and home with her auspices:

This spark is ignited in the present instant, in the name of Vesta, granddaughter of Gaia, daughter of Rhea and Kronos. I call upon the goddess of hearth and home. My lamps are lit in vestal reverence for the mysteries of fire, source of all color. I worship your immortality and grace, O lady of light.

Vesta, draw your eternal torch near, radiating your bright intelligence to warm and sustain this household. Appear veiled and glowing astride your donkey, attended by six dark-eyed Nymphae of the Levant, who devoutly foster your inferno. Stand your sisterhood of obscure vestal virgins along all of the corners and walls of my hearth. As they pour their corporal vapors from onyx urns, may they also decant a wholesome life into my fire.

By your Lares (fire spirits), guard and protect this portal of the underworld, permitting only good spirits to enter here. Entice the Panes (earth spirits) *to bless our pantry and lead our beloved Lares* (family spirits) *to the familial cupboard shrine. May all good-natured Panes and watchful ancestors around this residence receive my affectionate offerings with all due respect.*

With grace, daughter of the millstone, bake our bread in your precision, for it is sanctified by our labors and proven alone by your consent, sweet patroness of the banquet. Summon a sanctuary of knowledge and light in this place. Bright child of the earth, draw the vigor of wolves, bears, and lions to lay down in empathy for lamb, kid, and yearling. Becalm the restless spirits of the earth here and hallow our home as a place of peace. By my magic, fasten a sliver of your immortal life unto the confines of this hearth to consecrate our home.

O willful lady of fire, forever warm my kettle over your threshold of domestic harmony. By Saturn, bind fidelity and prosperity here. With an open heart I welcome collective family wisdom to warm my spirit and illuminate my mind by the cycles of the Moon. May all guests be made welcome to gather here, blessed by the light of the goddess Vesta, equal only to the Sun, in perfect love and perfect trust.

Vesta, keep our home fires burning; domum ignes custodiunt.

List the names of all who dwell in the home as well as any friends, coven members, or family members that you welcome frequently into your home in perfect love and perfect trust.

To activate the blessing, invite someone 'round for a long chat over tea or coffee; remember to serve bread and to place Vesta's favorite offerings at her feet.

Use your mantel as a sacred altar for family magic and times of togetherness. Honor and observe it as a portal to other worlds by keeping it tidy. Choose to value your hearth as evocative of the mystery and wonder inherent in the powers of the goddess of hearth and home, and Vesta will live well with you and yours.

Resources

Chambers, Mortimer, Barbara Hanawalt, Theodore K. Rabb, Isser Woloch, and Raymond Grew. *The Western Experience.* New York: McGraw-Hill, 2002.

Hulse, David Allen. *The Western Mysteries: An Encyclopedic Guide to the Sacred Languages & Magickal Systems of the World; The Key of it All, Book II.* St. Paul, MN: Llewellyn, 2000.

Nagle, Betty Rose, ed. and trans. *Ovid's Fasti: Roman Holidays.* Bloomington: Indiana University Press, 1995.

Nova Roma. "Gods and Goddesses of Rome." Nova Roma. Last modified August 31, 2013. http://www.novaroma.org/religio_romana/deities.html.

Singh, Upindar. *A History of Ancient and Early Medieval India: From the Stone Age to the 12th Century.* Delhi: Pearson Longman, 2008.

Singhal, K. C., and Roshan Gupta. *Ancient History of India, the Vedic Period: A New Interpretation.* New Delhi: Atlantic, 2003.

Tresidder, Jack. *The Complete Dictionary of Symbols.* San Francisco: Chronicle Books, 2005.

Whitcomb, Bill: *The Magician's Companion: A Practical & Encyclopedic Guide to Magical and Religious Symbolism.* St. Paul, MN: Llewellyn, 2002.

Midsummer, the Sun, and the Fairy Folk

by Jason Mankey

The summer solstice is a truly magickal occasion. It's a celebration of the year's shortest night and the power of the Sun. Over the centuries it has been associated with the Fey (fairy folk) and epic battles between the Oak and Holly Kings. It might also be *the* original magickal holiday, with some of those magickal traditions being passed down for millennia.

One of the oldest representations of the Sun is the solar wheel, a perfect circle with two intercrossing lines running through its center. Solar wheels appeared in a variety of different ways in ancient art. Most often they served as the wheels of chariots driven by solar deities, but they also sometimes appeared on the decks of ships when a boat was used to illustrate how the Sun made its daily journey through the sky.

What's most interesting about the solar wheel is just how long it's been venerated in summer solstice celebrations. In the 1400s written accounts of people lighting wheels on fire and rolling them down hills on the summer solstice began to show up in Northern Europe and Great Britain, but the practice is probably much older. Accounts of flaming wheels have been a part of the historical record since the fourth century CE and seem to be an ancient pagan tradition.

A good harvest was thought to be assured if the flaming solar wheel made it down the hill without toppling over. To ensure the wheel actually made it down the hill a long pole was inserted into its center with two people then holding each end and running with the wheel as it went down the hill. But that wasn't the only time fire was a part of Midsummer celebrations.

Ancient pagans believed that fire could be used for both purification and protection, and both of those ideas were incorporated into how fire was used on the summer solstice. To drive out negativity, bad spirits, and to ensure a bountiful harvest, people would run through their fields of crops with lit torches, the fire and smoke doing the heavy magickal lifting. Bonfires were a part of Midsummer celebrations, too, and were used to chase bad spirits and fairies away. The bonfire as a way of celebrating the solstice lasted well into modern times as well, though today they are often lit by Christians on the Feast of Saint John.

These ancient practices can be easily adapted for use in modern solstice celebrations. Lighting a "bonfire" in a grill or portable fire pit (and if you live in a spot where you can light a real bonfire, all the better!) is an easy way to practice a little ancient magick. Simply throw whatever you'd like to get rid of in your life into the fire and ask your favorite solar deity for assistance in manifesting that change. If what you want to get rid of can't be easily represented by a physical

item, simply write whatever it is down on a piece of paper and burn that.

Like pagans of old, I like to use Midsummer for cleansing, though I often cleanse my house instead of crops. As the Sun sets on the year's shortest night, I light up a big bundle of sage and use the smudge smoke to purify the biggest problem areas of my home. Some of those problem areas are mundane (my television makes me lazy) and some are a bit more magickal. My ritual room tends to attract spectral "visitors." Many of them are unwelcome, and a little purifying smudge will generally get rid of them.

My wife won't let me run with any flaming solar wheels, but I've thrown paper ones into our Midsummer fires over the years while asking for a productive year. An alternative idea is to bake a loaf of bread in the shape of a solar wheel. While eating the "solar bread," think of the Sun's power entering your body and powering you through the next six months. Solar loafs also make nice offerings, and I always share a little bit with the Goddess and God and the fairy folk who live in my backyard.

The Fey

The Fey have long been associated with Midsummer, and in both a positive and a negative way. Until relatively recently the fairy folk were seen as a "bad presence," and fires were lit on the summer solstice to keep them away from people and crops. As time passed the Fey were increasingly seen in a positive light, and while their presence wasn't always requested, they came to be associated with Midsummer celebrations. Much of that association is probably due to Shakespeare's *A Midsummer Night's Dream* (which dates back to the 1590s).

There are some disagreements on just who or what the fairy folk are. Some people see them as an ethereal race of beings existing parallel to humankind. Others see them as "nature spirits," but no matter how you perceive them,

Midsummer is a great opportunity to interact with them and pay them homage. The Fey are said to live anywhere there is a bit of nature—for most of us that probably means our backyards or a local park—and they usually exist in secluded spots. In my backyard they occupy a space between our fence and lemon tree. Figuring out where the Fey call home in any specific place is a matter of belief and intuition. They aren't going to tell you where they are: you just have to trust your instincts.

At Midsummer my Witch coven often leaves them small shiny gifts; glass beads seem to be a favorite. They also like sweets, so instead of ritual bread, we generally have ritual cupcakes on the summer solstice. Alcoholic libations, especially wine, are another good choice. Midsummer is also a good night to present them with even more substantial gifts, such as a fairy house. (You can either make your own or buy a small wooden dollhouse at an arts and crafts store.)

We also sometimes ask for their assistance near Midsummer. On the night before the sabbat we leave small trinkets outside next to their spot in our yard and ask for their blessings upon them. If you choose to ask the fairy folk for a favor be sure to leave them a small gift. While it's unlikely that they are going to destroy this year's harvest, they can be mischievous and even a bit spiteful. It's always best to say thank you just in case.

The Sun: A Companion in Magic

Most modern books about magick spend a great deal of time on Moon magick. Such tomes will tell you that if you are putting a spell together for gain you should wait until the Moon is waxing (getting bigger) in the sky. For operations such as getting rid of a bad habit they advise to wait until the Moon is waning to begin your spellwork. The Moon is a mighty companion in magick, so I understand the emphasis, but the Sun is just as strong. It's just a little bit different.

The power of the Moon is subtle. Over the course of twenty-eight days its light gradually grows and shrinks in the sky. This cycle is then repeated about eleven more times a year. The Sun is something else entirely and has two distinct stages.

Most Pagans and Witches are conscious of the bigger stage. We call it the Wheel of the Year, and it's the yearly cycle of the seasons and, by extension, the Sun's waxing and waning energy. Yule (the winter solstice, about December 21) marks the shortest day, but also the point from which all days begin to increase in length over the solar year. Midsummer is the longest day of the solar year and begins the shortening of days until Yule rolls around again.

Many Witches and Pagans use holidays such as Ostara (the spring equinox, about March 20) as a time to bring things into their lives. As the world grows in light, warmth, and greenery, they tap into those energies so that they might manifest in their own lives. To use a cooking analogy, using the cycles of Sun in magical work for gain or to be rid of something is a lot like using a slow-cooker or simmering a soup: the results are generally extraordinary but not so great if you really hungry now. Sometimes we don't have time to wait, which is when the Sun's second cycle comes in handy.

The Sun's daily rise and fall is an often overlooked tool in magickal practice and is easy to work with. From sunrise until solar noon is a time of gain, ideal for money magick or trying to bring new things into your life. For example, when I'm trying to stretch the dollars in my wallet, I leave my billfold in a sunny spot in the bedroom to tap into the Sun's "growing" energy. The hours directly before and after solar noon feature the Sun at its strongest and most intense; when the magick needs to be especially powerful, this is the time to work. Afternoon and until sunset are the best time for getting rid of things

My wife and I were once hexed by a bad Witch in our area (they don't all follow the Wiccan Rede) and needed to take some quick action. I didn't have time to wait for a waning Moon or even for the Sun to set (we had both had a pretty rotten day). Instead I took an ice cube out of our freezer, held it between my hands, and chanted the name of our local bad Witch along with the words "go away." When my hands couldn't stand the cold anymore I threw the ice-cube out into our yard and asked the earth and the Sun to take her bad energy away from us. As the Sun set the bad magick decreased, and as the ice melted that energy was absorbed into the ground.

Sunset is an especially powerful time for magick, and those evenings when the Sun is chasing the Moon are perfect for love spells. Sunset is also a liminal time, existing between the two extremes of night and day. I find it an especially appropriate time for communing with my deities (both in and out of ritual space) and for reaching out to the Summerlands (the world of the dead).

The Sun is often associated with male deities and masculine energies in magickal circles today, but that wasn't always the case. History contains just as many Sun goddesses as it does Sun gods, which means the energy of the Sun is capable of serving a variety of purposes. No matter your intent or working, the power of the Sun is capable of producing some truly magickal moments.

Water Magic

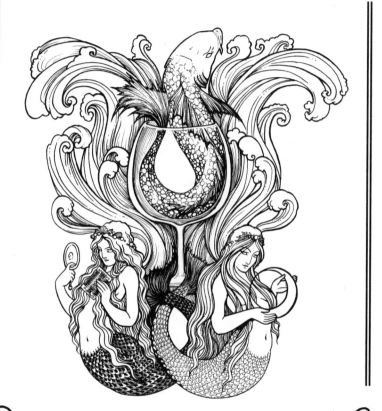

Divine Timing:
Aligning and Harmonizing with the Rhythm of the Universe

by Tess Whitehurst

In the magical world, we hear a lot about timing, from Moon cycles to seasons to days of the week. But making friends with time in general—so that it's our ally rather than our opponent—brings amazing benefits to our magic (and to everything else in our life).

Because let's face it: there is a lot of time resistance going on in our culture. If you listen to the phrases we so often use ("crazy busy," "killing time," and "not enough hours in the day," for example), you'd think we were each pitted in a constant battle against the clock.

But if you stop to think about it, this is a little nutty. After all, we're all right smack in the flow of time: in this present life experience, there's no escaping it. As the saying goes, it just keeps marching on.

And if you let your thoughts go even deeper and wander into the realm of physics, you'll realize that time is not quite as solid or unbending as our clocks and modern vernacular would have us believe.

Einstein Time

In *The Big Leap,* Gay Hendricks writes, "Newtonian dualism pits us against time. . . . We think of time as the master and us as the slave." He goes on to define what he calls "Einstein Time": a way of perceiving time that is more in alignment with post-Newtonian science and the theory of relativity. Because the truth is, in this more modern scientific paradigm, time actually emanates from the place where it is perceived. So it is actually

emanating from each of us, individually, as we perceive it. Hendricks counsels, "Quit thinking time is 'out there.' Take ownership of time —acknowledge that you are where it comes from— and it will stop owning you. Claim time as yours, and it will release its claim on you."

It sounds a little too simple, doesn't it? But as magical practitioners, we know that our concepts about things, and the stories we tell ourselves about them, have everything to do with how they manifest in our lives. And even though our cultural story about time being in short supply is a powerful one, we can begin to shift it in our own minds just by setting the intention to do so. The following ritual might also help.

Time Ownership Ritual

On a day when the Moon's sign is the same as it was at the moment when you were born, purchase or find a small calendar and a watch or small clock. (You might try a dollar store or secondhand store to keep costs low.) Burn white sage around them to cleanse their energy, and then tie them together attractively (rolling up the calendar into a scroll if appropriate) with a length of white satin ribbon. Also tie a tag onto them that says "Property of: (your name)."

While holding this charm in both hands, say,

I now dissolve and demolish the outmoded, Newtonian idea of external time. I now choose to step into the new, more accurate paradigm that demonstrates that time is emanating from me, and that it behaves in accordance with my expectations. In truth, I am the owner of my time, and I now claim this ownership in full.

Visualize yourself being the master of your own time. See and feel yourself having plenty of time for everything you want to do and easily arriving everywhere you want to be in perfect timing.

Place the time charm on your altar and leave it there for at least one Full Moon cycle.

The Inner Speed Limit

We all know when we are getting ahead of ourselves or behaving outside our most ideal and natural rhythm. You might call this a violation of our own "inner speed limit," a term I'm borrowing from author and Buddhist monk Tsoknyi Rinpoche. In his book *Open Heart, Open Mind*, he defines the inner speed limit as "a comfortable margin of activity that allows us to complete the tasks with which we're faced on a daily basis without receiving a mental, emotional, or physical speeding ticket."

You'll notice he doesn't define it as slowing down to the point where we barely get anything done—rather, just to the point where we don't rush around so much we create unnecessary stress or end up spilling our coffee. (Especially considering that both of these would defeat the purpose of rushing around in the first place, as stress causes us to be less effective in the long run, and spilling our coffee would cost us all that extra time cleaning it up and brewing a fresh cup.) Not to mention, our magic suffers when we violate our inner speed limit. By getting ahead of our natural rhythm, we get out of sync with the cosmic and planetary energies from which we derive our power.

Of course, those of us who have a lot on the agenda—possibly too much—are the ones most prone to violating the inner speed limit. So we have to be extra mindful of two things: first, of going at a pace that feels appropriate; and second, of releasing activities, relationships, and obligations that are not for our truest good.

Inner Speed Limit Meditation

A morning meditation can be a great time to align harmoniously with your inner speed limit and the timing that will most benefit your day. If you have trouble finding time, set your alarm clock five minutes early. When it goes off, hit the snooze button for five extra minutes and then lie in bed, flat on your back. Simply notice your breath as it goes in and out. When your mind begins to wander, bring it back to the breath. (This harmonizes you with your natural internal pace.) When the alarm goes off, finish up your meditation by calling on Archangel Metatron—the angelic expert on organization and time management—to assist you in managing your time and activities in the most ideal and harmonious of ways.

Kairos

Kairos is a Greek philosophical concept appearing in a number of ancient philosophies, including Pythagorean and Biblical writings, that can roughly be defined as the ideal timing or the opportune moment. While *chronos* is Greek for measured, human time, *kairos* describes transcendent, divinely orchestrated, and harmonious time.

According to Hunter W. Stephenson in *Forecasting Opportunity*, classicist R. B. Onians explained that there are "two meanings most commonly associated with kairos—namely, 'right timing' . . . and 'due measure.'" These two meanings "are derived from two different roots": archery, in regard to "the moment in which an arrow may be fired with sufficient force to penetrate the target," and weaving, in regard to "the moment in which the shuttle could be passed through the threads on the loom."

We all know when we are operating in kairos rather than chronos. When we turn on the radio, it's naturally playing a song that feels precisely right for the moment. When it crosses our mind that we'd like a latte, we turn a corner and behold a coffee shop. Wherever we happen to be going, we arrive at the precisely perfect time—even if it isn't the time initially agreed upon—and we never find ourselves stressing about it in the least. It's as if we're a sailboat and time is the breeze, blowing at the perfect speed and in the perfect direction. Sounds kind of amazing, right?

But how do we get in alignment with kairos? Watching the Moon cycles and seasons for one, and timing our magic and other activities accordingly. Changing our paradigm from Newtonian to Einstein time will also help, as will following our inner speed limit. Additionally, the following activities will go a long way toward aligning us with this most magical version of time:

Clutter clearing. When we release everything from the physical plane that we don't love, use, or need, we repair energy leaks and harmonize ourselves with the rhythm of the spheres. Not to mention, finding things will be easy, and cleaning house will take half the time.

Abstaining from time-related complaints. If you can purge your inner and outer monologue of time complaints ("I'm way too busy," "There just aren't enough hours in the day," "I'm always late," etc.), you'll be more likely to come into sync with time than believe yourself to be in opposition to it.

Speaking, thinking, or writing time-related affirmations. Instead of complaints, begin to populate your stream of consciousness with phrases like "I always have plenty of time," "Everything is occurring in perfect and divine timing," and "I am fully nourished by the present moment."

Kairos Alignment Candle Spell

During a Dark Moon, carve the word "kairos" into a purple pillar candle. Place it on a candleholder and sprinkle mugwort and silver glitter around the base. Light and chant,

> *My timing is right, my future is bright.*
> *I am in the flow, I am in the know.*
> *My struggles now end, for time is my friend.*

Burn the candle all the way down, extinguishing and relighting as necessary for safety purposes. (This may take an entire Moon cycle or more.)

Divine Timing Chakras

There are two chakras (or energy centers in the body and aura) that correspond with divine timing and our most harmonious personal rhythm. The first is the sacral chakra, located in the lower abdomen or womb space. This energy center is specifically important for those with a feminine personal essence or with a greater degree of femininity than masculinity. We feminine-leaning folks can bring our awareness to this center and discover quite easily what pace feels right for any given activity and even what activities will be in alignment with our life's most ideal unfolding. This is because the womb is the space of creation, and the space that is naturally synchronized with the rhythm at the core of the planet.

To tune in to this area, try placing your hands lovingly on your lower belly and breathing into it. Then, gently shift your thinking process from your head area down to your womb. It will be as if you are contemplating with your womb rather than your brain. By doing so, you will very likely instantly tap into a wealth of information and guidance.

Those with a masculine essence or a greater degree of masculinity will find it more effective to tune into the chakra located above the crown chakra, about six inches above the top of the head. By doing so, masculine-leaning folks can transcend the myopia perpetuated by the ego and enter into the bigger, more cosmic

picture, where the most effective and ideal action (as well as its ideal timing) is obviously perceived and easily acted upon.

To tune into this area, simply elevate your point of conscious perception from your brain to the area about six inches above the top of your head. Dwell here in consciousness for a moment as you relax your body and consciously breathe in and out. It will be as if your awareness is hovering at a vantage point just above your head. Once you've experienced this for a bit, remain at this vantage point as you consider your actions and the most ideal timing of your actions. You'll find that this exercise will make it surprisingly easy to gain clarity about the best way to proceed in any given situation.

Of course, we each contain a unique balance of masculine and feminine energies. So go ahead and experiment with both chakras to see what works best for you in various situations. Intellectual activities and planning, for example, might benefit from tapping into the chakra above the crown, while activities related to emotion, connection, healing, or present-moment action might be more enhanced by tuning in to the womb area. And many situations will benefit from tuning in to both.

Everyday Adventures

So often when we do a travel spell or carry a travel charm, our intention is really about divine timing: everything flowing smoothly and harmoniously, without us having to worry about or struggle against the clock. So, naturally, when we are proactive about getting into a positive alignment with time, all our travel adventures—even everyday adventures like a trip to the grocery store or a casual gathering with family and friends—benefit. And when hassles and annoyances no longer rule the day, life in general feels flowy, joyful, and fun.

Resources

Hendricks, Gay. *The Big Leap: Conquer Your Hidden Fear and Take Life to the Next Level.* New York: HarperCollins, 2009.

Rinpoche, Tsoknyi. *Open Heart, Open Mind: Awakening the Power of Essence Love.* New York: Harmony Books: 2012.

Stephenson, Hunter W. *Forecasting Opportunity: Kairos, Production, and Writing.* Lanham, MA: University Press of America, 2005.

A Tale of a Modern Magical Wedding

by Ellen Dugan

When two people meet and fall in love, there's a sudden rush of magic.

—Tom Robbins

It started out quietly enough. Our daughter brought a date to the family's annual Halloween bash. He seemed like a nice-enough guy. He was quiet, polite, and, hey, he was cheerfully holding his own among a coven of Witches and still seemed to be enjoying himself. *That's a good sign,* I thought. Then I watched the two of them and realized something was different this time. By the following October they were still going strong even though she was out of state at grad school. By the third turn of the Wheel back to Samhain they were officially engaged. And that's when things crazy— because, OMG, we were now planning a wedding!

All weddings are magical events. But for some of us the challenge becomes incorporating our Pagan traditions and still being respectful of the other family's religious beliefs. There, that sounded so nice and dispassionate . . .

Planning a Nontraditional Wedding

The truth is we found ourselves planning a wedding ceremony and reception that would be outside of the norm of what most people would come to expect. In this case "most people" meant our relatives *and* the family of the groom. In other words the bride and groom wanted a "nontraditional wedding." And I had no idea how much that phrase was going to become a part of my life.

My daughter and her fiancé had their hearts set on a Sunday morning semiformal event. I had my heart set on giving the bride whatever she wanted . . . within budget. She wanted the local antique greenhouse, a popular place for ceremonies, because it gives you a garden look all year long no matter the weather. The space was intimate, romantic, and magical. The groom agreed it was a wonderful space, so off we went to tour it. The question of an officiant was never really a question at all: within hours of my daughter having a ring on her finger she asked a friend of mine who heads up an international Witch school to officiate. The groom was comfortable with that; after all, he knew my friend.

Soon it was time to meet the future in-laws. My daughter identifies as Pagan; her fiancé identifies as Christian. His family is from Texas; ours is from the

Midwest. Our family is loud, unbreakable, and demonstrative; his is quiet, soft-spoken, and reserved.

We invited the groom-to-be's parents to our home, so we could all meet for the first time. My daughter was humming "One Normal Night" from the musical *The Addams Family* as we set up, and I rolled my eyes and kept my mouth shut. Because, hey, everyone's got to have a dream. You want normal? Define "normal."

The eyes of the future in-laws were huge when they arrived, but taking advantage of the holidays, I'd invited them over when the house was lavishly decked out for Yule. It took less than ten minutes for his family to relax. Yes, they knew their son was marrying into a Pagan family, and, yes, they knew about her mother, the Witchcraft writer . . . but they soon discovered we were a loving, fairly normal bunch of folks. While the groom's mother and I discussed the perks of a nontraditional wedding, everyone smiled, laughed, got to know each other, and had a nice time. It probably didn't hurt that I was pretty free with the wine.

Then next thing you know, the bride and groom picked out a date. My daughter pored over lunar calendars and finally chose the day of Ostara. It would fall on a Sunday, the Moon was almost full, and she loved the idea of working with the magick of the sabbat. I put a deposit on the ceremony venue, and then my husband and I took them to tour a ballroom for the reception. The bride and groom held hands and looked around the reception space with tears in their eyes. My husband and I held on to each other for dear life, trying to play it cool, and looked around the space with tears in *our* eyes . . .

While my daughter was talking about the brunch menu and table arrangements with the event coordinator, I looked at my son-in-law-to-be. "Would *you* like *your* reception to be here?" I asked him quietly. After all, it was his day, too. We wanted his opinion. He simply nodded yes and grabbed me up in a big hug.

On a funny note—when the event coordinator asked if we wanted an open bar, the kids tried to refuse. "Oh, that's okay. It's too expensive," they said. "Mom, Dad, we don't *need* an open bar."

My husband and I answered in unison, "Yes, we do!" So we got the open bar, and I got out my checkbook.

Dressing the Part

Next step: The. Gown. While I figured she'd go for a long black gown (because, hey, black wedding dresses are en vogue), my daughter threw me yet another curveball. Nothing long, she announced. She wanted the dress above the knees and absolutely not white.

Imagine the look on the salespeople's faces when we went looking for a short wedding gown. Tea length, sure, but short? They were horrified and confused, and finally I whipped out my catchphrase and simply said that she was a nontraditional bride. I'm a Witch mom: obviously, I can handle nontraditional. But her grandmothers . . . not so much. It took a little convincing, but pretty soon both grandmothers were on the "short dresses are fashion forward" bandwagon.

Next hurdle: Every short wedding gown we did find was white. As the bride has that Irish milk-pale skin, putting her in white would have been a bad choice. I agreed with the no-white rule, but finding a *short, not-white* wedding gown in the Midwest? There was the challenge. I actually lit candles to whatever gods of fashion there might be.

I prayed, I cast spells to help us find something the bride would love, and then we found one! A short, gorgeous confection in a nude—almost a pale peach—color and it sparkled and shimmered. She ordered some killer gold shoes and a custom-made gold headpiece. All in all it wasn't as expensive as a long gown. Until I added in the accessories. Gulp. I got out my checkbook and wrote more checks.

Next task: Bridesmaids dresses. Off to the big bridal store we went. It ended up that our consultant was a Witch. (Seriously, how awesome was that?) My daughter took one look at the consultant's purple hair and pierced nose, and they started talking about their love of retro fashion and black bridesmaids dresses. We found some great gowns, and the bridesmaids loved them because these were actually dresses they would wear again. For the tuxedos, the bride and groom wanted all black again. They also decided upon a best woman and two groomsmen standing with the groom, and the maid of honor, bridesmaid, and a bridesman standing with the bride. Why not? Let's mix it up!

The flowers were all in neutrals of white and softest peach. Music, food, centerpieces, candles, and on and on it went.

Then came the day of the bridal shower when I overheard the groom's family asking, "What exactly is a handfasting ceremony?" The groom, without skipping a beat, smoothly told them it was an ancient Irish wedding ceremony.

"Ooooooh, how romantic," replied the groom's mother and sisters. Well played, son. Well played.

The Ceremony

Time raced by, and then we were at the big day. The first day of spring! The redbuds were blooming, the magnolias were pretty pink cups, daffodils danced in the breeze, sunrise broke on the festival of Ostara . . . and it snowed like crazy!

Huge puffy snowflakes came down. It snowed, and it snowed some more. I panicked, and the bride was thrilled. She loves snow. With her hair and makeup done, I helped the bride and bridesmaids all get dressed. The bride slipped on a golden-hooded cloak to protect her hair and gown, and we were driven to the ceremony venue and secreted away for first looks. The bride and groom braved the snow and did pictures in a spring garden dusted with snow, posing under a big clear umbrella. The photographer happily went nuts over how gorgeous it was outside, and my daughter came shivering and beaming back to the bride room to warm up and wait for the start of the ceremony.

Guests arrived and looked around the venue with delighted surprise. As Erin was the first grandchild *not* to get married in a church, there had been some raised eyebrows. We ignored it, knowing what would happen when everyone arrived on the big day. The ceremony started, the bridesmaids walked down the aisle, and there were gasps as the bride and her father entered.

I know I'm her mother, but she looked like an elfin princess. As in Tolkien. My girl walked in on her dad's arm tall, slim, sparkling, and gorgeous in that short nude-peach colored gown with her long hair falling down her back and a band made of delicate gold leaves across her forehead. I don't know how she managed the shoes. My theory is that she floated.

My father, who is an old curmudgeon, took one look at her, pressed a kiss to my cheek and whispered to me that *his* granddaughter's dress was perfect. I'd managed to hold it together until that moment. Then I cried, too.

As the ceremony commenced the light coming through the glass roof slowly changed. As the bride and groom exchanged rings, the Sun came out, and I swear a beam of light illuminated the bride and groom.

There were more gasps. The photographer scrambled
to change lenses and settings on his camera. Some
people looked around nervously, while the Witches in
attendance just smiled.

When the bride and groom stepped outside after
the ceremony, the cobblestone streets were dry, the Sun
was shining, and the snow had disappeared. Magic?
Maybe. But then again, love is its own sort of magic.

My brother-in-law came through the receiving line
and gave me a hug. "The light changed when they
exchanged rings," he whispered to me with very large
eyes. "The Sun came out at the perfect moment."

"Yes, it did." I said with a smile.

He slanted me a look. "I knew that was you."

"I'm not the only Witch here, you know," I said seriously. I'm not sure if my statement comforted him or
not.

At the end of the day, the ceremony and reception went off beautifully. The bride and groom enojyed their brunch and folks devoured the food—eggs, bacon, and fruit, or ham, green beans, and pasta. People gleefully dug in and went back for seconds. Then after the first dance came the cake pops, another huge hit. People loved them. Again, because they were unexpected. I lost track of the number of times I heard comments about how lovely the ceremony had been, so romantic and Old World. How different, how special, the event had been. Nontraditional was fun. Nontraditional was trendy and cool.

And that, dear readers, is the point. It's okay to do something different and—dare I say it again? *Nontraditional.* We found a way to do a wedding that was inclusive and friendly to all the attendees. People were so swept up in the atmosphere and the romance of it all that, honestly, most of the Pagan elements went right over their heads. We made sure that the day was all about the bride and groom. It was what *they* wanted; it was what my husband and I gave them.

May they live happily ever after.

Evolving a Ritual Circle

by Dallas Jennifer Cobb

Have you ever attended a large ritual and felt enveloped in magic, only to return home and wonder how to create your own magic and where to start? Or perhaps you have attended a ritual that was awkward, stilted, and seemingly scripted, and it made you question "what went wrong"?

We can be drawn to the Pagan path and not know how to enact magic in our own lives nor how to gather together in community and really make a ritual magical. Understanding that magic can be learned, evolving a ritual circle is about that process—moving from interest to involvement, from solitary to collective, and from muddled to magical.

A successful ritual requires lots of dreaming, brainstorming, planning, organizing, and hard work. It all starts with a few individuals who form a ritual circle or organizing group and work together to create a multidimensional event to celebrate the season, which brings people from the community together. Like a drop of water, an effective ritual circle sends ripples out ever increasing in size, their magic growing and spreading.

There is lots of Pagan literature available describing the format of a ritual but very little that actually speaks to the magic of making magic as a community, the hard work that takes place behind the scenes, and the nitty-gritty details of how a ritual circle evolves. While rituals generally follow a format, a successful ritual is far more than that. Making magic requires the careful weaving of ideas, energy, and intent in order to bring the format to life.

While the format is the structure that guides how the ritual progresses, the ritual circle includes the catalysts who initiate the alchemy of changing words and ideas into feelings and intention. The ritual circle members "priestess" the ritual, bringing individuals together to function as a whole, moving the group from the general to the personal and from the mundane to the magical.

But how do ritual circles evolve?

The Seed

While I was young, I lived in a city and read Starhawk's *Dreaming the Dark: Magic, Sex and Politics* as part of a women's studies course. Entranced by the idea of taking activism into the realm of spirituality, I sought out writings by other Pagans, from Margot Adler to Z. Budapest. I became a solitary practitioner conducting awkward rituals, reading as I followed a format in a book and relying on what was written.

I found a Pagan store and through it connected with large, vibrant Pagan rituals. A bystander, I marvelled at the intricately crafted happening, recognizing the format that held it together as similar to what I was practicing in my awkward, beginner manner. I went to Witch camp, learned more Pagan practices and skills, and took place in massive community-wide rituals each evening. I marveled at how many of the skills I learned during the day were magically woven into different parts of the ritual: chants, dance, drumming, readings, storytelling, and symbology.

Back at home, I started a Full Moon circle. We met regularly, using many of Starhawk's ideas and many Reclaiming practices to guide us. Those stumbling early steps took enormous concentration, time, and energy, but slowly we got our feet. We practiced nonhierarchy, encouraging everyone to take turns at every aspect of the organizing so that we all had access to information and leadership. We attempted consensus decision-making, often sitting a

long time to come to an agreement. Together we learned how to structure a ritual, and we took turns casting a circle, calling in the directions, and greeting the God and Goddess.

But despite all the effort and good intention that went into our Moon rituals, it never felt transformative. We cast a circle but never really created sacred space. We ritualistically did work associated with the Full Moon, but I had few feelings of growth or change. Eventually I left the group because I felt like I was missing out on the "magic."

Rooting

These days I live in a sparsely populated rural area, close to nature, on the edge of the great Lake Ontario. When I moved here, my magical practice changed. I made up my own rituals to mark the sabbats, thinly veiled as other more acceptable holiday celebrations. On Halloween I told my daughter the story of Demeter and Persephone, and after trick-or-treating we made offerings of treats at the crossroad near our home. I brought more of "me" to the rituals and shaped them around my life and my little growing family. They felt more real and more significant: I was teaching and sharing with my daughter, and our time together felt quite magical. There was more meaning for me and more personal connection to the work.

I expanded my online community and met other isolated Pagan solitary practitioners. I wrote about my Pagan practice and through publishing made worldwide connections. On my own I held solitary Moon rituals, walking on the beach, writing in the sand, or plunging into the water to release the old and arising into the light. I found myself quivering as I experienced the transformation of my energy. I found the work powerful and moving. As Dion Fortune said, "Magic is the art of changing consciousness at will." And I was learning how to do that. I began to trust that I knew what I was doing, that I could make magic in my own life, and that I had magic to share.

Shoots

Slowly, I connected with other local Pagans, women who were also drawn to the Pagan path, and many who had been solitary practitioners. After attending a few community-based rituals, I heard the organizers welcome anyone interested in helping to plan the rituals to join them, and I leapt at the chance. I joined four women who, for the most part, organized the events. They planned and priestessed four sabbat rituals per year.

Through this involvement, I have experienced the transformational power of weaving the web with other women, designing rituals for our community, and making magic together. I have seen our ritual group evolve and grow as we have begun to spin more magic among ourselves and within our rituals and community. Magic ripples outward with increasing effect.

Within our ritual circle there is great diversity. We each bring a wealth of spiritual practice, learning, literature, knowledge, and experience to the circle. We have many similarities: we're all women who identify as feminists and are for the most part well-educated and articulate. We have enjoyed feminist activism, education, and community involvement and have experience with nonhierarchical organizing and consensus.

We have a range of ages, experiences, and backgrounds. Some have been Pagans for thirty years, others for just a few. One defines herself as a Goddess Worshipper, another as a Wiccan, and still another as a Pagan. We have different levels of confidence and comfort with public speaking. Our differences are perhaps what make for such potent magic among us. We come from different paths and identify differently, so we bring diverse tools and techniques to the circle. Together we have developed an accepting, pan-Pagan practice as we "cross-pollinate," each of us enhanced by the others.

Flowering

Sharing, learning, and teaching within the ritual circle, my confidence has grown as I have started to express my own individual form of magic and recognize that I bring a lot to the group. I have evolved from feeling like I had to disguise my Pagan practice to feeling confident and knowing I have lots to offer. I have felt excited by hearing different perspectives, learning new tools, and growing.

As a result of accessing more tools through my circle, my personal magical practice has evolved, deepening my awareness of magic at work in my life, and I feel supported to go deeper and do more meaningful magical work.

I also see the other women evolving, taking new ideas, new ways of working magic and new resources from each other. They are evolving individually, and collectively.

My evolution is linked to the evolution of these women, and we all contribute to the evolution of our organizing group. Spiralling outward, the rituals we organize have also evolved. No longer noisy, chaotic drum circles around a fire, we work through consensus; choose a theme; brainstorm chants, drumming, music, readings, and storytelling to build energy; and weave our individual magic together. Our rituals have evolved into elaborately crafted magical ceremonies with deep meaning and the opportunity for deep magical work.

Making Magic

The setting of a ritual is crucial. It must be accessible, safe, and welcoming to people of all abilities and mobilities. The considerations include physical accessibility, comfort, creating safe and sacred space, and having suitable facilities for feasting and cleaning up. I've been to rituals held in fields, in an empty industrial building, and many in private homes where the space was uncomfortable, cramped, and, at times, unsafe.

While outdoor spaces can be used when the weather cooperates, indoor is better. There are no rocks, uneven ground, sand, or mud to impede mobility. Ideally, there are doors wide enough for wheelchairs, washrooms adjacent to the main meeting area, and a hospitable space for storing feast food.

We found a fantastic space for holding our rituals. It's accessible, accommodating, centrally located, and well maintained. It has great acoustics, a built-in sound system, and lots of big comfortable chairs that can be moved into a circle. The floors are hardwood and invite barefoot dancing. There are washrooms and a kitchen, garbage cans, a water dispenser, and even folding tables to use for the feast foods.

We hold our rituals in a church.

Not in the basement or in an adjoining room but in the main chapel. It is physically suitable and imbued with lots of its own spirit. While some were opposed to holding Pagan gatherings in a Christian space, we held long discussions about it, and many points of view arose. Finally, we were swayed by the idea that the church was open to us, so we should be open to the church. And, if the minister of the church wanted to attend our rituals, she should be welcomed warmly. It was our chance to further cross-pollinate.

Our Vernal Equinox Ritual

Our standard ritual structure is this: setting the altar, cleansing/smudging, creating sacred space, casting the circle, calling in the directions and center, raising energy, performing magical work, making a covenant, grounding, farewell to the directions and center, closing announcements, and opening the circle to feast.

Here is our vernal equinox ritual, a beautiful example of how our ritual circle has evolved:

Sacred handwashing at the door cleanses/smudges each participant.

While people are milling and chatting, the crones sweep the ritual space with their besoms.

Circle member V plays the didgeridoo, calling us to circle.

A single bell is rung, signaling the sweepers to sit.

S circles, distributing a bell to each person and inviting them to ring it. The sound passes around sequentially; the circle is cast. People are invited to stand.

The directions are called by four different women, each detailing the significance of the direction and element, hailing and welcoming it. R calls in center, above and below, shoots and roots, stating that we are between the worlds and that what happens between the worlds affects all worlds.

M invites everyone to welcome the ancestors and the absent ones by calling out the names of those we want to bring into the circle in spirit, and then leads the chant:

We all come from the Goddess.

When it draws to a close, I rise. I speak about the significance of the vernal equinox, the themes of light and dark, balance, youth, sprouting and potential, starting over, seeds cracking and sprouting, shoots and tender roots.

I chant lyrics from Leonard Cohen, a rhyming set of lines that reminds us that where we are broken is where the light gets in. The first repetition is done slowly and loudly so everyone can learn the lyrics. On the second repetition bells are added. Over five repetitions the volume, cadence, and energy of the chant increases. B begins to drum, and the pitch rises to ecstatic. And then comes the signal to stop.

V steps to the center of the circle and quietly introduces the work, speaking of waking the seeds within, that which lies in our unconscious, what we are unaware of, what needs to sprout in our lives now, and how we will water and nurture these seeds, bringing them into the light in the days following the equinox.

Breaking the circle into four quarters, each of us has a group and leads the process of clearing energy from each person, one at a time:

We ring lightly at the feet, to clear old stuff. We ring near the heart center to awaken love and creativity. We do this as a community. Clearing and healing one another.

Moving up the body and over their crown chakra, people are encouraged,

Let go. Compost what is falling away and dying, and let it nourish your new seeds.

We finish with each of us putting a hand on the person, blessing them and saying,

Be free, be strong, be yourself.

The process is repeated for each person. The bells are collected and placed into a basket on the altar. People sit down.

R reads "And the Great Mother Said" by Linda Reuther.

B passes the chalice, urging each person to take one chocolate egg, make a covenant, and commit to the work.

I rise to walk around the circle, saying,

Join me. Place your hand over your heart. Slowly tap twice, making the heartbeat sound. Thump-thump.
My heart beats. Thump-thump.
Your heart beats. Thump-thump.
And I know I am not alone. Thump-thump.
We are in this together. Thump-thump.

The chest thumping and heart beating goes on for a short while, grounding the energy and bringing people back into their bodies. A single bell signals the end.

R bids farewell to center and asks each direction, "What gift will you leave us?" The directions are released.

M gives thanks, reminds people to take their dishes home, and welcomes anyone interested in helping organize to leave their e-mail address.

The circle is open, and the feast begins.

Blessed be.

We Are Nature:
A Ritual for Inner Healing

by Justine Holubets

After suffering from pollution in my small, overcrowded city and spending most of my time in a seventeen-meter room with my parents, with the huge gray wall of a factory as my window view, it was no wonder I was anticipating my next journey. The chance to go to Italy was a gift from Destiny. I was intoxicated by the crystal-clean air; the vast spaces of forest of the villa; an intricate labyrinth of wood paths; an ardent Italian Sun; the incredible mix of woods, grass, and flower aromas; and the omnipresent harmony of humans and nature. I was a guest of an international exchange program and enjoyed living at the most beautiful accommodation: a medieval palace with its spacious rooms, wide passages, and numerous frescoes with idyllic pictures of seventeenth-century life.

Villa Buri is an old and romantic edifice lost in the woods and hills of Northern Italy. It possesses an incredible charm that fascinates the imagination and awakens forgotten magic of medieval times. The two-story building, in a simple and elegant classical style with arched windows and spired turrets, was buried in the verdure of a splendid, magnificent park. Nowadays, the villa's rooms and outhouses host plenty of people. Along the approaching lane, instead of idle beauties in luxurious dresses, you will see mothers in jeans on bikes, bringing their kids to the school that now is located here. Instead of Vivaldi's violin music coming through the windows, there are modern pop tracks, which resound from a small restaurant. Instead of hoof sounds, you hear the gravel crunch under car wheels and boot steps. Managers, teachers, builders, cooks, and cleaners hurry to perform their everyday duties; for them, the villa is their job. For three long months, I became one of those people who trampled down the gravel of the park's paths; as a volunteer at an ecological project, I was involved in many gardening and simple construction jobs. However, for me the villa was a place of initiation and worship, where the breath of nature could free my spirit and harmonize my heartbeat with her rhythms.

Hearing the Voices of Nature

Everyone who deals with earth or building work can try to establish their own healing techniques, which can be spoken aloud or in one's head. I elaborated my own. While sweeping wet and dry leaves away from the alleys, I was sweeping away all doubts, troubles, and lack of self-confidence, which blocked up my freedom. While burning the heaps of dry wood, I was burning illusions and nightmares, prejudices and obsolete aims. While releasing trees from tenacious ivy, I was getting rid of fears that paralyzed my free will. I

pressed the cutting pliers so hard that corns appeared on my palms, and I wondered how such thin and tender ivy could withstand so many efforts to eliminate it. When pushing away big stones from park paths, I was surprised to find their similarity with human pride and vanity. Heavy and monolithic, they block our smooth walking along the path of life, and to get rid of obstacles we have either to bend and clear our way or go on constantly stumbling until it would be impossible to walk.

I understood that I am like the tree, river, park—I am them, I am nature. My body can be bound and captured by diseases, weight, and pimples, just like trees are covered by thin yet tenacious ivy threads. My heart is lapping with emotions, just as the river carries its waters from unknown source to unknown mouth. My mind is perfect soil for seeds of wisdom or nonsense, just like same earth gives life to flowers or weed.

While gathering the harvest, I remember how a strange thought struck my mind: what is a sweet and so long-awaited reward for people is death for nature. The fruit is cut and taken away from the place it was born and nurtured for so long. It dies in order to give life; it shares its accumulated light and sun and its own juices for no reward. It's an example of the sacred deed of giving, which has been always before our eyes since the beginning of the world. Isn't it our mission to give and sacrifice our victories, achievements, and labor to someone who is taking care of us—to life, a god, or nature?

I once heard Sufi wisdom that prescribes "to kill yourself first" in order to gain any knowledge. It didn't sound ridiculous but rather struck me as an all-reflective truth that can be felt with the heart. How would a new fruit appear if the previous one doesn't make way for it? How would my dreams come true if I didn't give them space to appear? Nature always recreates herself, never stops cleaning and transforming, thus supplying the eternal process of creation and recreation with the necessary intermediate phase—death. In her ordered and interwoven processes of birth, life, and death is her eternal youth; in enveloping the smallest creature into such a global process is her majesty. That's why we are as small as the leaf on the tree and as big as the ages-old oak. Merging with her, turning into her, and submitting to her laws, we join the eternal harmony of creation. What was new for me was feeling the practical value of all these known truths. I felt them as something that can be applied to my mind, body, and soul.

The Song of the Storm

After examining my own connection with nature, this revelation inspired a desire to harness nature's power for my own inner change. My main goals were to release profound phobias and stress, to get rid of some depressing fear or dependence, to purify my mind from losing strategies, and to clarify my life path and set up the goals. Another sub-aim was to lose weight and make the process fast and effective. The ritual didn't take away my weight overnight, but it definitely helped take my laziness away and enabled me to alter my food and daily routine forever.

The night of Halloween and Samhain was approaching, the mysterious, frightening, and dark night. I felt that it was tremendously important for me to perform special actions at this November feast in order to complete my spiritual initiation. Villa Buri was buzzing with a busy modern life till sunset, but when all the people left and the gates were closed, it seemed that spirits of the past returned—the villa was surrounded by soaring, bodiless dancing sylphs and dryads. The last beams of autumn sun tangled in the thick leafage of the trees soon disappeared, and light lost its power. The darkness seemed thicker due to heavy rain clouds, which covered the sky. The wind was howling throughout the dark woodland, and it seemed the spirits began their ominous songs. Sharp lightning sparks were cutting the dark, and the branches waved and creaked like an old pirate ship deck. The showering rain dampened other sounds, but I felt voices all around me: the song of the storm, the ancient song of water, fire, and leaves.

Earth Transformation Ritual

Perform this ritual when you feel the need for transformation and profound inner change. It is essential to feel an affinity with the weather and surroundings. Rain, clouds, wind, or any other revelations of nature may help you tune in to the turbulent yet powerful spirit of the ritual. Thunderstorms, as a combination of fire and water, passion and healing, are perfect weather. As for time, it is better to plan it during the waning Moon, in the second half of the lunar month. The lunar rhythms help you tune in to the rhythms of nature, and the tone of releasing is perfect to free yourself. The best days are two days before and two days after the New Moon. They are called "the days of Hecate," the goddess of crossroads and the netherworld who traditionally hunts with her dogs and brings not only fear but release, freedom, and wisdom. In fact, these darkest days of the month may be called "the small Halloween," an analogue to this night of the Great Hunt. During dark periods, we become more sensitive and intuitive and can see clearly our own subconscious.

You will need:

Candles to represent fire. Try dark blue or violet for transformation, netherworld, and spirit.

Aroma to represent air. I recommend wormwood or celandine to purify the space around you.

Stones for earth, or a bowl of water to attract healing spirit and enhance energies' conductivity.

An image of your deity to center your request. Strict and even harsh gods work especially well. The tarot offers a wide range of images that help mobilize your spiritual power and determination, for these are very needed! Try Justice, the Hermit, Temperance, or the High

Priestess; they call for the refusal of temporal pleasure for the sake of a higher aim.

Establish your deity image and burn a candle. If it is unscented, add aroma to your ritual with incense. Pray and talk to your deity, expressing all any frustration, pain, doubts, fears, disappointments, and disillusions. But remember: true magic doesn't demand a lot of things. The main components are concentration and imagination.

Chant,

Be free through love, feel unity with nature.
'Cause we are one, and it doesn't matter
Where you go, through rain or sun,
Inside you always follow nature, 'cause we are one.

Enjoy complete solitude and take off the mask of contentment and happiness, releasing all tension. I recommend using a tarot deck too to perform some spreads afterward, seeking clarification on your path ahead.

The next step, performing a symbolic action, will be different for each person. Timing does not matter. Whatever you may feel is right to do, do it—this ritual is about reclaiming your agency and transforming yourself. Your symbolic action should reflect or model the solving of your problem. In my case, it was cooking pancakes that night and destroying them as the representation of my weight and fears. I took them to my secret place at the river, and there, wreaking my anger and frustration, tore them to small pieces.

With symbolic things and a symbolic action, you have to put emotions into the process and feel the victorious joy in the end.

Feel your ritual and observe your reality afterward: see, smell, and feel, and I am sure you will feel changes.

My Transformation

When I woke the next morning, I felt tired and my body was aching. That day and afterward it was easier to restrain from overeating and apply myself to work out. The ritual returned my inner power, which in turn altered my practical reality in a very interesting way. First of all, I could easily lose weight and, with time, gain a nice and healthy body. Unexpectedly, I got an invitation for a project in Morocco, and difficulties with the embassy were solved easily and quickly. In critical situations, I felt strong support and practical help from both friends and strangers.

Nature and my Samhain ritual taught me a lesson: things come at their time, and it's beyond the human power to control their arrival and descent. We cannot keep people, possessions, and events. We can just meet them, live with them, and gratefully let go when the time comes.

Drawing Down the Sun for Seasonal Depression

by Stacy M. Porter

The darker months of the year, autumn and winter, are as cold as they are mysterious. This time of year, when the nights are longer and death surrounds us, is when we are meant to grieve, reflect, and turn inward. We mourn life as the trees lose their vibrant leaves. We reflect on the past year and all we have experienced. And we turn inward to work on ourselves and learn from everything that has happened.

I actually love autumn. I love bringing out my hoodies and sweatpants, my fuzzy socks and cute scarves. I love pumpkin spice lattes and vegetable soups and broths. I love curling up on the couch with a good book or spending hours binge-watching my favorite shows, not feeling any guilt because it is far too cold for me to even step outside. I also love the first snow. It is beautiful and sparkly. It makes me think of the faeries, as I believe they are the ones who meticulously craft each snowflake to be truly unique.

However, the cold months of the year lose their charm, at least for me, after a while. My muscles are stiff, my body aches, and my mood slumps. I get a bit of cabin fever, which spirals into the winter blues. Physically, this is because our bodies aren't receiving the same nutrients from the Sun because of the Earth's position in the cosmos. We have moved farther away from the Sun, out of reach of its warm embrace.

And, to be honest, the snow doesn't seem as pretty anymore once you have had to dig your way out of your house a dozen times. It turns all brown and gross from car fumes. And we've all fallen because of ice at least once in our lives, right? After all that, we are all ready to kick winter to the curb. Sadly though, winter seems to cling and drag on. At least, that's how it feels to me sometimes.

Seasonal Depression

Seasonal depression, or seasonal affective disorder, is a type of depression that can occur annually for a lot of people, generally starting in the fall and lasting all the way through winter, leaving them feeling drained, moody, and generally low. We all have a bit of darkness in us. It's a shadow that makes us human, able to experience everything that this life on earth has to offer. It's not necessarily a bad thing. The shadow is sadness, grief, and anger. It might not be fun, but I know from experience that we cannot truly be in the light without first knowing the dark. One cannot exist without the other, as is the balance of life. However, that doesn't mean that we should bask in it. Being sad all of the time isn't healthy. And being happy all the time could be considered annoying. It's all about balance.

The problem starts when the darkness seeps in, pooling in us. It starts like a drizzle, a soft rain that just touches our skin, but it can gather in a puddle and overflow into an ocean, making us feel like we're drowning. This is when the shadow, when sadness, becomes depression. This is when we start to feel lost and numb, worthless and alone. This

is when we need the Sun more than ever. It seems out of our reach during the darker months of the year, but I can assure you that the Sun is still there, shining for us all. We just have to invite it into our lives. That may seem oversimplified, but all magic in this world starts with an intention. Almost everyone has heard of drawing down the Moon. That is when we invoke the Goddess and align with her, her message, and her powers by basking in the light of the Moon (usually the Full Moon, when she is at her most powerful). This is a sacred practice, but there is another practice that is often forgotten about that is just as meaningful. Drawing down the Sun invokes the God, the bright and brilliant Sun. By standing in his light, even when it looks or feels dim during the fall and winter, we are inviting the courage, passion, and warmth of the Sun into our bodies and circle. We are inviting his strength, resilience, and hope into our lives when we need it the most during these dark times.

Drawing Down the Sun Ritual

Before You Start

Many people practice drawing down the Sun in partnership with drawing down the Moon. It can be done during a ritual, particularly during a sabbat, by the coven's priest. However, I think it's equally important to have your own personal experience with the Lord and Lady, with the Sun and the Moon. Since we are using this ritual as a way to recharge ourselves during the dark times of the year, this ritual can be very personal. I have designed this version of drawing down the Sun to be rather informal and special. You can definitely wear your pajamas while performing it, or you can dress up. It all depends on how you feel and what needs you have.

There are two times to best perform this ritual. You could do it while sipping your morning tea or coffee while the Sun is rising. This energy is about renewal and transformation. It's the perfect time to set new intentions or to help you wake up, open your eyes, and finally see the world around you, as seasonal depression often makes everything feel weird and distant. You can also perform the ritual around noon or 3:00 p.m., when the Sun has reached its peak and is at its strongest. This energy packs a powerful punch: this is the hottest time of the day, so the Sun is more prominent and relevant in your environment. It's the perfect time for cleansing, healing, and igniting a fire within yourself. Because it's so hot—because you can actually feel the Sun's warmth at this time—it will help remind you that you still have that same fire, that same light within you.

Whenever you draw down the Sun, no matter the time, know that the ritual is a way to empower the body, mind, and spirit. This time of year, when seasonal depression is clinging to our lives, we feel like we're standing in a field of fog, unable to see or move. But the Sun is literally what breaks through fog. It clears the path and ignites the soul. So don't worry too much about trying to align with the cosmos or sacred times. Good intention really does mean something, with any type of magic.

It's best to perform this ritual outside, so there's nothing between you and the Sun. However, if that's not an option, you can always find a window to stand in front of. Just make sure that the Sun is in your path. Stand so that you can see it and so that its light is also shining on you.

When You're Ready
Find a place you feel comfortable, where you are in direct visual and physical contact with the Sun. You can light a candle or draw a circle. Prepare however you feel is best for you and your needs, whether that means brewing a cup of tea or coffee so that you can feel heat in your palms or calling the quarters and making this a big and beautiful ceremony. Nothing is right or wrong here.

Standing in the Sun, keep your eyes open. Trace the design that the rays of sunshine are making in the sky without gazing directly into the Sun. Let your creative mind take over. Watch as the golden light dances through the sky and visualize it making its way straight to you. Once the light has made it toward you, close your eyes and imagine it literally wrapping around you, embracing you in its golden warmth.

The light will dance around you, getting stronger, until it completely surrounds you in a comfortable, safe, and secure cocoon. Then, your skin will begin to absorb that energy until you are completely made up of light.

Feel that energy fill your body, mind, and soul and let it take over for a moment. Forget life and responsibility. Instead, let the Divine Masculine be the voice in your head for a moment. Let that energy be your conscious, your instinct, and your guide. You might receive a message, words or a visual, but mostly you will be gifted with

feeling. You are safe, you are warm, and you are loved in this moment.

Take as long as you need, whether it's a few seconds or an hour, simply breathing into that light, making it stronger and more vibrant. Let the light cleanse the darkness inside you, let the light chase away the shadows, and let the light offer you comfort and joy. It will make you stronger, so long as you embrace it.

When you are ready, open your eyes again and watch as the Sun expands out of your skin and dances into the air around you, warming the earth and lighting up your life.

The light is not leaving you, for the light you saw and felt was already there. You were just bringing your attention to it, remembering it, and honoring it.

Take a deep breath and feel your shoulders relax as your body, mind, and soul strengthen with passion and heat. Thank the Lord, thank the Divine, and thank the universe for this day. If you have tea or coffee, pour a little bit on the earth as an offering. Then, release your quarters and circle, if you drew them, and go on about your day knowing you can call on the light you found whenever you need it. After you're finished, I recommend having something to eat to help you ground.

You can practice this small guided meditation every day, every Sunday, or just whenever you feel the need.

Sungazing

My personal practice of drawing down the Sun is strongly influenced by a practice referred to as sungazing. Sungazing is a very ancient practice and has been found, in some way or another, in almost every culture all over the world. Sungazing is meant to supercharge the brain, to activate our brain cells so that we can reach our highest potentials as humans. By doing this, we can heal the body, uplift the spirit, and raise our vibration to literally become one with the divine energy all around us.

Traditionally, the safe sungazing hours are in the hour before sunrise and in the hour after sunset. Staring at the Sun will damage your eyes, so be cautious when attempting this exercise. The first time you gaze into the Sun, you do so for twenty seconds. Then you add ten seconds every day after that. This is when we stand barefoot before the Sun and gaze into the light to find healing, transcendence, and divinity without anything separating us (windows, glasses, etc.) from the Divine. It's meant to be a daily practice for nine-month periods, but I have heard that everyone who tries to do this practice, no matter how regularly or irregularly, finds some kind of success. It's all about the intention and how much belief you have within the practice.

Whether you practice drawing down the Sun, sungazing, or a mixture of the two, you are tapping into a sacred energy that will ignite something very sacred inside you. You are telling the universe that you are willing to show up for yourself and you are telling the Sacred Divine that you are showing up for them. Everyone and everything is connected. Once you open your heart to the Divine, they will open their arms to you. Sometimes you just need to take the first step and open your eyes to the light. And sometimes something as simple as opening your eyes can be just what you need to remember that you are the light.

Brightest blessings!

A Guided Visualization through the Ring-Pass-Not: Recycling Emotional Energy

by Barbara Ardinger

In her book *The Cosmic Doctrine*, originally written in 1923–24 as channeled from the Inner Planes, British occultist Dion Fortune (1890–1946) describes the Ring-Pass-Not, which is the ultimate outer limit of the universe. Fortune tells us that the Ring-Pass-Not (which was also described, but in a different way, by Madame H. P. Blavatsky) is a purely abstract ring of energy that protects our universe from the demons in other universes. Primal atoms also exist at the Ring-Pass-Not.

I have long believed in recycling. I take copious amounts of paper, for example, to our recycling bin every week. Not long ago, I started to think about other, more abstract kinds of recycling. How, I asked myself, might we recycle emotional energy? Just as at the end of a ritual we sometimes send the energy we raised down into the earth to be recycled (I think maybe it comes back up as flowers. Or weeds.), could we also leave our emotional burdens and negative feelings at the Ring-Pass-Not? How can we carry our emotional burdens there and let them disintegrate among the primal atoms? They could regroup as, say, a breeze or a bubble of kindness and come back to our world. If we do this kind of recycling, can we also come back to the world as clearer, cleaner people? As better Pagans?

My apologies to Dion Fortune for oversimplifying her doctrine. Her book is highly cerebral and abstract, whereas my intention in this guided visualization is not thinking but feeling. I want us to be good, grounded Pagans.

When we do a magical visualization, we work at a level of reality where anything is possible. Let us therefore move into a solar system that looks like our own but is a solar system filled with magical energy. So fasten your seatbelts. Here we go.

Guided Visualization

Sit comfortably with your spine straight and take two or three deep, easy breaths. As you feel your body relaxing, know that if there's an emergency, you can quickly return to consensual reality and deal with it. Know that as you travel magically, you are safe and your energy is safe. As you breathe deeply, your body relaxes more deeply and your mind becomes more alert.

Take two or three more deep, easy breaths and feel yourself in lift-off. Look down and see Earth as the astronauts see it, small and blue. Know that you are now outward bound in a magical starship, in the hold of which lie your emotional burdens. The hold has a transparent door. Look through it at your emotional burdens. What are they? Jealousy, prejudice, hatred—none of which you didn't know you were carrying? Guilt for something done or not done? Fear of

something or someone? What form do your emotional burdens take in "real" life? Do they keep you from doing things
you like to do? Do they make you say hurtful things to people you'd rather not hurt? Look into the hold again. What
do your burdens look like? Maybe they're big, ugly, lumpy
things with sharp teeth and claws. Take another deep, easy
breath and make sure that door is locked. Also make sure
there's an outer door or airlock that you can open to dump
those heavy burdens.

Take another deep, easy breath and imagine you have
landed on the planet Venus. Remember, this magical solar
system looks like our real one except that the planets are
colored and you can breathe while you're there. Venus is
an emerald green planet. Go outside and stand on Venus.
You are perfectly comfortable. The energy of Venus is love,

pleasure, and harmony, especially the harmonies of nature—plants and trees. Feel the energy of Venus flowing into you and wrapping itself around you. You are more loving (but not overemotional) than ever before.

Take another deep, easy breath and imagine you have landed on the red planet Mars. Before the Roman god Mars was conflated with the Greek Ares (who is a berserker), he was an agricultural god who defended his people and his land. His energy is strong and assertive. It's filled with fortitude and individuality. Go outside and stand on Mars. You are perfectly comfortable. Feel the strength of Mars flowing into you and wrapping itself around you. You are stronger and more assertive (but not aggressive) than you have been before.

Take another deep, easy breath and imagine you have landed on a huge purple planet. This is Jupiter, and the great planet's energy promotes justice, enthusiasm, optimism, and expansion. Go outside and stand on Jupiter. You are perfectly comfortable. Feel the energy of Jupiter flowing into you and wrapping itself around you. You are more just, generous, and optimistic than you have been in the past.

Take another deep breath. Now you find yourself on another huge planet, this one as black and quiet as the night. This is Saturn, whose energy gives you your sense of duty and responsibility. It also gives you discipline and balance, the necessary balance to Jupiter's energy. Go outside and stand on Saturn. You are perfectly comfortable. Feel the energy of Saturn flowing into you and wrapping itself around you. Now you know that there are reasonable limits. You feel more balanced than you did when you were hauling those old emotional burdens around.

Take another deep breath. Now you find yourself on an indigo planet. This is Uranus, whose energy pushes you to evolve and awaken to your freedom so you can cope with the unexpected events of life. Go outside and stand on Uranus. You are perfectly comfortable. Feel the energy of Uranus flowing into you and wrapping itself around you. Uranus's energy is the energy of the visionary, the one who sees ahead. What can you see ahead? Can you see both expansion and reasonable limits? Can you see yourself changing and becoming freer? Are you beginning to see the edge of this magical solar system?

Take another deep breath. Now you find yourself on Neptune, an electric blue planet whose energy brings creativity and helps you understand how to dissolve the old and imagine the new. Go outside and stand on Neptune. You are perfectly comfortable. Feel the energy of Neptune flowing into you and wrapping itself around you. You're beginning to understand how to really dissolve old things—like those ugly, negative emotional burdens—and imagine a new, freer state of being.

And now take the big leap to the very edge of the universe. Feel your starship speed up and shift into hyperdrive.

You're going where no one has gone before, past science fiction, past books with good advice, past burdens like unproductive anger (though you still know that righteous anger can be useful), past guilt, regrets, hatred, and prejudices. You're speeding along now, faster than the speed of light, too fast for useless emotions to keep up.

And here you are! Here is the Ring-Pass-Not. What does it look like to you? Is it a waving black curtain like the aurora borealis? An endless dark wall? An impenetrable wall of light? An endless river of energy, darker and deeper than any earthly river? A black hole that looks like a huge, hungry, velvet donut?

As you gaze in wonder at the Ring-Pass-Not, you feel your starship safely entering it and flowing with it. This is where you understand that you can safely release those old, ugly, lumpen heaps of negative energy that you've been carrying around for so many years. You understand that you don't need them anymore. Those negative emotions are useless. They're harmful to you and every other person you ever meet. It's time to let them go.

Move the lever that opens the outer door of the cargo hold. Move another lever that slowly but surely pushes those emotional burdens out the door. Move a third lever that kicks them right into the Ring-Pass-Not. Watch the Ring-Pass-Not swallow them up.

Sit quietly and watch your emotional burdens float away in the Ring-Pass-Not. Say,

> . . . And so it's time to part,
> my dearest loves:
> the angers and the hurts
> I have cherished for so long,
>   fed you,
>   borne you,
>   grown comfortable with you.
> I have nourished you well.
> I have held you in my heart.
> And when you grew too strong . . .

I hid behind you.
But now I fear you—
I fear the power you had over me.
Go! Go into the Ring, flow with the Ring,
be absorbed by the Ring.
> *Go now.*
> *Be gone.*
> *Release your useless energy.*
And when you come 'round again,
come 'round as peace,
> *as humility,*
> *as understanding,*
> *as kindness.*
I release you to transformation.

Sit quietly with the words of this poem in your mind. When you're ready, let the words go, too.

Now it's time to return to Earth and consensual reality. With another deep, easy breath, turn your starship around and drive it out of the Ring-Pass-Not. Shift into hyperdrive again and speed back home. Come home with the speed of magic and thought. Come home without those old emotional burdens.

Just before you land back in your living room (or wherever), just before you open your eyes, remind yourself that the burdens are gone. Open your eyes and look at a new day.

Meditation for the Incredibly Reluctant

by Deborah Castellano

If you are anything like me, the idea of "relax and let your mind become a distant observer" is anathema. Let's start even sooner than that—let's start with someone else ordering you to "let your eyes drift shut." The basic functions of your brain and body should be something you have sovereignty over, not be at the command of some yoga-toned near-stranger barking orders at you and forcing you to relax against your will.

I have been forcibly resisting meditation for nearly my whole experience as a Witch. I think in part because I was constantly being told I *had* to do it (pass), in part due to being a type-A doer, in part due to my indifference to enlightenment, and in part due to my anxiety. Let's go over these examples as reasons why you, too, may be resistant to meditation.

"If you don't meditate, you can't do magic."

So let's start at the beginning with that one. If that was the case, none of my magical work up until the last two years or so has been effective. Now, obviously, it's hard to concretely point to one's magic and say, "Yes! That's what made This Thing go!" But I think just going by the number of years I've been practicing Witchcraft, it's safe to assume that something at some point worked.

If you were a Witch in the Woods/Edge of the Village–type historically, do you think you had a whole lot of time to meditate? Probably not, as you were trying to survive. Not from persecution most of the time most likely, unless you had a particularly choice little piece of land that someone wanted to put their grubby hands on. Mostly, in the boring ways— you had to grow food, store it, and possibly deal with animal husbandry along with the thrill of medieval laundry. So that's not a terribly true statement. Does it *help?* Of course it helps. You know what else helps? Eating a healthy diet of lean meats, vegetables, and whole grains without delicious sugar. Are you doing it all the time? Probably not. Meditation won't promise you an impressive magical career, but not meditating will not promise you that either.

"If you don't meditate, you'll drop dead."

My Aunt Jeanie is ninety-four years old and recently shook off a heart attack like an annoying head cold. She cusses, she smoked up until the last ten years or so, and she only agreed to go into a retirement home because she was bored at home all day. Aunt Jeanie is a total type-A proto-badass and she's never meditated a day in her life.

Would it help you manage your stress level? Of course it would. Do you know what else would help with that? Not getting so stressed out by by modern living. Does that sound unhelpful? Because it is. It's really difficult when you are a type-A psycho like myself to not engage in stressful activities and even harder to want to dedicate large swarths of time *not* doing. We're a group of hypermotivated Parvatis, always wanting to make sure the universe keeps turning by the sheer force of our activeness. You may be like my Aunt Jeanie and just have fantastic genetics, or you could meditate every day of your life and be genetically predisposed to cancer. Meditating doesn't guarantee you a long life, but you aren't guaranteed a long life by *not* meditating either.

"You will never achieve personal enlightenment without meditation."

Meditation seems like a pretty reasonable path to enlightenment in many traditions, but saints in other traditions seem to get enlightened through austerity and trance work. Mary Magdalene was enlightened enough to give resurrection a whirl and wait it out even when the boys had given up on it, even though she had never witnessed it. There are many arguments to be made that Mary Magdalene was enlightened through her work with her teacher, but that's another story for another day. At the very least, there seems to be many paths to enlightenment, depending on your personal belief structure.

But let's put that aside for a moment to contemplate: "Am I terribly interested in becoming personally enlightened?" This question seems like it has an obvious answer of yes, of course. Because shouldn't we all want to be? But I feel like if we really, truly wanted to be enlightened, we'd all be working a lot harder at it. So it's worth investigating if that's even of particular interest to you.

"You will never achieve a lack of anxiety without meditation."

There are lots of ways to get a generalized anxiety disorder under control through the use of therapy, medication, cognitive behavioral exercises, and alternative medication and healing practices. If me becoming less anxious hinged solely on meditation, I would have been in for a really rough past two decades. Like all of the other examples, does meditation help? Yes. It does help.

Then why bother?

As you have probably picked up, the point of all of these examples is you can lead a fully functioning, happy, magical, type-A existence with an anxiety disorder that's reasonably under control (or whatever your specific reasons are for not wanting to meditate) without meditation. However, meditation is a really good tool to add to your preexisting tool box of Witchcraft and coping skills. It doesn't have to be your only tool or even a tool you use that often. But it will help you focus your will faster in magic, it will help you destress, and it will calm and center you. Not perfectly, not every time. But coping skills and magic don't work perfectly every time either, so having one more trick up your sleeve for your magical and practical repertoire can only help you.

A Repetitive Meditation

In Hinduism, when you say a mantra 108 times while focusing on your intention (whatever magical work you are attempting to accomplish, a favor, a prayer for yourself or someone else, and so on), it's called a *japa* practice. You would usually use prayer beads to keep track of your counting, though there are tricks to use only your fingers. I have never been able to pick up how to only use my fingers correctly, so feel free to do further research on that on your own if that's of interest. If instead you decide to go with prayer beads, you can buy a set either at your local India Cash and Carry or on eBay. Making them yourself would also be an option. In-person purchase is ideal, so you can find beads that move easily through your fingers and make sure there are actually 108 beads by counting them.

When you use prayer beads, they are always to be held in your right hand regardless of which hand is dominant. When you are moving the beads through your hand, you use your thumb and middle fingers. You never use your pointer finger. You start at the tassel of the prayer beads and you work your way around them until you come back to the tassel. You may want to practice the motion before actually performing japa.

Generally, when working with goddesses in the Hindu pantheon, there are mantras that have to be given to you and could have repercussions if done incorrectly, and then there's everyone's seed mantra. The seed mantra is the equivalent of calling someone on the phone and saying, "Hello, is Name here? May I please speak to them?" Even if you mispronounce something, no one is going to get all that upset because you got their "phone number" out of the seed mantra "phone book" and everyone has a copy of it.

Shiva is an excellent deity to do mantra to. He's married to Parvati (for all our type As here), and while Parvati is the "doing" part of the universe, Shiva is the "being" part of the universe. If you are trying to get more in touch with your own "being," he's the one to talk to. When he's not being a householder with Parvati and holding the universe together with her, he's smoking pot in a cremation ground hanging out with his cremation ground bros, the *ganas*.

His seed mantra is ॐ ह्रीं नमः शिवाय, or *Om Hrim Namah Shivaya*.

Om: *Oooooooh-mmmm.* The sound starts in your belly and shoots up through your throat and then through the top of your head. It's the universal sound of creation.

Hrim: *Hah-reem.* The sound starts in your throat and then shoots out the top of your head. It's Shiva's and Shakti's sound, and it lifts the veil of illusion for you to reach Shiva (or Shakti).

Namaha: *Nah-mah-hah.* A salutation where you are honoring Shiva.

Shivaya: *Shee-vah-yah.* Shiva's formal name. You are calling him directly but also your inner self that is "being."

So you would practice this meditation by first focusing on your intention and then holding that intention while you intone your mantra once for every prayer bead, starting at the tassel and then ending at the tassel. Usually, the last mantra is said more slowly, so you and the deity you are talking to both know you are finished.

Building a Tiny Astral Home Away from Home

When you build an internal shrine inside yourself and you maintain it, you are building a tiny safe haven for yourself on the astral plane. Kabbala, Gnosticism, and Hermetics all have some version of this. If you don't have a lot of experience or a mentor, this is a good way to get your feet wet in working with the astral world, and it's in the borderlands between meditation and trance work, which makes it interesting. Obviously, anytime you do magic there's an element of risk involved. Use your common sense and critical thinking skills here—don't juggle hedgehogs or chainsaws. If you don't feel ready to do this, then you should not do it.

Your astral home is a good place to do magical work and to work with spirits and goddesses you already have a good working relationship with. Treat your astral shrine as you would treat your actual home: you likely wouldn't invite a bunch of random strangers into your house, you wouldn't give an acquaintance who doesn't live with you a spare key to your house to come and go as they please, and you would have a general set of rules about how you expect people to act in your home. The same rules apply to your spiritual shrine.

Create Your Shrine

1. Take some deep breaths until you feel grounded and centered in yourself. If it would make you feel more protected and you are not Wiccan, put down a salt circle around you and four white candles (one to one of your sides, one to the other side, one to your front, and one to your back). If you are Wiccan, you can always cast a circle according to your tradition's ritual outline.
2. Imagine yourself in a cave. You are holding a torch. You see a set of stairs leading down. Follow the stairs and walk until you see an exit from the cave.

3. When you step outside the cave, what do you see? An ocean, a valley, mountains? Walk until you see a clearing. Wait until you see an omen that it's okay to construct your shrine there.

4. Construct your shrine however you see fit, furnish it however you see fit, landscape however you see fit. Make sure it's something you can remember easily, especially if you aren't a visual thinker. The more consistent you can keep your structure, the better a foothold it is for you.

5. When you are done spending time in your shrine, follow the path back to the cave and take the stairs back up. If you had cast a circle, open it back up. Resume normal life.

6. Visit your shrine regularly. Make sure it's kept the way you want it to be kept. Entertain visitors you've prevetted. Eat food there, read there, do whatever you like to do in your physical life. The more time you spend in your shrine, the more of a hearthstone it can be for your astral work.

About the Authors

BARBARA ARDINGER, PHD, is the author of *Secret Lives*, a novel about a circle of crones, mothers, and maidens, plus goddesses, a talking cat, and the Green Man. Her earlier books include the daybook *Pagan Every Day, Goddess Meditations, Finding New Goddesses*, and *Quicksilver Moon*. Her day job is freelance editing for people who have good ideas but don't want to embarrass themselves in print. To date, she has edited more than 300 books, both fiction and nonfiction, on a wide range of topics. Barbara lives in Southern California with her two rescued Maine coon cats, Heisenberg and Schroedinger. Visit her at www.barbaraardinger .com and https://www.facebook.com/barbara.ardinger.

ELIZABETH BARRETTE has been involved with the Pagan community for more than twenty-seven years. She served as managing editor of *PanGaia* for eight years and dean of studies at the Grey School of Wizardry for four years. Her book *Composing Magic: How to Create Magical Spells, Rituals, Blessings, Chants, and Prayers* explains how to combine writing and spirituality. She lives in central Illinois, and her other writing fields include speculative fiction, gender studies, social and environmental issues. Visit her blog *The Wordsmith's Forge* (http://ysabetwordsmith.livejournal.com/) or website PenUlti- mate Productions (http://penultimateproductions.weebly.com).

MIREILLE BLACKE, MA, is a registered dietitian, certified dietitian- nutritionist, and addiction specialist residing in Connecticut. She is obsessed with the city of New Orleans, the various works of Joss Whedon, and her Bengal cats. Mireille worked in rock radio for over two decades before shifting her career focus to psychology, nutrition, and addiction counseling. She has been published in *Llewellyn's Moon Sign Book, Today's Dietitian*, and *OKRA Magazine*.

Mireille is an adjunct professor at the University of Saint Joseph, is a clinical dietitian at Bristol Hospital, and is working on several titles, including *Life and Times of the RadioWitch*. Find Mireille at rockgumbo.blogspot.com, radiowitch.com, and on Twitter at @RockGumboRD.

BLAKE OCTAVIAN BLAIR is an eclectic Pagan, ordained minister, shamanic practitioner, writer, Usui Reiki Master-Teacher, tarot reader, and musical artist. Blake blends various mystical traditions from both the East and West along with a reverence for the natural world into his own brand of modern Paganism and magick. Blake holds a degree in English and religion from the University of Florida. Blake lives in the New England region with his beloved husband. Visit him on the web at www.blakeoctavian blair.com or write to him at blake@blakeoctavianblair.com.

DEBORAH BLAKE is the author of the Baba Yaga paranormal romance series (which includes *Wickedly Magical, Wickedly Dangerous, Wickedly Wonderful,* and *Wickedly Powerful*), as well as nine books on modern Witchcraft from Llewellyn. She has an ongoing column in *Witches & Pagans Magazine* and was featured in *The Pagan Anthology of Short Fiction*. When not writing, she is the manager and cofounder of the Artisans' Guild, a not-for-profit artists' cooperative shop where she also sells her jewelry. She can be found at www.deborahblakeauthor.com.

DEBORAH CASTELLANO (www.deborahmcastellano.com) is a frequent contributor to occult/Pagan sources such as the Llewellyn annual almanacs, PaganSquare, and *Witches & Pagans Magazine*. She blogs at *Charmed, I'm Sure*. Deborah's book, *Glamour Magic: The Witchcraft Revolution to Get What You Want,* was published with Llewellyn in the summer of 2017. She resides in New Jersey with her husband, Jow, and their cat. She has a terrible reality

television habit she can't shake and likes St. Germain liquor, record players, and typewriters.

DALLAS JENNIFER COBB practices gratitude magic, giving thanks for personal happiness, health, and prosperity; meaningful, flexible and rewarding work; and a deliciously joyful life. She lives in paradise with her daughter, in a waterfront village in rural Ontario, where she regularly swims, runs, and snowshoes. A Reclaiming Witch from way back, Jennifer is part of an eclectic pan-Pagan circle that organizes empowered and beautiful community rituals. Contact her at jennifer.cobb@live.com.

MONICA CROSSON is the author of *The Magickal Family: Pagan Living in Harmony with Nature* (Llewellyn). She is a Master Gardener who lives in the beautiful Pacific Northwest, happily digging in the dirt and tending her raspberries with her husband, three kids, three goats, two dogs, two cats, many chickens, and Rosetta the donkey. Her garden was featured on Soulemama.com's 2016 virtual garden tour. She has been a practicing Witch for twenty-five years and is a member of Blue Moon Coven. Monica is a regular contributor to Llewellyn's almanacs, calendars and datebooks. She also enjoys writing fiction for young adults and is the author of *Summer Sage*.

RAVEN DIGITALIS (Missoula, Montana) is the author of *Esoteric Empathy, Shadow Magick Compendium, Planetary Spells & Rituals* and *Goth Craft*. He is a Neopagan priest and cofounder of an Eastern Hellenistic nonprofit multicultural temple called Opus Aima Obscuræ (OAO). Also trained in Eastern philosophies and Georgian Witchcraft, Raven has been an earth-based practitioner since 1999, a priest since 2003, a Freemason since 2012, and an empath all his life. Visit www.ravendigitalis.com, www.facebook.com/raven digitalis, www.opusaimaobscurae.org, and www.facebook.com /opusaimaobscurae.

ELLEN DUGAN is the award-winning author known as the "Garden Witch." A psychic-clairvoyant, she has been a practicing Witch for over thirty years. She is a Master Gardener and teaches classes on writing, Witchery, psychic development, and magick. Ellen is the author of sixteen books published by Llewellyn Publications. She recently branched out into paranormal fiction with her popular Legacy of Magick series. You can find Ellen on Facebook, Pinterest, and Twitter.

MICHAEL FURIE (Northern California) is the author of *Spellcasting for Beginners, Supermarket Magic, Spellcasting: Beyond the Basics* and more, all from Llewellyn Publications. A practicing Witch for more than twenty years, he is a priest of the Cailleach. He can be found online at www.michaelfurie.com.

EMBER GRANT has been writing for the Llewellyn annuals since 2003 and is the author of three books and more than fifty articles. Her most recent book is *The Second Book of Crystal Spells*. She also sells handmade crafts and enjoys nature photography. Visit her online at EmberGrant.com.

JUSTINE HOLUBETS is a Solitary Wiccan practicing ancient Egyptian sacred traditions living in Lviv, Ukraine. She holds a tarot certificate from and is a consultant for the British & Astrological Psychic Society and works as tarot and lunar rhythms/astrology consultant for Zodiaclivetarot.com in the UK. A published author, she currently studies psychology at Roehampton London University online and prepares courses to help women maintain healthy, dignified intercultural relationships. She also explores sacred architecture and symbols, Greco-Roman mythology and psychological archetypes, and chakra and energy healing. Visit her at http://www.zodiaclivetarotreading.com/tarot-reader?id=129.

JAMES KAMBOS writes and paints from his home in Ohio. He frequently writes about Greek folk magic and Appalachian folklore.

SANDRA KYNES is an explorer of history, myth, and magic, and a member of the Order of Bards, Ovates & Druids. Her inquisitiveness has led her to investigate the roots of her beliefs and to integrate her spiritual path with everyday life. Her work has been featured in various Llewellyn publications, *Utne Reader, Sage Woman, The Portal,* and *Circle* magazines. She enjoys connecting with the natural world through gardening, hiking, bird-watching, and ocean kayaking. Visit her website at www.kynes.net.

TIFFANY LAZIC is a registered psychotherapist and spiritual director with a private practice in individual, couples, and group therapy. As the owner of the Hive and Grove Centre for Holistic Wellness, she created two self-development programs focused on teaching inner alchemy and intuitive tools from around the world. She is an international presenter and retreat facilitator, is the founder of Kitchener's Red Tent Temple, and serves on the Council of the Sisterhood of Avalon. Tiffany is the author of *The Great Work: Self-Knowledge and Healing Through the Wheel of the Year.* Visit Tiffany at www.hiveandgrove.ca.

NAJAH LIGHTFOOT is a freelance writer and a happy, contributing author for Llewellyn Publications. She is a priestess of the Divine Feminine, a martial artist, and an active member of the Denver Pagan community. She keeps her magick strong through the practice of Hoodoo, Pagan rituals, and her belief in the Mysteries of the Universe. She finds inspiration in movies, music, and the blue skies of Colorado. Find her online at www.twitter.com /NajahLightfoot, www.facebook.com/NajahLightfoot, and www .craftandconjure.com.

LUPA is a Pagan author, hide and bone artist, naturalist and eco-psychologist in the Pacific Northwest. She is the author of several books, including *Nature Spirituality From the Ground Up* (Llewellyn,

2016) and she is the creator of the Tarot of Bones. You can find out more about her work at http://www.thegreenwolf.com.

JASON MANKEY is a Wiccan Witch, writer, and wannabe rock and roller. He has been a part of the greater Pagan community for over twenty years and has spent nearly half that time teaching and speaking at Pagan conventions across the United States and Canada. He has written two books for Llewellyn Publications, *The Witch's Athame* (2016) and *The Witch's Book of Shadows* (2017), and is also the channel manager of Patheos Pagan online. He lives in Sunnyvale, California, where he and his wife, Ari, help lead two local covens. Because they don't want to be outnumbered, Ari and Jason only have two cats.

MELANIE MARQUIS is the creator of the Modern Spellcaster's Tarot (illustrated by Scott Murphy) and the author of *A Witch's World of Magick, The Witch's Bag of Tricks, Beltane, Lughnasadh,* and *Witchy Mama* (coauthored with Emily Francis). She is a local coordinator for the Denver Pagan Pride Project and is a frequent presenter at magickal gatherings around the country.

ESTHA K. V. McNEVIN (Missoula, Montana) is a priestess and ceremonial oracle of Opus Aima Obscuræ, a nonprofit Pagan Temple Haus. She has served the Pagan community since 2003 as an Eastern Hellenistic officiate, lecturer, freelance author, artist, and poet. She offers classes on multicultural metaphysical theory, ritual technique, international cuisine, organic gardening, herbal craft, alchemy, and occult symbolism. In addition to hosting public rituals for the sabbats, Estha organizes annual philanthropic fundraisers, Full Moon spell-crafting ceremonies, and women's divination rituals for each Dark Moon. To learn more, please explore www.opusaimaobscurae.org and www.facebook .com/opusaimaobscurae.

Susan Pesznecker is a writer, English teacher, nurse, practicing herbalist, and hearth Pagan living in Oregon. Sue holds an MS in professional writing and loves to read, watch the stars, camp, and garden. Sue has authored *Yule: Rituals, Recipes, & Lore for the Winter Solstice* (Llewellyn, 2015), *The Magickal Retreat* (Llewellyn, 2012), and *Crafting Magick with Pen and Ink* (Llewellyn, 2009) and contributes to the Llewellyn annuals. Visit her on Facebook (https://www.facebook.com/SusanMoonwriterPesznecker).

Stacy M. Porter has studied politics in Africa, survived a Russian winter, touched a Michelangelo sculpture in Italy, and saved sea turtles in Nicaragua. She holds a degree in international studies with a minor in English from Juniata College, is a second-degree priestess in the Ravenmyst Circle Tradition, and is a certified yoga instructor through Bodhi Yoga Academy. Stacy is currently making magic in Orlando, Florida. You can follow her adventures on Instagram at www.instagram.com/stacymporteryoga and on Facebook at www.facebook.com/StacyMPorterAuthor.

Suzanne Ress runs a small farm in the alpine foothills of Italy, where she lives with her husband. She has been a practicing Pagan for as long as she can remember and was recently featured in the exhibit "Worldwide Witches" at the Hexenmuseum of Switzerland. She is the author of *The Trial of Goody Gilbert*.

Rev. J. Variable X/0 lives in Portland, Oregon, and holds degrees in English, digital media production, and arts and letters. As a professional psychic advisor, Variable often has to encourage clients to let go of centuries-old superstitions, assumptions, and faulty logic before they can understand how mysticism and magical practices can actually help them in the real world. Please visit http://www.reverend-variable.com for more information.

Charlynn Walls resides with her family in Central Missouri. She holds a BA in anthropology with an emphasis in archaeology. She